Double Standards

Double Standards

M.B. Malik

Matador
9 Priory Business Park,
Wistow Road, Kibworth Beauchamp,
Leicestershire. LE8 0RX
Tel: 0116 279 2299
Email: books@troubador.co.uk
Web: www.troubador.co.uk/matador
Twitter: @matadorbooks

ISBN 978 1785891 649

British Library Cataloguing in Publication Data.
A catalogue record for this book is available from the British Library.

Typeset in 11pt Bembo by Troubador Publishing Ltd, Leicester, UK

Matador is an imprint of Troubador Publishing Ltd

Dedicated to my beloved late father, who taught me everything I know. Papa, you are missed daily - it is all for you. For my mother, to whom I owe everything., and my motivation – my niece – Ilyana.

Contents

Preface

February 9th 1988

State dinner at President House Lahore, Pakistan

Few would reminisce a more high-powered dinner table than Pakistani President General Muhammad Zia-ul-Haq and the Ruler of UAE HH Sheikh Zayed Al Nahyan. The important men were busy devouring the main course of traditional Lahori mutton kebab tikkas, fish and biryani, while the President's staff were on standby to refill any plate that looked as though it was nearing depletion.

Just as dessert was about to be served, one of Sheikh Zayed's aides whispered into his ear at which point he promptly wiped his mouth with the embroidered silk table napkin, abruptly stood up and made his way towards the exit of the state dining hall.

At this point the entire table, including General Zia-ul-Haq stood up and were in shock as to what grave insult or culinary crime had been committed that could have offended His Royal Highness. Less than a minute later, the President's personal advisor whispered into his ear, which caused him to immediately excuse himself from the table and he also made his way out of the dining hall.

Suddenly the pin-drop silence turned into a hurried frenzy as the president's protocol officers gathered their personnel to escort the high-powered leaders and their entourages to their destination which was unknown to the rest of the table until the leaders had left.

Rumours were beginning to spread but security officers kept everything very hush. The destination: Sheikh Zayed Hospital Lahore.

The whisper into Sheikh Zayed's ear "Your Highness, Mr. Abedi has suffered a severe heart attack and is in critical condition" Who was the man who caused the State dinner to end and led the world's most powerful men to be by his hospital bedside within a matter of minutes?

His name was Agha Hasan Abedi, the President of one of the largest banks in the world.

Humble beginnings

Pakistan is indeed a funny place. For it nurtures an uncanny knack for disgracing its fallen heroes and shaming them constantly. It's almost as bad as my mother's obsession with me, being the only son, although without the nostalgic claustrophobia attached.

Now being a British-born Londoner with parents of Pakistani descent, I somewhat found myself warming to this 'troubled' nation of 180 million people. As a kid growing up, I would be supporting the green shirts in almost all the Cricket matches where England were not the opposition. The litmus test of my Britishness was however in the summer of 1992 when Graham Gooch's boys were up against Imran Khan's cornered tigers at the World Cup Cricket Final in Melbourne. My loyalties came under immense scrutiny by my fellow nine-year-old school buddies at St. Martin's Prep School in Northwood, a quiet green and leafy suburb in North West London. As the great Khan lifted up the cup, a nine-year-old me was jubilating up and down the corridors of Prep School with my milk and biscuits (pre-Thatcherite babies will understand) dribbling all over the place.

It is at this time I began questioning my own self, regarding identity and belonging in a nation where I had never lived and the only ties I had were my parents and the language we spoke at home. Then at the tender age of thirteen I was sent off to a place to be further confused in this identity crisis: A quintessentially-English boarding school in a predominantly Jewish inhabited area of North London. At first, I used to burst out in Oscar-winning tears most nights on the phone, blackmailing my poor old parents, branding them 'cruel' for the crime of sending me to 'prison' as I would term it. My emotionally-wrecked mother then having to send me home-cooked meals on almost a daily basis, circumventing the strict rules of parents visiting on Sundays only. Unfortunately, we were the only school in the vicinity to have conscripted Saturday school which constituted morning chapel service followed by afternoon sporting activities. The rationale that our Headmaster gave was that 'there isn't enough time in the conventional week to fulfill our full academic and extra-curricular programme'. Bollocks – was my initial reaction. "We are all going to become Prime Ministers and leaders of our generation" said Simon Ratzker, a fellow housemate who was celebrated to become our future Olympic hero.

I later realized that our headmaster at the time was quite correct. As I look back and seeing the world I live in today, the boarding-school days were probably the best days of my life. I didn't quite fit in at the beginning while sharing a dormitory with twelve other bright-eyed thirteen year olds. I was a typical and indicative 'Mummy's boy' as it were, who was too shy to speak to girls (this changed very rapidly as girls were introduced to the school in the sixth form). To add to my socially-reclusive demeanor, I despised alcohol ferociously. So much so that the slightest smell of alcohol seemed repugnant to me, which is why I found it difficult to socialise at parties after rugby and cricket matches that we played in. I remember distinctly when I got selected to play for the First XI cricket tour to Barbados in 1996. I was merely thirteen and was playing with the senior squad in the West Indies, which to me was an enormous boost to my self-confidence as well as a real shot at the Under nineteen Middlesex County selections later on. On the very same trip, one evening we were all out in Bridgetown, Barbados's capital, and the boys put all their efforts in trying to make me drink, going as far as tipping the most beautiful waitresses to send me drinks for free. But all their attempts failed which is when I knew that the years ahead would be quite tough indeed.

However at the time I didn't know that those same people with whom I shared an incommodious space with in bunk beds, would grow on to become the closest and most cherished friends I possess. Even later in life, I learnt the paradigmatic saying 'it's the quality of friends, not quantity that counts' to be very true.

I very much doubted some of my peers' abilities to be PM, however the older I got, I became acutely aware of the privileged environment that had been bestowed upon me. The nineties were a great time to grow up in, as many would agree. *Spitting Image* was a family television fixation with a blue-faced John Major being humiliated on a weekly basis and the joke never got old. In any case, even the thought of the idea of boarding school was daunting, with the older boys flushing my head down the toilet on my birthday and filling the bathtub with all sorts of liquid and then throwing me in.

However at the ripe old age of thirty-two, entering my first phase of mid-life crisis and imminent financial squeeze in the midst of the worst quadruple-dip financial mess this world has ever seen, suddenly I realize that those five years spent at boarding school were unquestionably the best years of my life. Things changed considerably when the school's board of governors decided to introduce the opposite sex into the sixth form which saw a variable impact on our A-level grades. This in turn led me to ditch the coconut oil for hair gel and I also stole my dad's aftershave to take with me in my dormitory. Those really *were* the days!

Going back a few years, 5th July 1991 was a memorable day for me as a nine-year-old spoilt brat. I returned home after a gruelling day at Prep School with a perdurable and beaming smile on my face as it was the last day of term which welcomed two months of glorious summer holidays for me, but hell for my parents.

Normally summer holidays were looked forward to. The first couple of weeks were spent abroad, usually across the pond to either Canada or the USA to visit countless numbers of 'uncles and aunties' whom I can't even remember the names of. My cheeks would inevitably be pulled incessantly by elder women not realizing how sore they became after a while. As I grew older, I wanted to get revenge and pull theirs in return, however the one and only time I did it, my fingers were tainted with excessive make-up powder and so I refrained.

This summer holiday of '91, however was different. Very different. I came home making a huge racket as usual and demanding that my mother take me to the department store to buy me the new 'LA Gear' or 'Reebok Pump' basketball shoes that had come out. It had been over a week since they had been released in the UK and I was the only one out of my classmates who didn't own a pair and this had become a matter of huge embarrassment for me. How shallow and spoilt I was back then! I know. Forgive me.

I continued to pester my mum who kept making me quiet because she said my father was on a very important phone call upstairs and we don't want to disturb him. I began to get even more rowdy as I wasn't getting my way and refused to eat supper until she agreed to take me to the store to buy the shoes. The funny thing was I never even played that much basketball, those shoes were just the 'in' thing and 'a must have' for all nine year olds at the time.

Once the crying and feet tapping started, my father called my mum from upstairs asking her what the noise and fuss was all about and reminded her that he was on a very important phone call. He sounded quite stressed and worried. I hadn't really heard his tone like that before but at the time I didn't really care about anything else except for my Reebok pumps.

"Nothing!! So sorry. He is just making a fuss over those shoes he wants, get back to your phone call, I'll make sure he is quiet!" shouted my mum.

"No no that's absoloutely fine!" yelled back my dad. "I got worried as to why he was crying, are you sure everything is ok?

Why don't you just take him out and buy him whatever he wants. Go on, I'll see you both when you get back," he added.

My mum gave me the worst look the world had ever seen and taunted me all the way to the department store of how I had disturbed my father while he was busy and basically probably told me how I was an ungrateful little imbecile.

She wasn't to blame though. The poor soul had been through the toughest six months of her life as my father had recently undergone his second life-threatening coronary bypass surgery and was making a steady recovery at home. In those days, the surgery was still a big deal and doctors had advised him to rest at home and not go to work for at least two months. This proved to be an extremely tiresome ordeal for my father, who throughout his life thrived and prospered only by getting up at 5am daily and going to work. Even his imminent retirement which was approaching that same August after a month's time was something he dreaded as he wouldn't know what to do with himself post-retirement. His entire life was his job and career as the case is with many people.

To be honest, I didn't even know or understand what my father did until after I left Prep School. I only knew that he was a 'banker'. On all official documentation, from school forms to bills, his designation was simply written as 'Bank Executive'. Thanks to the Almighty, I received the best childhood and unconditional love from both my parents with a roof over my head which is all that one could ask for. The basics of which is denied to so many in this world unfortunately.

We got home from the department store and my misery had now doubled as the shops had sold out of Reebok Pumps in my size. I was livid. I threw a tantrum and demanded that my mum take me to another store. She somehow managed to strap me in the car and take me home while I continued my immature and foolish tantrum. I was nearing a slap as we entered the front door as my mum warned me to stay quiet and not disturb my father as we went in. I reluctantly agreed to stay silent, but as soon as we walked through the door I ran upstairs to my dad at bionic speed and jumped on his bed to cry and complain about my mum. He was still on the phone and told whoever it was on the other line that he'd call them back. "What's the matter beta?" ('beta' means 'son' in Urdu) he said. I kept crying and he couldn't understand a word I was muttering as he became occupied in wiping my tears while hugging me. Meanwhile my mum had caught up with us and he looked at her asking for explanations for my tears. "The shops had run out of the shoes he had his heart set upon and I tried explaining to him but... listen forget it, I'll handle it, you get back to your phone calls and don't stress, I'll handle it, give him to me," she said.

"No, leave him," he said calmly. He then turned to me, wiped off my last tear and said "Shhhh, there there! No more tears ok? Papa will buy his son the best pair of brand new shoes next week, whichever ones he wants, ok? Happy?"

"Next week???" I exclaimed in despair, thinking I would have to wait an entire week for my beloved pumps. "Yes, next week beta. Papa is taking you all away to Florida next week and I'll get you the shoes which none of your friends have either, I promise".

With those words, suddenly my pathetic, ill-minded, senseless and lousy tantrum ceased to a halt and was replaced with teeth showing my braces and a massive hug for my dad. My mother just sat on a chair opposite the bed and shook her head. My dad patted me on the back while I hugged him and winked at my mum while asking her to put the kettle on as there was a very uncomfortable chat ahead.

The reason was soon to be revealed as to why my mum was so worried and why my dad was on the phone the entire day.

Since he had been recuperating at home following his heart surgery, he had been in constant touch with his work via telephone on a daily basis – something which his doctor had advised him not to do. Nevertheless he called the office every morning and got updates and delivered instructions to his staff as per usual and also wanted his retirement to go smoothly so he could hand over his duties to the incumbent. His retirement package among other savings, were deposited in a bank as one normally would do in his position. The problem was, however, and the reason for his worry, was that the bank which he chose to deposit his money and his life savings was no ordinary bank.

The remainder of the day saw him frantically making and receiving calls as the mainstream media began reporting the headline that authorities in the UK, USA and Luxembourg had passed a court order to liquidate the Bank of Credit and Commerce International (BCCI), effectively freezing my father's and another one million customers' hard-earned money. This also meant making 14,000+ employees redundant around the world. For my father this news was a huge blow, as hard as it was for him to retire from his job, but to discover that you may also have lost your entire life savings, pension fund and retirement package in the institution which you trusted for eighteen years was heartbreaking. The worry for my mother however was not the fact that we had lost every penny we owned but her only concern was the potential risk this awful news bought to my father's ailing health. The doctors had specifically requested him not to take on any stress and such news would undoubtedly trigger further complications to his weak heart. However, the courageous and valiant man he was, not only did he withstand the terrible news of losing his livelihood and his life savings – but he also never for a single day allowed his wife and children to feel or notice any difference or change in their environment from that moment onwards.

He kept his cool and took control of the entire situation financially and emotionally in every aspect. As children aged nine and twelve respectively, my sister and I never felt any hindrance or impediment in our upbringing after my father had retired. In fact, we feel we were blessed as we now had our father at home with us as we didn't get to see a lot of him earlier due to his extraordinary work schedule and commitments. We felt humbled and lucky to spend as much time with him as possible, and vice versa. It was a blessing in disguise maybe as I look back, with him no longer being around, I wonder if he was still working – then I might not have got to spend valuable time with the one person on this earth who I struggle to live without to this very day.

This is not to undermine the stark fact that BCCI's abrupt and unfair closure had a devastating effect on thousands of people both financially and emotionally. I am just spinning our own personal circumstances into a positive light. Unfortunately many others were not as fortunate as me and it is with them that my thoughts and prayers lie. For the closure broke many families far and near. The utter devastation and financial turmoil was clear. The ripples are felt to this very day. Vast amounts of Asian families had also kept their savings in BCCI as it was the bank of choice for those ethnic minorities living in the UK. Shop owners, small businesses and councils all kept accounts at the bank and were devastated at the news of the closure. Hence since childhood I had a fascination with the bank and was eager to find out what exactly happened. The fascination however soon turned into intriguing investigation and inquisitiveness after the 2008 world financial crash which led to a number of banking scandals being exposed. I began to dig deep and my curiosity developed into a passionate thirst for information and diligent research. This led to the present-day scenario of being able to compile a thorough and honest analysis of the topic in question.

Chapter One

Early days

When I was growing up, being the only son and having an elder sister, I would almost always get the stick for being....Well, just being myself really. The fact that my sister could get away with murder if she wanted to really ate me away from inside, even more so the fact that my parents always thought that she could 'do no wrong'. On one occasion I turned the sprinklers on in the garden, ran through the water a few times until I was drenched. The following hours saw the wrath of my mother and the out pour of anger and concern as she dried me off preventing her 'trophy son' from falling sick.

My sister on the other hand did exactly the same thing with my cousin the following week, and didn't get reprimanded. I was at an intellectual loss to understand how there could be one rule for her and one rule for me. It was beyond me. But then again it was petty sibling rivalry and animosity. One would never expect this type of differential treatment to be a benchmark practice in modern world capitalist economies. Of course not. One rule for them and one rule for us?

Nonsense! Or is it?

Those young financial aficionados amongst you who have yet to inherit the perfidious grey hairs on your heads, will probably not remember a man by the name of Agha Hasan Abedi.

He is a man to whom thousands of people are indebted all over the globe.

Mr. Abedi or 'Agha Sahab' as he was affectionately referred to by friends and colleagues was born in the pre-partitioned Indian city of Lucknow on 14th May, 1922. He came from a humble but educated Shi'ite Muslim family background. Although later we will discover, that Abedi was probably more a 'Sufi' than a Shia Muslim.

His father ran the affairs and estate of the Raja of Mahmudabad which included an excellent library where Abedi would spend many hours fascinated by literature. Due to the passion for literacy and culture in the family, Abedi received the very best education that was on offer at the time and studied Law at Lucknow University followed by a Masters in English Literature. His next direction was tricky because he had no interest in doing the traditional bar exams to become barrister and neither did he opt to take on a teaching route. He was however, mesmerized by the world of banking and finance from his college days. He wanted to learn more about it as he didn't have a formal financial or banking-related degree. Hence in 1946 he joined the Habib Bank as a trainee officer which was his first exposure to banking and the start of a fascinating career spanning five decades.

He diligently climbed up the corporate ladder at Habib Bank and rose through the ranks becoming one of the most notable successes the bank had ever seen in a very short span of time. He became instrumental in securing and maintaining the account of Muhammad Ali Jinnah's Muslim League party in Bombay whereby he would personally go and collect cash from Jinnah at his party headquarters. Jinnah would be vigorous in the counting of the money and Abedi would make every effort to return to the Habib branch to deposit the money in Muslim League's account immediately.

Habib Bank, at the time was the largest bank in pre-partition India. In 1947 at the time of India's independence, Pakistan was created under the vision and leadership of Jinnah. The young and optimistic Abedi left for Pakistan as many of his generation from the Urdu speaking community did from Lucknow, and became a 'Mohajir'. The word 'Mohajir' simply means 'migrant' in Urdu but also sometimes is used to refer to people of the Urdu speaking community.

Even in his early days in the newly created Islamic Republic of Pakistan, Abedi created a niche for himself as a charismatic and dynamic banker, always thinking of new and innovative ways to banking and banking methodology which was alien to the region at the time. There was one instance where he would transport surplus cash from a small branch of Habib Bank to another one in Rawalpindi via horseback carriage called 'taanga'. It is almost unthinkable to do such a thing in modern day Rawalpindi, a city close to the capital Islamabad because of the sheer danger and threat of looting or theft of the money. However those were the golden days of Pakistan that my parents spoke of, where everybody was so honest and noble and the thought of somebody robbing you wouldn't even cross your mind.

Another story relayed by the late Altaf Gauhar, renowned journalist and former Secretary of the State Bank of Pakistan, was that in 1957 there were hundreds of financial transactions that took place on a daily basis at the Karachi Municipal Corporation, yet there was no banking facility on the premises of the KMC. This triggered a sudden solution in the eyes of a young opportunistic Abedi whereby he approached Gauhar and offered his services from Habib Bank. When he was asked how long it would take for the branch to set up, the reply was 'tomorrow morning'. Lo and behold, the very next day saw the opening of Habib Bank in the KMC building foyer with a table, small safe, cloth and banner with a few chairs. Where the National bank of Pakistan had demanded unrealistic terms for opening a branch, Abedi had spotted a potential opportunity and made it into a business relationship with the KMC. This was the beginning of a revolutionary and visionary career and a small glimpse into his wit and wisdom.

By 1959 Abedi felt he had reached his saturation point and was not being challenged enough in his career. He had learnt a great deal about banking during his years at Habib along with some valuable connections which he used to his advantage. Hence with his experience and networking skills at play together

3

he decided to create the United Bank Limited (UBL) with the backing of the well-known Saigol family. Mian Yusuf Saigol who was impressed with Abedi's plan for a new bank that would break the norms in Pakistani banking, agreed to invest the first twenty million rupees that would give UBL its first breath. By the mid-1960s UBL was the second largest private sector commercial bank in Pakistan going head to head with the Habibs. This was the first great success for Agha Sahab who gathered together some of his like-minded colleagues from Habib and convinced them to join his bank, which they did and prospered as a result. Amongst the early recruits were great bankers of the time like Abdus Sami and Jamil Nishtar who later became Senior Vice President of UBL. Some early commentators report that even the esteemed Sher Ali Mundrawala joined Agha Sahab after much convincing and dithering. Mundrawala, however was more of a conservative banker who didn't like too much change. Agha Sahab wanted to change and revolutionise banking in Pakistan altogether – and that he did. As we can see, UBL is now one of the largest banks in Pakistan. It has 1200 branches in the country, numerous representative offices and branches overseas (including UAE, UK, USA and Switzerland) and boasting assets of over 747 billion rupees. UBL offices and branches, from the very beginning, would always stand out as being distinctive with marble floors and glass exteriors. Abedi bought the first IBM 360–40 computers to Pakistan and installed them in UBL's first computer division which handled and processed the 'Fauji' Army foundation accounts, one of the biggest accounts of the country.

Even by seeing this success, others in the Habib clan didn't join Agha Sahab until a much later stage like Mr. Ibne Hasan Burney and Mr. Ameer Siddiki who was Senior Vice President of Habib Bank around the time Agha Sahab left and founded UBL. The delicate distinction between those who did join Agha Sahab from the beginning and those who joined later was one of prudence. Agha Sahab's ambitious and speedy nature was not everyone's cup of tea as banking still was at that time a conservative, prudent profession and still in its infancy in Pakistan. But Agha Sahab was always a man in a hurry, which we will discover more clearly a little later. When he had thought of an idea, he didn't want to waste a single moment. Others were very sceptical and somewhat afraid of this hurried approach. Although many of his colleagues didn't fully understand the scope of his vision and ambition until the bell tolled for UBL and all private sector banks in the winter of 1971 as Zulfikar Ali Bhutto became President of Pakistan.

The winter of 1971 was another watershed moment in the history of Pakistan as they lost the war to India and also lost East Pakistan which became an independent Bangladesh. To add insult to injury, Bhutto brought in a wide range of Economic and social policies which some would argue had a detrimental and lasting effect on Pakistan's Economic and political stability. One such move was the decision for his government to take control over all of the banks in the country in a rampant and shrewd nationalization programme. In addition, many notable businessmen, politicians and public figures were either humiliated by being dragged to prison – or put under house arrest. Agha Sahab fell under the latter category and his passport was also confiscated.

However Abedi was always one step ahead of the game by predicting beforehand what was about to happen. He knew that UBL would fall victim to this brutal act of state authoritarianism which would eventually be a death sentence to private enterprise.

He hatched his cunning and brilliant brainchild, the birth of a truly international bank which no state could nationalize, while under house arrest in Karachi. This is when the initial concept of the Bank of Credit and Commerce was conceived. I have highlighted this point for the reader's attention and for those who still believe the false notion that Agha Hasan Abedi had criminal intent while conceiving BCCI. Those who think so, are gravely misguided.

Chapter Two

From desert sands to the city – The birth of BCCI

The birth of BCCI is intricately connected to the relationship of Abedi and Abu Dhabi, namely the late HH Sheikh Zayed bin Nahyan Al Nahyan who was the founder and President of the United Arab Emirates. Their relationship and humble beginnings is a beautiful story in itself. For without Sheikh Zayed, there would be no BCCI.

In the same vein, many say that Agha Hasan Abedi played a vital role as a sound and loyal financial advisor to the Sheikh and the UAE. Sheikh Zayed was a visionary and fine leader. A thorough gentlemen but a religious and devoted Bedouin tribal leader at heart. His most noble attribute was that he was a very simple man. Despite being a man with substantial means, he hardly ever spent on himself but was known to be extremely generous to people around him and found it difficult to say no to people. This was partly due to the fact that he *knew* people knew that he had money and hence he had an equally big heart.

The Arab sheikhs traditionally had a soft spot for Pakistan from the very beginning. It was considered a brotherly neighbour and friend in every aspect. The Arabs were very fond of Pakistani people too and still are, to a certain extent. Their admiration extended to Pakistan's armed forces, educational infrastructure and political know-how. Many of the young princes and sheikhs went to study at some of Pakistan's academic institutions in the early sixties and thus developed a love of the nation and its people ever since. In return Pakistan always had the Arab State's back in terms of military support and training. This was particularly true for the former Trucial States who did not have the military expertise or system in place to train

6

their own armed forces and so the Pakistani Army did the honours. Few people also know the fact that at one point the national flag carrier Pakistan International Airlines (PIA) was commissioned by the UAE to train and develop systems and staff for the creation of the now world-renowned Emirates airline. In addition, PIA helped with the establishment of Malaysian and Singapore Airlines. It is a fact that I sometimes find difficult to believe due to the current poor and fledgling state of PIA in current times.

The seven Emirates which now make up what we know as the United Arab Emirates used to be called the Trucial States during colonial British rule before gaining independence. Oil exploration had not yet reached as far as the Emirates, but there were inklings that there was oil to be found in the region however nobody would ever have imagined the scale of which to be discovered later. Only Abedi was one of the very few who knew what this small tiny region on the coast of Arabia was worth and the potential oil wealth it would deliver in times to come. Therefore, much before the idea of BCCI, Abedi set out to develop and nurture a meaningful relationship with the Arab world and their leaders. As early as 1965 when Abu Dhabi had nothing and not many had heard of Sheikh Zayed, Abedi and a trusted aide flew a hired aircraft to gain an audience with the Sheikh. Knowing the importance of gifts and hospitality in the Arab culture, Abedi took with him a beautiful hand-woven Persian rug, which he carried himself and presented to the Sheikh. The beautiful element was the fact that neither could Abedi speak Arabic nor could the Sheikh speak Urdu/English. They both communicated *through their eyes*.

His initial mission was to provide banking services to the Gulf region. However due to Agha Sahab's charming and charismatic personality, Sheikh Zayed developed a strong warmth for him and they developed a strong trust which would prove mutually beneficial for both in the future. From the start both men had lots in common – humble modest beginnings, honest noble intentions, love of poetry and rugs to mention a few. But the catalyst in this relationship remained the fact the Sheikh had enormous increasing wealth but lacked the financial knowledge to cultivate this wealth. In the sixties the entire region was a desert and so it was common for the Sheikh to store his money under beds and carpet flooring or store cash in the palace rooms. This was a huge dilemma for the Sheikh as there were no banks in the region or near the palace. If the Sheikh wanted to inspect his wealth in person then it would be a great ordeal for his workers to transport entire containers of gold and cash for him to inspect. Naturally being a seasoned financier, Abedi provided a solution for all the Sheikh's problems and began to handle all of the ruler's financial matters. From 1967 onwards Abedi was effectively acting as Sheikh Zayed's personal finance manager and banker as well as having the authority to invest the Sheikh's money overseas. Such was the nature of friendship and mutual trust between Agha Sahab and the Sheikh. It was around the same time in 1967 when Agha Sahab sent a team of dynamic aides to each Trucial State to establish and develop a relationship with the late HH Sheikh Rashid Al Maktoum, Ruler of Dubai. This bustling smaller Emirate was an hour away from Abu Dhabi and known as the trade hub for the shipping industry and other businesses. It was a far cry from the modern and glitzy Dubai we see today with hardly a high rise building in sight. The seaport city was always more cosmopolitan than the quiet capital of Abu Dhabi which is more conservative and traditional in comparison. Ashraf Nawabi was sent to Dubai initially for six months to source out further business opportunities but he soon wanted to return to Pakistan after his assignment was drawing to end due to the difficult and primitive living conditions in those times. It took considerable persuasion by Agha Sahab to make him stay and assure him of the fruits that the region would bear in the near future. He was spot on and Mr. Nawabi never looked back nor regretted that decision to stay on.

The ties between Abedi and Sheikh Zayed were strengthened further during the Sheikh's frequent trips to Pakistan for 'hunting' and holidays. Abedi left no stone unturned for his important guest and his entourage on these hunting trips and even established a protocol department at UBL which would cater for the Sheikh's each and every need. From the building and upkeep of the Sheikh's palaces in Pakistan, to travel and entertainment – even the red carpet at the airport was provided by Abedi and his colleagues at UBL.

It is important to repeat here, which very few people recollect, the fact that Sheikh Zayed and the Trucial States were largely unknown abroad in those days. Even after gaining independence, Sheikh Zayed was denied the importance and status that would normally be attributed to a leader of an independent and developing nation. He felt mostly sidelined and complained that he wasn't given the attention that was bestowed upon leaders of neighbouring Arab States. Consequently he praised and favoured Abedi as it was he who first extended VIP State protocol and reception to the Sheikh when nobody even knew who he was. Due to Abedi's efforts and introduction of the Sheikh to consequent Pakistani leaders such as Field Marshal Ayub Khan and Yahya Khan, it was then Pakistan which became the first country to honour and give recognition to the newly created UAE by inviting the Sheikh on an official State visit.

One of Agha Sahab's nephews, who resided in his family home in Karachi back in the late sixties, described to me how Abedi transformed the area and land near his home for a place befitting the arrival of a King. He would arrange a fleet of Mercedes limousines and Land Rovers for the Sheikh and his entourage that would take them hunting which was a passion for the Sheikh. This relationship of Sheikh Zayed with Abedi and Pakistan strengthened even further in years to come.

Abedi became more involved in the financial matters of the Sheikh as his personal wealth grew. Therefore Abedi was the perfect man to handle this wealth and provide efficient banking services to a region that was alien to this concept. The personal wealth of the Sheikh along with the wealth of the region was to rocket and rise to tumultuous levels from 1971 onwards, which was when the UAE was established officially and the oil prices began to rise.

Abedi was frustrated and irate in 1971, with his passport confiscated by Bhutto's Government and UBL months away from being destroyed, but was hell bent on trying to meet Sheikh Zayed to seek his backing for a new bank. However in order to do that he needed to get out of the country.

According to Pakistan's federal secretary at the time, Abedi checked into the Intercontinental hotel in Rawalpindi and told his colleagues to pull strings to get him an appointment with Bhutto's Finance minister Mubashir Hassan. Naturally given the unorthodox measures Bhutto had recently placed, Abedi's team were unable to secure a meeting with the Finance minister. Abedi was intrigued to find out why this was the case and inquired as to what exactly was said during the refusal. It was then relayed to him by his team that Mubashir Hassan had explicitly and most rudely refused to meet Abedi in an arrogant manner. Upon hearing this news, Abedi sought Mubashir's residential address and positioned himself outside his gate the very next morning. As the Finance secretary's car left for the office, the arrogant man looked at Abedi (who was patiently waiting outside) through his car window but sneered at him angrily and ignored him. This episode would be repeated over the next several mornings until one morning Mubashir asked his driver to stop the car and while pulling down his window asked Abedi: "What is it that you want and what is needed to get rid of you?"

"I want to speak with you for ten minutes only" Abedi replied. Mubashir Hassan granted Abedi the meeting which took place at his office in Rawalpindi and it lasted for over an hour. Abedi left the Finance secretary's office with his passport and excitedly jumped on a plane to Abu Dhabi.

The UAE had been created and Sheikh Zayed was King and absolute ruler. Agha Hasan Abedi was his trusted confidante and had made the Sheikh a very happy man over the years. It was uncommon for the Sheikh to say 'no' to people who were dear to him and especially to somebody as close to him as Abedi. During this trip, Abedi described to the Sheikh the unstable state of affairs in Pakistan and pledged to him the idea of a new international bank that would not be controlled or hindered by any local government but would be focused on helping the developing countries as well as bridging the gap between the Third World and the West. The Sheikh was onboard and pledged full support to Abedi's new bank which would be truly international in nature.

Abedi was elated and for the next few months focused his efforts to find an established partner to give his bank credibility and stature of international calibre.

For him, there would be no better partner than the American powerhouse – Bank of America. In February 1972, having carefully crafted an enterprising business proposal with the backing of one of the richest men in the world, Abedi flew to New York and secured a meeting with Roy P.M. Carlson (head of Bank of America's MENA region) at the famous Waldorf Astoria Hotel on Park Avenue. Abedi on future numerous occasions had termed this as the 'historic meeting' which he also described as destiny and the 'will of God'.

The meeting was a success although Roy Carlson said he needed some time to give a final decision after consultation with other directors at the Bank. However only after a couple of months of waiting, Roy Carlson delivered the epic news that Bank of America had agreed to inject the initial $2.5 million capital needed to give life to BCCI. Why did the Bank of America agree to this relatively unknown financier from Pakistan? The answer is simple: Bank of America was trying desperately hard in recent years to establish a presence in the Middle East with little success. Their competitors and other American banks had already established some presence in the Gulf region and Bank of America also wanted a piece of the cake. Naturally, Abedi's proposition was enticing for them to invest the initial capital in return for a 30% stake in this exciting new venture as it would undoubtedly bring access to Sheikh Zayed along with a slice of the Gulf-oil boom money that was on its way. In fact, the Bank of America were so desperate for a foothold in the Middle East at the time that they agreed to Abedi's distinctive condition that all management and control of the bank would lie solely with him. So the deal was a win–win situation for both sides. Abedi gained his credible American partner and Bank of America got Middle Eastern access.

On September 22nd 1972, Abedi joined his new fellow colleagues at Bank of America's rooftop headquarters in San Francisco for a celebratory luncheon which was hosted by Roy Carlson. The mood was festive as Abedi had registered and incorporated the Bank of Credit and Commerce International S.A. (Societe Anonyme) at Luxembourg.

Luxembourg is a tiny Duchy state in the heart of Europe and was known for its banking and tax friendly status. It also allowed Abedi to let BCCI be free of foreign control and Governmental hassle which he experienced with UBL at the hands of Pakistan's former Prime Minister Zulfikar Ali Bhutto. He wanted BCCI to be a truly international bank with no single home country. This was a reality in essence but also came with its disadvantages like not having a single regulatory body and thus having to deal with multiple instead. However the new bank was set up and the educated banking elite from all corners of the world, especially from Pakistan started to join the BCCI as staff.

Abedi took the cream of his first bank UBL with him to BCCI. The initial seventeen bankers, who were the first batch of BCCI staff were handpicked from UBL by Abedi and taken to Beirut in Lebanon in August 1972 for a roundtable meeting at the Phoenicia Hotel. In the meeting, Abedi explained the plans for the new bank and handed over the blueprint details whilst delegating duties to his deputies. Many ex-UBL staff were reluctant to join BCCI at first as they were fearful that they would lose their benefits of completing ten years of service with UBL. Mr. Abedi reassured all his colleagues that the benefits that they would attain from employment at BCCI would be tenfold of those which they received at UBL. One such loyal deputy was Mr. Swaleh Naqvi who many have known to be Abedi's 'right hand man'. He was the most loyal colleague anybody could ever ask for with an impeccable character and excellent banking credentials. He stuck by Abedi through thick and thin till the very end and became BCCI's first Chief Executive Officer, whilst Abedi remained President.

With $2.5 million startup capital, BCCI began operations in a small office in the desert city of Abu Dhabi. It was hard times for the bankers who started there and they put up with tough living conditions at first, living in 'mess-type' flats at the very beginning. However this was a short-lived transition period whilst the city of Abu Dhabi, UAE's capital was also changing around them. New buildings and hotels were being constructed and the team at BCCI was adamant to solicit new business and deposits with an aim to become the UAE's biggest bank.

It is relevant to note that in none of my interviews with the initial employees of BCCI who were closest to Abedi, did they even hint towards any malicious intent or irregular activity during the setting up of the bank. This in turn automatically negates the notion of commentators and investigators who in the past have described BCCI as an institution that was set up specifically for crime and that Abedi had criminal intentions which were embedded in his management. Hassan Parvez, one of the first batch of BCCI officers who was posted at Beirut soon after the roundtable meeting in 1972 described how primitive and humble the beginnings of BCCI actually were. He used to have a small apartment behind the Yaldazar restauarant on Rouche Street. The living room was used as an office for BCCI and his first job, under the guidance of a senior manager by the name of Mr. Vilayat Hussein Abidi and Mr. S.M. Akhtar, was to produce stationery for the new bank. The designs for the various forms and documents had been conceived by BCCI executives while flying between Abu Dhabi, Beirut and London. In those early days, every effort was made to save costs and expenses. So, instead of renting a warehouse for the stationery, Mr. V.H. Abidi rented the basement of the apartment block where he was living and therefore very soon it was crammed full of registers, forms and documents. A few weeks later construction work started on BCCI's first flagship branch in Abu Dhabi. As stated earlier, things were so primitive in the desert city in 1972 that everything had to be imported from Beirut. Hence Hassan Parvez was assigned the task to buy carpets, wallpaper, furniture and fittings all to the specific tastes and requirement of the President. Once the procurement and shipping was complete, he proceeded to Abu Dhabi to join other colleagues as a trainee officer at the newly-opened branch.

It was evident and clear from the beginning that BCCI placed a heavy emphasis on marketing and even more so on personal customer service which was the priority. In the first few months of operation there were only a handful dozen or so employees based at the Abu Dhabi HQ. They were headed by Swaleh Naqvi, who at the time was general manager of the Middle East region who was strongly supported by Zafar Iqbal, Ashraf Nawabi, Dildar Rizvi, Bashir Tahir, Shafqat Bokhari, Azizullah Chaudhry, Iqbal Rizvi, Basharat Malik and Saleem Siddiqi among others. Mr. Naqvi began to divide his staff into marketing teams of twos. The commercial area of Abu Dhabi was split up into different areas and each team was assigned to an area. The teams were instructed to visit every office, every shop and every company in the designated area to offer the services of BCCI and win new business while introducing themselves. It was during these days that we can witness the dedication of the staff who worked honestly through sheer hard work and humility. All the people who were there at the beginning came together for a single goal and purpose to expand the bank's base. It is difficult to this day to find such love, sincerity, faithfulness and devotion to a single cause in a business-related environment whilst working as a team (and this happened over thirty years ago in the desert sands). Everyone at that first branch from the general manager down to the junior clerk had one desire and ambition which was to see BCCI grow.

This unity of purpose propelled BCCI in a few short years into the ivy league of international banks. To demonstrate this unity, one time the government of Abu Dhabi had announced a scheme of land compensation that amounted to millions of dirhams. The beneficiaries were several hundred private individuals, the majority of whom were local Emirati citizens. The cheques were to be given out at the Ministry of Finance, which at the time was housed in a very old, two storey building. A long queue formed outside the Ministry. Despite the great heat, there was no shade and no cover. The marketing teams caught this news and immediately mobilised themselves as they saw this as a fantastic opportunity to open valuable accounts and make new relationships. The eager and enthusiastic teams proceeded to the Ministry, taking with them a table, two chairs and a crate of cold drinks. They established their remote mobile BCCI branch outside in the open, in full glare of the scorching heat and sun. (This method is reminiscent of Abedi's mobile Habib Bank branch outside the KMC earlier in the fifties). As soon as someone had received his cheque, they offered him an ice cold drink to quench his thirst and invited him to deposit his money with them. On the first day of this initiative, the new BCCI marketing team opened forty accounts with a total value of approximately 500,000 dirhams (which would be equivalent to more than 100,000 GBP Sterling or $150,000 US dollars) which was a gigantic amount in 1972. Imagine this collection of deposits on the very first day of soliciting business in the desert heat. It was an unprecedented success. However, when they returned to the site on the next day, they noticed that officers from a rival bank had taken note of BCCI's success and had already set up shop and started soliciting deposits. The rival bank had about five tough and imposing looking staff who were seemingly surrounding and hounding clients who came out the Ministry and guided them to their table where they were strongly encouraged to open an account. The BCCI staff quickly calculated that they could not compete with those aggressive figures and so immediately sent for reinforcement in the form of an officer called Mr. Malik who along with being well known for his warm, friendly and jovial personality, was endowed with an impressive and imposing physique! Soon after his arrival at the site, most of the remaining beneficiaries opened their accounts at the BCCI table. Such was the marketing strategy in the early days of BCCI, where a smile, honesty, warmth coupled with immaculate customer service would go a long way. The false rumours of bribery, threats and illegal solicitation of clients was far from the truth. The method adopted was simple and honest which is how banking should be, but hardly ever practised in today's world.

From my interviews of ex-BCCI senior management and staff, I have heard many stories about the early days and there are countless such instances where we see the true humble intentions of all the staff led by the vision of Agha Sahab. The vast majority of the officers he recruited were from humble, educated and devoted backgrounds. The focus of recruitment was not the years of banking experience one possessed or how prestigious his alma mater and undergrad university was, but more interest was shown in the candidate's personality, family values, presentation and dignity. During one actual interview, Mr. Abedi hardly spent a moment reviewing the young man's qualifications or credentials. Instead he was exploring the psyche of the young man's mind and asking him pertinent questions regarding his personal tastes and interests. When one officer said he had absoloutely no idea about banking whatsoever, Mr. Abedi asked him "so tell me what do you know about then, what is your passion?" "Cooking" the young man replied. Mr. Abedi smiled and said "what is your favourite dish and describe to me how you cook it." The young man seemed puzzled and thought it was a trick question yet he continued to elaborate on how his favourite dish was 'maash ki daaal' (lentils), which also happened to be one of Mr. Abedi's favourite dishes so his eyes started to sparkle slightly as the young man described the preparation method. Once the description was complete, the young man walked out the office with an appointment letter to join the new bank as a trainee officer and BCCI would teach him everything there is to know about banking in addition to enrolling him on a prestigious global banking course. Mr. Abedi was a people's person and loved to probe into people's personalities whilst enriching their lives and enhancing their qualities and strong points. It is a quality that we should all incorporate in ourselves by focusing on our strengths always.

When we look back in retrospect, the timing of BCCI's birth was perfectly mastered by Abedi in lieu of events that were taking place at the time.

This can be clearly seen following the Bhutto nationalization programme and the Middle Eastern Oil boom that was soon to follow. BCCI was a benefactor of both and success was due more to the latter as Libya's Gaddafi tightened his fists. However the real impetus and catalyst came on December 22nd, 1973. The ministers of petroleum of six of the top oil-producing countries in the Gulf (now known as the Gulf Co-operation Council or GCC) gathered together in Tehran at the invitation of Mohammad Reza Pahlavi – the Shah of Iran. Cumulatively these nations were part of what we know as OPEC (Organisation of Petroleum Exporting Countries). Newspapers and media around the world were frolicking at the reports of further rises in the price of oil as in the last two months before the meeting, the price of a barrel of oil had doubled to $5.12.

The Shah held a well-attended press conference at 9am the same day and announced that the price of oil would double once more, hence quadrupling the price of a barrel in a space of a few weeks to $11.65. This would change the course of history, literally. That very press conference and announcement had almost shifted the realms of power from West to East in a matter of seconds and the following weeks saw hundreds of billions of petrodollars flow into the coffers of OPEC nations, their leaders and of course – filled the deposits of BCCI abundantly. The timing was excellent and this demonstrates how BCCI catapulted to new heights that were fuelled by the petrodollars of the Middle East and there was absoloutely nothing wrong with this. No illegal deposits, no bribery and no fraud. Just pure perfect timing and a spout of good luck coupled with God's will and excellent management. The downside was the obvious outside jealousy that came with such success and external forces came into play much sooner than expected. The traditional western powers were soon humbled by the Oil embargo and the unknown Sheikhs of the desert were suddenly turned into important and super-rich world leaders.

Not only did Sheikh Zayed get what he wanted in terms of international importance through the oil boom, but through the creation and apparent ownership of BCCI, he acquired the global prestige that came with owning a successful global enterprise which was the envy of the world.

A new global power had been born. The rest of the world watched with its tongue hanging out.

Chapter Three

Redefining banking

*"Conventional management is the development of work through people.
Real management is developing people through work"*
—*Agha Hasan Abedi, President – BCCI.*

Abedi's focus on developing people especially his staff at BCCI
was never-ending. Whilst he was accelerating and attaining great
success, he wanted his people to follow him and do even better.
The culture of BCCI was being developed along with its people.
The organisation was not known as a company and neither were
the people called employees. Everybody was part of the 'BCCI
family' where each and every individual could attribute themselves
to the success of BCCI in some form or the other. Everybody
had a special place in the bank, nobody was too big or small,
everybody was treated equally and everybody was coined as simply
an 'executive'. Apart from the obvious positions of President and
CEO, there were no hierarchies present at the bank and that was the
way Abedi wanted it. The culture of 'open-plan offices' and walk-
in glass offices for CEOs practised today was being practised long
before at BCCI in the seventies.

There was a reason behind the success of BCCI and the reason
was not criminality or dishonesty. It was the collective ambition
and tunnel vision of a leader and his staff combined with humility
that was the recipe for success. This model can be applied to any
organisation and I urge all managers to do the same.

BCCI's assets rose from $200 million in 1973 to over $2.2 billion
in 1977. In just those four years alone, BCCI's network of branches
increased from nineteen offices in five countries to 146 offices in

thirty-two countries. This figure quadrupled in the years to come. BCCI was growing faster than it had imagined and this was all part of Abedi's ambition for it to be the largest bank in the world. This speed of growth in hindsight, was probably not one of Abedi's best moves. However one can understand why he wanted to grow so fast. He wasn't getting any younger, hence his time was limited and his hunger for expansion grew. He was a man in a hurry and this sometimes worried his associates also however they never dared to question his opinion as they looked up to Abedi with reverence. He was an extremely wise and ambitious gentleman who had the uncanny knack of 'getting it right' most of the time and predicted financial outcomes of political situations. There would be the odd occasion when some of the bolder senior figures like the Head of Communications John Hilbery would voice their concerns on the question of opening operations in a certain politically-volatile country. Mr. Abedi would listen to everyone and take their opinions into serious consideration, however in the majority of cases he would continue nonetheless, and then when the bank's profits would prosper in that particular country or region, he would prove their reservations to be incorrect with a smile.

While Abu Dhabi was the main HQ and place of birth for BCCI, simultaneously operations were being set up in Luxembourg and London, the financial capital of the world. The first branch in the UK started up on the second floor at 60, Mark Lane which served as a regional office also. There were only twelve BCCI family members at the beginning and from the start they all worked tirelessly round the clock for months on end without a break. These long hours were not imposed on the staff but they did it out of choice to succeed as a team. Soon another branch was opened in Mayfair's most prestigious district at 25 Park Lane right next to the Hilton Park Lane Hotel and the location was handpicked by Abedi for strategic and logistical purposes. He knew the importance of attracting high net-worth clients and so made sure that BCCI catered to their every need. The early seventies saw an influx of wealthy Arabs and Sheikhs with pockets full of oil-cash descend upon their favourite destination, central London, like bees on honey. They went from insane shopping sprees at the world-famous Harrods store to all-nighters at the Sheraton Casino in Knightsbridge. Naturally they needed banking services at their disposal wherever they went, either to withdraw or deposit and BCCI was the bank of choice as they were familiar with them back home in the Middle East already and made good relationships with the bankers. Not only did BCCI come handy at providing an urgent personalized service 24–7 for these wealthy Arab clients, but they also facilitated the tycoons in buying up investments and pricey properties in and around central London to add to their bulging and ever-expanding portfolio. It is common knowledge that the Arab's love affair with London is an ongoing one and will not diminish anytime soon. It only takes a glance around the glitzy Mayfair neighbourhood to notice their presence which increases more so during the summer when we see London infested with Arab money as they spend millions on shipping their expensive cars to roam around the city and enjoy the best nightlife it has to offer before rushing back home to observe the Islamic holy month of Ramadan. Today we see the shops and the big brands taking full advantage of these wealthy men and women by luring them to their stores and hotels but back then it was BCCI who was the biggest player in this very lucrative game. Abedi had spotted this opportunity long before anybody else as usual and suddenly the British public saw BCCI branches popping up around the posh and exclusive locations of central London.

By 1977, in only five years BCCI had a strong network of forty-five branches in the UK alone (expansion was capped and limited at this number by the Bank of England which was a prejudice in itself but shall be addressed later). Each and every branch had the traditional trademarks of a typical BCCI branch that distinguished it from other banks which incorporated sleek and new designs, expensive and tasteful furniture and most importantly the most immaculately dressed and well-mannered set of personal bankers. By setting the bar so high in terms of presentation and quality, Abedi was revolutionizing banking in itself and by having numerous branches at most prestigious locations, he was also making a statement of BCCI's financial strength and making its presence felt – which it did quite profoundly. So much so in fact that rival banks looked at the BCCI branch network in awe and were gobsmacked at their growth. All BCCI staff were the envy and talk of the town at fashionable dinner parties and first class airport lounges. The point of the branches were to cater for the growing need of the customers and it was an excellent marketing strategy also since each BCCI branch was an advertisement of power, prosperity and success on its own. The interior decor and design of every BCCI branch around the world was comparable to a hotel suite and while depositing money one would think that they were sitting on the leather sofas with marble flooring of a five-star hotel foyer reception.

If you look around today at the receptions of distraught and ghastly-looking high-street banks that look as though they havn't seen a renovation in decades then you don't blame BCCI to be wanting to stand out from the crowd especially when they were handling such important clientele. I sometimes avoid going to my local bank branch as I get depressed just looking at the dullness of the place hence I am taking full advantage of online banking. On that note BCCI was one of the first banks in Europe to fully computerize all its systems and procedures, a step ahead of everybody else.

The luxury and personalized service was not limited to wealthy clients though, each and every customer of BCCI was offered VIP treatment which included a customary offer of a hot tea or coffee served by waiting staff while you queued at the cashier. This was a personalized banking service at its best and that too BCCI introduced in the seventies. Natwest and others in the UK have only recently started measures to help speed up queues at lunchtime and have longer opening hours on Saturdays. BCCI would always go that extra mile for their customers no matter who it was or how big or small their deposit was.

This concept of personalised service was introduced by Abedi from the origins of hospitality that was inbuilt in him and the Arabs alike. This was something that the West and traditional banking circles failed to understand and probably never will. In the Middle East when banking was still alien, people would trust individuals and not the bank/institution he worked for. Hence the stress on developing a personal relationship with all clients while offering them the best customer service that one could offer was the mission for the bank and the staff.

But again, the best advantage to the top-end clients was that they were never more than a few steps away from a BCCI branch. You step out of Harrods and directly opposite you would see a fabulous premium BCCI branch located at 171–175 Brompton Road, Knightsbridge (which currently is occupied by the Burberry fashion label). You step outside the Ritz hotel and you will see a branch directly opposite at 198 Piccadilly. In fact, there were almost four BCCI branches on the short stretch of road at Park Lane alone going from Marble Arch till the end of Hyde Park corner. Such was the impact and message that Abedi wanted to create that BCCI had truly arrived and was here to stay.

BCCI also constructed and commissioned its own buildings wherever planning permission permitted such as one of the first state of the art all glass buildings ever in the heart of London at Earls Court (249, Cromwell Road which now houses Metro Bank and formerly Malaysia airlines). It would not be unusual to see a fleet of Mercedes cars and limousines outside prominent branches that would be ready at the disposal of VIP clients and customers.

The BCCI family members i.e. the staff would also enjoy considerable benefits and perks that one would associate with a growing and successful international powerhouse. But it is to be noted that the salaries and bonuses, although excellent for those days, are nowhere near the unjustified amounts dispersed to investment bankers in recent times. Hence I found it laughable when journalists would write about the high salaries and perks of BCCI officers attributing them to wrongdoing, when we now have salaries which are multiple times that of BCCI staff today but they all seem to be doing 'legitimate banking practices'. Nobody for once pointed a finger at the high salaries of city workers as everybody wanted to be in their position. It was only after the Credit crunch and crash of 2008 that people started to snarl and stick their middle finger up at 'greedy' city bankers. Before the going got tough everybody wanted to be their friend!

BCCI's aggressive strategy for the UK region was also there for two more reasons which many believe to be the core reasons. First is the obvious one, which is that the UK and specifically London is seen as the financial capital of the world like New York and so it needed to have a substantial base there. Secondly, which many people underestimate was the important function of catering to the needs of the ethnic minority immigrant population based in the UK who were primarily from Pakistani, Indian and Bangladeshi backgrounds. The original BCCI branches brought together the vision of the United Bank and close links with the ethnic community it already had in place. These links were highlighted and strengthened by the location of regional branches in areas such as Bradford, Manchester, Birmingham, Southall, Leeds and East London who all have densely-populated immigrant communities. All of these communities needed a reliable and trustworthy bank to transport hard-earned money from the UK to their home country. This was also the strategy adopted in the Middle East where labourers from the sub-continent preferred BCCI to be their bank of choice as there would be BCCI branches in all the home countries hence making international transfers easy and quick. In those days not much trust was placed on Western Union and speed cash services but BCCI was a reputable and reliable organisation with presence in all corners of the globe which made such transactions worry free for the customers as their loved ones would simply collect the cash at their local BCCI branch in India or Pakistan or anywhere in the world. In addition the UK Asian community had a strong business community which comprised of many small businesses who took out loans on favourable terms with the bank and relied on them for their continued business. Many of these were shopkeepers and cash-and-carry owners which made up a considerable portion of the Asian market at the time.

However as the pattern of the Asian community changed with the influx of those from Uganda and elsewhere, the bank's pattern of clientele and operation also adapted accordingly. The activities began to broaden from being ethnic deposit orientated to providing fully-fledged commercial banking facilities for the whole of the community.

Once the network of forty-five UK branches had been reached and capped in 1977, the phase of rapid growth in branch openings had ended and the priority switched to consolidation and growth of individuals and branches alike. Kemal Shoaib was the first Regional General Manager of the UK region after Dildar Rizvi diligently set up the network there followed by Vilayat Hussein Abidi, Mazhar Abbas and Basheer Chowdry who all very adroitly and competently helped the UK region grow to be one the most efficient and profitable ones whilst adhering to the law and regulations of the UK banking system. The crown jewel however, was the state of the art and swanky UK head office of the group constructed at 100 Leadenhall Street which housed seven floors. Mr. Abedi shared the top floor with his senior executives who were all in open plan offices as he wanted to change the 'closed-door manager' culture.

Abedi was extremely meticulous about appearance and presentation through which he made his important first impressions and this was evident from the bespoke branches and sharply dressed bank staff. He even had a personal attendant who would be in charge of his desk and have the task of keeping everything in order given his obsession with spruceness and uniformity. One time he relieved his desk assistant of his position so that the young man could move to another role as he never wanted to keep anybody in one position for too long to avoid risk that it would hinder their personal development. A new candidate who happened to be an Englishman was selected and on his first day of reporting to work he was running slightly late due to London underground tube delays. He hurriedly rushed into the elevator while sorting himself out and at the same time another extremely well dressed gentleman entered the lift and stood beside him. The gentleman looked at the new recruit, who was busy fixing his jacket, and asked him if he worked at the bank. "Yes, in fact today is my first day, I'm running slightly late! I have a very crucial role to perform. I'm going to be in charge of the President's desk! Do you think I'm looking smart enough?" he said anxiously. The other gentleman stepped slightly forward and adjusted the young man's tie knot while patting him on the shoulder saying: "Yes you are looking very smart and I have a feeling that the President is going to like you". Having said that he left the elevator at his floor. The young man continued onto the HR department to collect his joining pack and to receive further instructions. Mr. Abdul Hafeez, who was heading the HR department received him and pointed out that he was late on his first day and the young man apologised as he was being led towards the President's office. As he entered the President's cabin, he was startled and pleasantly surprised to acknowledge that the man sitting at the President's desk was Mr. Abedi, the same gentleman who had fixed his tie in the elevator just moments earlier.

Here it would be fitting to clarify for those who assumed that the bank was a Pakistani Muslim institution and hired only their own kind or gave preferential treatment to Pakistanis or Muslims are gravely misinformed. The BCCI family was one of the most diverse and multicultural of its era. It is true, to start with, that the majority of the Senior Management positions were taken by British and Pakistanis but that was due to the origins and situation in which the bank was founded upon. Even at the early stage, however, the Bank of America also had advisory staff on the board of the bank and seconded their own staff. As the bank grew to other locations, whether it be the Francophone world under the late Iqbal Rizvi, the Americas under Khusro Karamat Elley or Shafique Ur Rehman and Far East Region under Dildar Rizvi, the utmost effort and preference was indeed given to accommodate and recruit local talent from those countries. This was in part fulfilling the aim of being a truly international bank with its roots or origins from the Muslim world.

Even for the sake of argument, if we take on the critics accusations as having some form of validity, then even then what is the harm of an international bank with a Third World focus in hiring staff from those ethnic minorities? There certainly was no evidence or case that surfaced at the bank of discrimination of any form amongst the employees and the recruitment was executed at all levels following a strict equal opportunities policy. Every nationality was given equal importance at all levels of seniority and management and promotions were awarded upon merit, not sucking up. There are many who even went so far as saying BCCI was predominantly favouring and handpicking employees from Shia Muslim backgrounds to prominence. The bottom line was the HR department never looked at the skin colour, race, religion or sexual orientation of an employee or client. The bank followed the simple principle that everybody is the same in God's eyes and everybody is very important. To confirm this, the head of HR in the UK was an English gentleman by the name of Alfred Oriss.

Abedi made a point at many meetings and conferences to make sure that each and every member present at the meetings felt that he/she was as important as he was. He spent hours delivering lectures on how the importance of 'being important' was. At one annual conference of international staff which was held in Geneva, Abedi sat at the front of the glorious historic hall and picked out individual managers and addressed them by name whilst asking them pertinent questions along with asking them how important they thought they were. On one occasion he asked a colleague "Mr. Banerjee. Are you important? I think you are very important. Do you think the gentleman sitting next to you is important?" And so on. In these conferences, which would last for hours and hours into the night, some managers would duck or hide behind brochures in fear of being asked a philosophical question by Mr. Abedi! He once asked Javed Ali Khan at another conference in Vienna: "What is the psyche of your mind and being?" This is not a normal question which any President of an international bank would be asking one of his managers at a meeting, but such was the style and charisma of Mr. Abedi which would make him distinctive and more revered by his followers.

The following of Abedi became almost like a cult. Every year these annual conferences would take place in the grandest of halls in the world's finest architectural masterpieces. The favourite venue was Vienna among others and BCCI officers would be flown in from all corners of the world to attend this three-day conference to hear their leader speak. Abedi would always be on the move travelling to visit regional offices and hold meetings. A more detailed look at the content of these meetings will be explored in a later chapter. However almost all ex-employees of the bank have mentioned to me that practically every aspect of their moral and personal aims were discussed apart from banking in itself. Banking and profit although an important part of BCCI's goals, was never the main focal point at any of Abedi's meetings. He was more philosophical and metaphysical in his speech, talking about humility and giving and the bank's moral purpose merging with its material purpose. His speech would not be fully understood by his colleagues at times, which they openly admit yet they still followed him.

A similar analogy would be during the fight for the creation of Pakistan, the Quaid-E-Azam Muhammad Ali Jinnah would be addressing masses of thousands of illiterate people at huge rallies, none of whom could understand a word that Jinnah spoke because his speeches were in English. However they always knew that whatever he was saying was the truth and that he was on the righteous path while fighting for justice and humanity. I used to find the same example in the political campaigning of cricketer-turned-politician Imran Khan, although his speech delivery in Urdu has vastly improved since he first started out.

At BCCI, employees found that they were part of something bigger. They were not just slogging out the nine-to-five working week. They would actively work longer hours out of their own will in order to achieve the greater collective purpose of BCCI and its regional offices. Everybody also believed and were experiencing the reaping of benefits which this hard work was producing and eventually paid off. They had all finally found a sense of security in a truly global organisation which was on a par with the international elite of banking and found a new 'family' and institution that they could call 'home'. It was a greater purpose for the bank, which transformed materially for themselves personally when they secured a mortgage paying regular instalments, drove a nice car, sent their kids to the best schools and went on regular family trips abroad. All of these 'material' comforts encompassed what we call 'living the dream' as it were, and BCCI was fulfilling it in full for its staff.

The secret of its operating success was of course well documented in interviews given by staff and on the odd rare occasion by Abedi himself. The main concentration was short term trade transactions, liquidity and people-orientated street banking of a highly professional and personalized nature.

The bank was also at the forefront of all innovative activities and banking practices being a step ahead of its competitors. A famous example was in the early eighties when Travellers Cheques were launched across the world by VISA International. BCCI was one of the first banks to incorporate travellers cheques into its UK operation and used it as a formidable marketing strategy which proved to be immensely profitable. Travellers cheques were an ideal product for the bank as they were easy to sell, highly profitable, risk free and frequently provided new leads to other business opportunities. They were so successful in marketing this product that a sales target was achieved in 1986 for over $1 billion which led management to set an even more ambitious target of $10 billion for 1990. Abedi termed travellers cheques as 'a profitful instrument of relationship'. In the UK, the bank established a relationship with British Airways and invited high users of the product to join an elite club which offered airline discounts and other perks. In March 1986, the bank signed an agreement with the authorities for the Commonwealth Games which were held in Edinburgh, Scotland. This agreement appointed them as the official provider of travellers cheques to the Games, which are the second most important games on the sports calendar after the Olympics. BCCI began its association with VISA International in 1977 when it helped launch their credit card and then came the travellers cheques. Visa's manager of international development said in 1982: "BCCI has developed and implemented a travellers cheque programme faster than any bank I have known. And they have done it with superb professionalism. The joint vision that such a strong element in BCCI's style is undoubtedly a major factor in their success. It seems to provide a motivation beyond what a commercial organisation can normally expect". Such was the impressionable impact the bank's marketing professionalism was having around the financial industry as a whole and it was growing from strength to strength.

Another little known fact was that BCCI was helping in the development of young bankers in helping them achieve professional status and success throughout the world. This was in the form of donations and sponsoring of various educational and charitable institutions around the world. One prominent example was the sponsoring of the Centre for the Study of Financial Development by BCCI at the famous City University Business School known as CASS in London. The objective of the department at CASS was to contribute to the understanding of financial development where students would concentrate on international financial systems, less developed countries (LDCs) and the financial history of developed countries. Dr. Zannis Res, a Greek professor of Finance who was the centre's director in 1985 said: "Our priority is to further our understanding of how financial development occurs. We want to understand the inter-relationships of countries and systems, for example the North/South relationship, the relationship of oil-rich countries with developed countries etc. In this context BCCI is so interesting. It is one of the very small number of Third World Multinationals that are working to integrate the Third World with the developed countries. Unlike older and established banks, BCCI is not seen as the agent of any government. It belongs to a new generation of institutions that is seeking new ways of doing business."

In early 1980, BCCI had also sponsored a lectureship in the centre for Banking and International Finance at City University. This was coupled with the prestigious 'Cambridge connection' which was initiated in November 1982 when Sir James Callaghan, former Prime Minister of Britain, told Mr. Abedi about the idea for a new trust at Cambridge University. Cambridge was provided substantial funding by the bank for scholarships and development by creating this special Trust. Earlier on, Britain at the time began to charge higher fees for overseas students wishing to study in the UK and thus this threatened Cambridge's continued commitment to open its doors to talent from all over the world to its world-class academics. The university responded by setting up the trust helped by funding from Abedi and BCCI to bring to the university outstanding students from the Commonwealth (which for its purposes included Pakistan, Sudan and Burma) and within the first five years the trustees had achieved the seemingly unattainable target of supporting over 400 scholars. The chairman of the trust was the Prince of Wales and notable trustees were: Agha Hasan Abedi, Sir James Callaghan, L.K. Jha, Dr. Kenneth Kaunda, Sir Shridath Ramphal and Professor Arnold Cantwell Smith. The

Cambridge connection was a strong one, as was the Callaghan/ Abedi relationship. The bank supported the trust even at the worst times of financial crisis, when funds were depleting and the project was in jeopardy, BCCI always came to the rescue. Together the bank and Cambridge set up over a dozen associated trusts in places like Zimbabwe where Abedi and Callaghan travelled together on 13th August 1982 to inaugurate the Zimbabwe Cambridge Trust under the chairmanship of Robert Mugabe. In my opinion this was the most enlightened philanthropy in the grandest of styles reflecting not only the bank's far-flung interests and its concern for the developing nations, but also its President's philosophy and vision, based on the principle of giving. Not many would know about these silent philanthropic measures, as this was the practice of Abedi and his closest associates like Swaleh Naqvi who till this day does phenomenal work with the Infaq Foundation (former BCCI Foundation) in silence. This is the true beauty of giving.

The bank's corporate communications, both internal and external, were far more advanced and efficient than any other organisation of its time. The in-house magazine 'BCC International' put together by former Bank of America Director John Hillbery, was designed specifically for keeping the BCCI family up to date with the Bank's activities as well as providing an effective internal communications tool across the organisation. Having worked for some of the largest companies in the Middle East of today's world, I am still struck by the professional outlay, design and content of the bank's publications from twenty years ago. They managed to produce high quality material with such intricate and thought provoking content cultivated to motivate the employees at all levels with limited technology at the time.

It was through Abedi's ability to befriend the world's elite and make influential connections in all walks of life which collectively catapulted the bank to further success and expansion throughout the globe. Whenever there was a new branch opening in a foreign country somebody from BCCI would know somebody who knew somebody who could introduce them to somebody who would be in a position of authority with powerful contacts in that location. Though actually in the case of licence obtaining or starting operations in the new country, the leader of the nation would be befriended as Abedi had political clout almost in every country.

From Jimmy Carter to Robert Mugabe and from Muhammad Ali (Cassius Clay) to the Pope – everybody was Abedi's friend. It is no coincidence that to this day, anybody who actually knew him personally has never had anything to say about him except for words of praise and fondness. HRH the Prince of Wales was a friend of the bank and signatory of the Cambridge Trust (in addition to BCCI's John Hillbery who produced a cheque of 250,000 GBP to help the trust at a time of dire need). He also attended functions of Project 'Fullemploy', a UK charity funded by BCCI that aimed to promote the involvement of minority communities in Britain's economic life.

To contribute to the booming health industry and also to cater for the increasing number of senior Arab citizens who flew abroad for medical treatment, BCCI established the renowned state-of-the-art Cromwell Hospital in the heart of London which to this day is still known as one of the top private hospitals of the world. Cromwell became a favourite of the royal families of the Gulf and is still used heavily by foreign patients seeking world class medical facilities and is seen as a symbol of excellence.

BCCI also helped set up the Prince's Youth Business Trust (PYBT as it was known then) and on December 6th 1989, Mr. Swaleh Naqvi handed over a cheque representing part of the bank's 500,000 GBP pounds covenant to the Trust. PYBT was established in 1986 by Prince Charles for his concern of young people's lack of opportunity to become self-sufficient within the UK economy. Hence the trust would give business loans and help young people aged eighteen to twenty-five and disabled people aged eighteen to thirty to set up their own business. This was an amazing initiative funded by BCCI to help young people in the UK as it was doing all over the world. In fact, the idea behind PYBT is more relevant in current times post the 2008 financial crisis. In the height of austerity with over 2.5 million unemployed in the UK. BCCI was effectively running a small 'Dragon's Den' style initiative but in a philanthropic and non-profit making manner helping young entrepreneurs. In November 1989, BCCI's Mr. B.A. Malik was seconded to the PYBT on a full-time basis as National Co-ordinator for Community Affairs as he could understand and assess the needs of the Asian community in the UK through his perspective. Nazmu Virani, one of the most successful Asian entrepreneurs ever of that era and one of the richest Asians in the UK at the time was also a big player in PYBT, linking it to the community as well as being a loyal customer of BCCI. He was of Ugandan origin but settled in the UK and had business interests in real estate, portfolio management, hotels and small business. He offered his services to PYBT with the blessing of Prince Charles and ran it from his office of Control Securities PLC. The BCCI/PYBT connection was definitely fruitful for the bank but again it was fruitful in terms of satisfying the bank's moral purpose and not to improve its public image as stated by critics. There were many memorable evenings and gala dinners in North London that the bank would host with esteemed guests such as the late Lord Tom Boardman (former chairman of Natwest) and his wife Deirdre. On other occasions the late Sir Angus Ogilvy (husband of Princess Alexandra of Kent who is the first cousin of current Queen Elizabeth II) would attend the dinners as he was also a trustee of PYBT. Kensington Palace was regularly holding banquets in honour of the great work that PYBT was doing and a lot of this can be attributed to the BCCI connection.

We can place former US President Jimmy Carter and former Prime Minister of Great Britain Sir James Callaghan in the same category. Where Abedi helped Callaghan with the Cambridge Trust, he also helped Jimmy Carter with the funding of a philanthropic and charitable venture called Global 2000 which was set up to improve agriculture to the poorest nations. He also contributed to the Carter Foundation and established the coveted Third World Foundation and Orangi Project.

During the eighties, President Carter accompanied Abedi on the BCCI private jet all over the Third World countries visiting the poor and setting up initiatives to help people living in poverty. Carter always said that Abedi and BCCI shared his vision of a prosperous Third World where we can see developing countries stand on their own two feet and be less dependent on foreign aid. In the same vein, he announced the Third World Prize which would be given to people who have made the world a better place in some way or form and contributed to the improvement of the developing nations through hard work and dedication. Nominees and winners of the Third world prize included Nelson Mandela, Bob Geldof, the International Rice Research Institute, Indira Gandhi and many others. The *South* magazine was also funded by BCCI and headed by Altaf Gauhar and his son Humayun Gauhar who is now a renowned journalist and author. The magazine would highlight Third World issues and promoted intellectual independent thinking. There is no doubt that these great initiatives were seen by BCCI's enemies as just a 'political façade' for Abedi to further his influence peddling in high places. However the truth was that his intentions were nothing but pure and these charitable foundations are still in existence today helping thousands of people with millions of dollars. Abedi's vision and persona was much greater than petty influence peddling and 'bribery' which his critics accuse him of. It was a vision of the Third World improving its own education, economy and infrastructure with great minds and financial backing (namely through his bank) so that an empire could be built purely to help people in need. This was clearly something which the enemies of the bank did not want, as clearly this was increasingly bearing the signs of a new world order funded by opulent Arab Wealth.

All these facts raised eyebrows in the West because effectively BCCI was taking over the roles of the World Bank and the

International Monetary Fund (IMF). Abedi started to use BCCI to help Third World nations financially with short term financing. Like when Peru, Jamaica and his home country of Pakistan needed assistance to stabilise their balance of payments then Abedi obliged. In fact some say that BCCI bailed out the Pakistan government against the security 'crop of the land and soil' on about three occasions. It was at this point that Abedi began to think of another offshoot bank called the 'South Development Bank' which would be specifically for this purpose. However the adversity and hostility that BCCI and Abedi were facing from the very beginning from the West was increasingly evident, especially when it came to the notion of expansion in the United States.

Chapter Four

Ruffling feathers in Washington

By 1982, BCCI was the second fastest growing bank in the world according to *'Euromoney'* and the financial press. The rate of growth was a concern for all who were on the outside but for Abedi and the BCCI family it was a moment of triumph and rightly so.

Much before that, Abedi made it clear about his intentions of making BCCI the largest bank in the world and this disturbed many people in high places looking down from Wall Street and Threadneedle Street. However in order to gain any form of success in the ivy league of banking, he knew that he needed to make it big in America. The USA had strict laws where no foreign entity could acquire a local US bank or its affiliates. Knowing the animosity he experienced with the Federal Reserve in the US and the Bank of England in the UK, he had a fair idea that the US would not grant him a full banking licence to operate as a normal commercial and retail bank. And he was right. BCCI was allowed to open branches in the US but only as an 'agency' and not a full-service bank.

The first branch was opened in New York and the location again handpicked by Abedi at 375 Park Avenue in one of the most prestigious and sought-after buildings in New York City. He had his eye on this particular location from the early days as it happened to be directly opposite the famous Waldorf Astoria hotel where Abedi had the 'historic meeting' with the Bank of America in 1972. The battle to secure the location was fought by Khusro Karamat Elley who was BCCI's representative in the USA and setting up of the branch was handled by Dildar Rizvi who made sure every aspect of the office including the interior was in line with the traditional BCCI high-quality standard. This 'branch' was actually a representative office as were all the other agencies of BCCI in California, Florida, Houston and Chicago. This is another example (in addition to the status of licenced deposit-taker in the UK) where BCCI was shown prejudice due to its Middle Eastern roots by not being able to establish real operating branches in the US at the outset.

The fact that the bank was not allowed to offer normal banking services restricted BCCI in many ways as it was not allowed to take deposits or offer loans, however it let the bank have a presence and footprint in the USA which enabled it to nurture important relationships and help broker lucrative deals.

One such deal was the takeover of a US bank by the name of Financial General Bankshares (FGB) which was later renamed as First American Bank (FAB). It was widely rumoured in the American media that BCCI orchestrated the takeover in the seventies and that it secretly owned one of the largest banking networks (FGB) in Washington, thereby breaking US Federal banking Law. The McFadden Act also forbade inter-state banking. This was probably BCCI's most vicious allegation and one which was used resolutely and robustly by the US authorities to back its unfounded case against the bank in later years.

Let us analyse and discuss this allegation in more detail but to do this we must look historically about what was known about Abedi's intentions for the US market and for FGB in particular. The first and foremost point to acknowledge is the fact that neither did Abedi nor BCCI ever have any intention to own FGB, either secretly or otherwise, and never did it have any direct handling of the transactions of the takeover of the Washington-based bank.

One article was printed in the *Financial Times* on 17th May 1978 which was maybe deliberately shoved into obscurity that outlined Abedi's intentions about the USA and where he discussed details about FGB in an interview given to the admirable late journalist Nicholas Colchester. In the article it is clear that Abedi had big plans for the USA as soon as Bank of America had sold its 30% interest in the bank (earlier reduced to 24%) which then allowed Abedi to have a greater footprint there. It was during the same year in 1978 that speculation was circulated about the bank's secret ownership of FGB and this was totally baseless. In the article Abedi stresses that his ambitions for the USA were mainly to expand BCCI's clientele base and to facilitate the deployment of Arab wealth in the region.

The BCCI/FGB story is one which may seem very confusing when one looks at it at first yet it has been magnified and exaggerated in false terms in various books that have been written to defame the bank. Let me explain the gist of the matter to those who were equally baffled as I was when I first started investigating the story.

We can trace the tale back to when Abedi met Bert Lance, who was a close friend of President Jimmy Carter and had helped Carter win the Presidential elections in 1976 hence becoming a White House aide. Prior to being appointed as director of the office of management and budget in Washington by Carter, Lance was a shrewd financier flourishing at Financial General Bankshares (FGB), a banking holding company which owned banks in many states. This was an unusual bank because the McFadden Act forbade American local banks to engage in interstate banking however the regulators had made an exception for some reason for FGB as the bank controlled only majority shareholdings in partnership with other local investors. Lance progressed further in FGB and became President of the National Bank of Georgia (NBG), one of its subsidiaries in Atlanta in January 1975. In June the same year he became Chairman of NBG after colluding with a group of investors including Jackson T. Stephens (a prominent financier from the South) to purchase NBG stock from FGB.

Later on in September 1977, he was pressured into resigning from his public office given to him by the Carter administration amidst allegations of financial misconduct and other pending investigations by the Office of the Comptroller of the Currency (OCC). Following his indictment in May 1979 on charges of violating federal banking laws, he became under severe debt of nearly $6 million as the price of his majority stock in NBG had fallen to disastrous levels. He was on the verge of bankruptcy until he met Abedi and they became friends through the good office and goodwill of Jimmy Carter.

Lance was desperate to sell his NBG stock and Abedi agreed to help him by introducing him to potential buyers from the Middle East thereby acting as a middleman to broker the deal. This is what normally happens in the general sphere of investment banking deals whereby there is a buyer and a seller and an intermediary between the two who receives a cut of the cake from the proceeds for arranging the transactions and aligning the two parties. In this particular case, Abedi had two incentives and reasons to help Lance out of his financial mess. Firstly he was best friends with the US President Jimmy Carter and this would be beneficial to the Carter/ Abedi relationship later and enable Abedi to further his Third World Foundation initiatives and philanthropy. Secondly it would allow Abedi to execute his aim to deploy Arab wealth into the United States with seasoned investments and simultaneously nurture special relationships to market BCCI services to a wider audience which would inevitably lead to expansion.

Hence Abedi introduced Lance to Ghaith Rashad Pharaon, a well-connected Saudi tycoon who already had varied business interests (including banks) in the United States and was also one of BCCI's most influential customers. In May 1978 Pharaon bought all of Lance's NBG stock via funds from his personal investment company GRP Inc. coupled with a loan from BCCI among other sources. There was much noise over this transaction and much later First American asserted that it was BCCI that had obtained control and secret ownership of NBG in the above deal.

There was no evidence to support such an assertion and one must explore that *even if* such a notion was deemed to be true, then it wouldn't really make a substantial difference to BCCI as the NBG stock was not even on BCCI's balance sheet as assets. What benefit would BCCI derive from such a takeover which would have been branded as illegal by the regulators anyway? The main and sole role BCCI played in the NBG deal of 1978 was merely that of an intermediary and to offer a routine banking loan for one of its most important customers for a private investment.

Let's for the sake of argument, pretend that Pharaon had received a substantial loan from Citibank in Washington DC to finance his investment in shares of NBG. Would there have been headlines in the *WSJ* or *FT* that Citicorp had conspired a secret and illegal takeover of NBG and planned to attack FGB (the parent company) next? It sounds quite ridiculous when you think about it. Then again, most of the unfounded allegations upon BCCI and its senior management are laughable in the grand sphere of what is happening in the banks today.

The fact that Abedi, who happened to be the President of BCCI, made the introduction between Lance and Pharaon is the reason why the deal occurred in the first place is paramount to this dilemma. Had the CEO or another broker of another investment bank made the deal or found Lance a buyer for an ailing NBG, then would the story have been any different? So since Abedi made the deal, it is only natural that he would want his bank to be the bank of choice for a loan to one of its most coveted clients. In the same vein, it only made sense for Pharaon to turn to BCCI for a loan to make up the remainder of his capital to make the purchase of shares. Quite simple really… yet the Peter Truells of this world like to sensationalise everything, much like how I exaggerate about youths vandalizing my car on Halloween 'trick or treat' nights.

Therefore Lance had been saved and Abedi was successful in brokering a deal that bought benefits to both parties but this would lead to Lance setting his eyes on an even bigger takeover battle in the form of Financial General Bankshares. Earlier I explained why FGB was attractive given its unique exemption from the interstate banking law and also of its prime location on Capitol Hill and headquarters overlooking the White House at 740, 15th Street, Washington DC.

Due to various reasons and disagreements at board level and with the Federal Reserve in the US, large amounts of FGB stock was made available from 1977 onwards and then plans to sell the entire stock on the open market were announced. This was a golden opportunity for Bert Lance and a group of other prominent wealthy Arab Investors including Sheikh Kamal Adham (Former Saudi Head of Intelligence). The board of FGB were unhappy to see by the end of 1978 that Bert Lance and the Arab contingent had bought approximately 8% and 20% of FGB stock respectively. The board were adamant to resist the Arabs taking over such an important American bank as they looked upon the group of investors with suspicion and malice. This was evident from various mainstream press coverage during that period of the takeover battle which dug deep into the background and financials of the Arab investors who were interested in buying FGB stock and painted a less favourable picture of the group. Undoubtedly such media reports of the potential buyers would discourage the public from supporting the takeover too and divide opinion among the management.

During the same period, FGB board of directors issued a scathing and misinformed press release to the media that the board "has reason to believe that possibly in excess of 15% of its outstanding common stock has been purchased recently in a series of transactions". They further added that FGB "has been informed that the purchases have been made by a foreign bank which may be seeking to obtain control of the Company." This statement was baseless and then caused a flurry of headlines across the American newspapers insinuating that BCCI was the Middle Eastern bank that was orchestrating the takeover. BCCI's Dildar Rizvi spoke to the press and categorically denied any involvement in the deal as did Bert Lance who also maintained that the group of Arab investors were acting in personal capacities and not from BCCI's instructions. BCCI had nothing to do with it!

The FGB board then took a further drastic move to resist the full takeover from the Arab investors and sued the group including

Bert Lance, Jackson Stephens (his investment banker friend), Abedi (who had nothing to do with it) and the Arab investors. The allegations for the litigation were that Lance's boys were acting as a group collectively to buy FGB stock from October 1977 onwards and this would then be in breach of securities laws as they failed to disclose the required schedule 13(d) to the SEC (which demanded that any investor who buys 5% or more of a publicly listed company must make a disclosure). The man who came to the rescue for Lance's group and BCCI to defend their case against the unfounded allegations (and to disassociate BCCI from the entire deal) was super lawyer Clark Clifford, one of the most respected men in Washington.

Clifford was a man of great moral standing within the judicial and political circles, having held high government office during critical and contentious periods of American history. When Abedi met Clifford, the two began to develop a warm and cordial relationship and Clifford was joined by Robert Altman who was his associate and protégé. Clifford on many occasions spoke highly of Abedi and that he was a man of unhindered integrity and importance. Had Clifford not been satisfied with the background, integrity and character of Abedi and his Arab clientele, then there would have been little chance of him taking on the case given his stature and position. He was a man that could not be bought or bribed and he was a man whom nobody could deceive or influence. Hence he always went by his sound judgment based on credentials and valid references as evidence.

The accusations against BCCI in this highly-publicized takeover battle was that the bank adopted a 'nominee' scheme whereby they put forward nominees as investors to purchase FGB shares on their behalf and secretly take control of the American bank illegally. There has been no solid evidence to suggest that these allegations were true except for the same fact described earlier that BCCI extended credit facilities to the investors in the forms of bona fide loan agreements.

Furthermore let me clarify that the notion of adopting 'frontmen' or 'nominees' is a normal practice in the Middle East which is widespread especially among the more wealthy businessmen or sheikhs. There are practical as well as security reasons for this. For example, even Sheikh Zayed himself would regularly get people to purchase property or other items on his behalf simply to get a better deal as the price would undoubtedly rise if the vendor would discover that the sheikh's name were attached to the deal. Hence even if the allegations were true, the incorrect labelling of BCCI adopting nominees to carry out the secret FGB takeover was no sinister or evil deal on paper.

Secondly as stated earlier, BCCI did not use any nominees to take over FGB as those shareholders acted collectively as a high-powered Middle Eastern contingent, independent of BCCI's opinion, in order to purchase a majority shareholding in the Washington-based bank. There was never any intention by BCCI or its senior management to take over FGB later known as First American Bank (FAB).

Clifford and his competent team at Clifford & Warnke managed to negotiate a swift settlement with the SEC and the Arab contingent even went so far to compensate the ex-FGB stockholders up to $1 million to compensate them for selling their stock below $15 a share. The reason for this was had the sellers known openly that the buyers were a group of some of the most wealthy Arabs in the world then inevitably the stock demand price would have gone up.

The media had a field day and went on a full-blown assault on BCCI and its Arab clients perpetrating and planting the idea in the public's mind that the bank was illegally trying to take over FGB while publicly mud-slinging the Arabs involved. Despite the hostility faced, the Arab investors continued their fight for the bid for FGB until January 1979 when the Federal Reserve ruled that they could not take over FGB on the grounds that Maryland's Attorney General had issued a legal opinion (under pressure from FGB's board) that FGB's Maryland bank could not be purchased.

The Arabs believed this ruling to be unconstitutional and launched a counter attack by collecting together potential candidates who could be elected to the FGB board under the direction of Clark Clifford. Clifford then lobbied the candidates, one of whom was Stuart Symington (a former Senator) to be elected to the board in the hope that if they get enough people elected then their party would have majority control in the board of FGB and hence the resistance to the takeover would cease. The plan was cunning and it worked. Clifford, Symington and Elwood R. Quesada (a property tycoon) were elected to the FGB board.

This was also Clifford's first official entry into the banking industry for commercial purposes and a company was established in the Netherlands by Clifford's team called Credit and Commerce American Holdings N.V. (CCAH) – a Netherlands Antilles corporation which included numerous high-profile Arab shareholders for the purpose of the takeover. CCAH was the parent company of its sole subsidiary called Credit and Commerce American Investments B.V. (CCAI). The CCAH shareholders consisted of (but were not limited to) the following:

1. His Excellency Ali Mohammad Al-Shorafa is the former Grand Chamberlain (Director) of the President's Court, and Director of Presidential Affairs for the United Arab Emirates.
2. HE Sheikh Kamal Ibrahim Adham, Saudi Arabian businessman and former head of security for the Kingdom of Saudi Arabia.
3. Abdul Raouf Khalil. Khalil was previously Minister of Communications and Deputy Chief of Saudi Intelligence, and the former Executive Administrator to Sheikh Kamal Adham. He was also a close business associate of the sheikh.
4. Faisal Saud Al Fulaij, former chairman of Kuwait Airways.
5. HH Sheikh Sultan bin Zayed al Nahyan (son of Sheikh Zayed).
6. Abdullah Dawaish, financial advisor to Sheikh Zayed and his son HH Mohammed bin Zayed.
7. Mohammed Hussain Qabazard, Sheikh Zayed's aide.

So these investors and others were collectively known as 'CCAH'. Most of them seemingly had connections to BCCI and therefore some of them were important BCCI customers, however it is to be noted that BCCI was not in charge of CCAH, neither was it involved in this takeover. The accusations that were made on the bank could also be attributed to other financial institutions or companies that the CCAH shareholders had affiliations with. I am certain that BCCI was not the only bank that the above named individuals used for their business interests. Why were those other organisations not accused of taking over FGB?

Abedi was the main link here and since he was the man who introduced Lance to the investors, the FGB and the media ran a story to malign his bank and accuse it of the takeover simply because they wanted to resist the 'Arabs' taking over a large Washington bank. The story line was plausible and to some extent made sense, but was nevertheless still incorrect.

Even after the FGB was filled with key people that would allow the takeover to go through, there was still the Federal Reserve to convince that was increasingly reluctant to give in to the Arab bid. Finally after much deliberation and assurances by Clifford and Symington, a covenant was made to the Federal Reserve that FGB would be effectively controlled by US citizens and distinguished Americans with an added clause that BCCI would have no ownership of shares under any circumstances.

Finally following intense discussions in April 1981 the takeover was completed with approval of the Federal Reserve but with its strict conditions that the Arabs would simply be passive investors and American bankers who were well regarded and experienced would run FGB. This was the deal that was agreed and that was the original plan and intention from the very beginning!

In hindsight it doesn't even make practical sense for BCCI to be involved with FGB in the first place and that's why they never actually were in control of the American bank. Abedi always said that BCCI would only be an advisory to the board of directors which included Clifford and that was the only stance. Of course Abedi wanted to expand in the USA, however he could have done that anyway and he did, to some extent successfully without any need to get into a messy illegal takeover battle. Who would want that sort of negative publicity? The risk would've been too fatal for him even if he wanted to do it since the American media were already out for his blood. It would've been too damaging for BCCI to be involved in such a high profile takeover amidst such scathing allegations. The allegations and negative press came nevertheless even though BCCI had no hand in the transactions or shares of the takeover.

Once the details were final, Clifford spoke to the media and emphasized the USA's need to engage in financial dealings and accept lucrative investments from the Middle East as it was in their best interests. He also added that this deal would bring important petrodollars back to the USA in the form of jobs and prosperity for Americans. Indeed this was Abedi's aim too — to help people and distribute wealth. Another accusation which supported the opposer's argument that BCCI was behind the deal was that the name of the company CCAH: 'Credit and Commerce American Holdings' as it had the words 'Credit and Commerce' in it which was similar to BCCI's name of Bank of Credit and Commerce! Clifford maintained that this was merely a coincidental and convenient name which the Arabs were familiar with back home in the Middle East and it held no legal correlation with BCCI at all. Makes sense! If the company set up to make the takeover was called JP Clifford Chase, would the press go mental and accuse one of the largest investment banks (JPMorgan) in the US of taking over FGB? I think not.

My agreement with the regulators in this whole affair lies in the fact that traditionally such a takeover of an American bank would be executed where the buyer is a strong conventional bank or even a partnership of banks. However in this case CCAH was effectively an investment vehicle to purchase shares of a bank and wasn't a bank itself. Therefore my concern would not have been the fact these were foreign investors trying to buy up chunks of America, but my concern would be the *ability of the Federal Reserve to efficiently regulate* and monitor the group. However these days we see everybody from the Qatari Investment vehicles buying up everything from Barclays Bank to Harrods and there seems to be no trouble.

The final hurdle was the New York State approval which was also given in 1982 after Clifford's intervention and then he delivered on his promise to install a prominent and reliable seasoned banker to head FGB by the name of Robert G. Stevens who was former CEO of a Columbus-based bank. The real power however always remained with Clifford and Altman who were merely advised by Abedi and BCCI on banking and investment related issues. This was also confirmed by BCCI's Khusro Karamat Elley who sat in meetings with Mr. Swaleh Naqvi, Mr. Abedi, Mr. Clifford and Mr. Altman and maintained that at no point was there any involvement of BCCI in the day-to-day dealings of FGB. Khalid bin Mahfouz, the late owner of National Commercial Bank (NCB), Saudi Arabia's biggest bank, also invested heavily in FGB and other ventures during the eighties.

In 1987, First American Bank (FAB) as it was now known, purchased the National Bank of Georgia again back from Ghaith Pharaon. Clifford & Warnke, the legal firm dealt with all the legal documentation pertaining to this deal.

In all fairness, looking back it seems the entire FAB/FGB takeover deal was meant to be a regular routine and simple investment by a group of wealthy businessmen. It was unfortunate however that BCCI's name was dragged all over the press for no reason whatsoever during the battle, as the foul taste that was left behind with the regulators and those in the corridors of Wall Street would remain for a long time and they would later dig the knife into the enemy sooner than expected.

Chapter Five

Under Attack

Late in the night on 9th February 1988, following an extensive trip from New York to Lahore (in anticipation of Sheikh Zayed's arrival) with stopovers in London and Abu Dhabi, Agha Hasan Abedi suffered a heart attack while staying at PC hotel in Lahore, Pakistan.

In the early hours of the morning his brother-in-law, Zahid Kasim rushed to the hotel as soon as he heard the news. On the way to Abedi's room, he passed by the top-tier management of BCCI in the corridors who were all in a state of shock as to what had happened to their leader and mentor who they all regarded as a father figure. The ambulance was apparently on its way to whisk Abedi off to the Sheikh Zayed Hospital in Lahore but he was in full consciousness and eloquent as ever as he gave instructions to his brother-in-law to execute on his behalf while sitting up straight on the edge of his bed. "Zahid, I have had a massive heart attack" he said whilst still perched upright on the side of the bed.

There was not even a single wheelchair in the hotel in Lahore where Abedi was staying. The senior management of the bank were just standing there in shock as if they were paralysed and hardly anybody was acting as if there was a real emergency. When the ambulance finally arrived, they too did not have a wheelchair! Stupidly then, they headed back to the hospital to fetch a wheelchair therefore doubling the transit time! Now frustrated at the incompetence of all present, Kasim managed to source a wheelchair after words with hotel staff. To save time, Abedi was taken to hospital in his private car.

The ICU medical team at Sheikh Zayed Hospital Lahore took

over and Abedi was eventually in a stable condition but it was evident that his heart attack was severe. Requests to visit him started almost immediately and as a result HH the late Sheikh Zayed and former President General Zia-ul-Haq came to see him whilst still in ICU. Meanwhile Zahid Kasim began contacting Abedi's personal physician Dr. Khalid Hameed in London however he was somewhat difficult to get hold of at the time.

Dr. Hameed took some time to reach Lahore and meanwhile the Lahore doctors were handling Abedi but many were not entirely content with the standard of medical treatment he was receiving. He was soon transferred to a private room from the ICU and then more officials and dignatories started to line up to visit him including the then former Chief Minister of the Punjab province and current Pakistani Prime Minister Nawaz Sharif and the cricketer-turned politician Imran Khan.

By this time the British Cardiologist Dr. Somerville had also arrived from the UK with Dr. Hameed. A few days later Abedi suffered a second more serious heart attack which left him in a more fragile state. He was rushed to the ICU again but this time none of the expert foreign cardiologists were at hand to treat him immediately hence the local more junior doctors took over.

Zahid Kasim made efforts to track down Dr. Hameed who was at a dinner at a prominent Lahori family's residence.

Abedi survived the second heart attack but was still unconscious. Ex US President Jimmy Carter personally telephoned the top doctors he could get his hands on in order to persuade them to fly to Lahore immediately to evaluate Abedi. Hence he sent the renowned pioneer of the heart transplant Norman E. Shumway from California. Zahid Kasim received Norman Shumway at Lahore airport so he could be taken to Abedi for consultation.

Shumway concluded that Abedi's heart had been 90% damaged and he needed a new heart. The only capable facilities available were in London at the Cromwell Hospital (which ironically Abedi himself founded with funding from BCCI and Sheikh Zayed). A new problem was that it was logistically difficult and dangerous to transport him in his fragile state as doctors were unsure whether he would survive the journey to London and time was ticking.

Hence the then Crown Prince of Abu Dhabi Sheikh Khalifa bin Zayed Al Nahyan (current ruler of Abu Dhabi) converted his private jet into a makeshift ambulance and Abedi was flown to London the next day. Luckily a matching donor was found and the very same evening the world famous Sir Magdi Yacoub performed the heart transplant on Abedi at the Cromwell Hospital on 9th March 1988.

The transplant was successful but there was a momentary lapse of oxygen which caused some complications. The next day on the 10th March 1988, Abedi was escorted to the Harefield Hospital in Middlesex where Magdi Yacoub's team looked after him during his recovery. Following a long stay at Harefield he followed up as an outpatient until December 1990 when he finally moved to Karachi.

I would be correct to say that post his first heart attack in February 1988, Abedi relinquished operational control of BCCI and handed it over to Mr. Swaleh Naqvi, his second in command, who was formally appointed as Chief Executive Officer of the BCCI group by His Highness Sheikh Zayed Al Nahyan at the Dorchester Hotel in London while Abedi was still in hospital. A new Central Management Committee was set up to steer the group into the correct direction after the President's departure and it was led by Naqvi, but the ceremonial figure head was still Abedi in absentia but he played no major role in the affairs of the bank due to ill health. Many say that the bank's fortunes took a turn for the worse soon after Abedi was out of the picture. This may be a practical accuracy given that BCCI was Abedi's conception and much of its success and growth can be wholly attributed to Abedi's visionary leadership, hence the lack of such a central figurehead and similar persona could have left the group essentially rudderless. However there are many claims by insiders who believe this not to be the case. Where they did feel the absence of Abedi was felt substantially, they also found the leadership of Mr. Swaleh Naqvi to be no less remarkable. Bearing in mind the circumstances in which he took over as CEO and the vacuum of power which he had the tumultuous task of fulfilling amongst the political turmoil which was brewing within the top tier, everybody still respected Naqvi tremendously.

Meanwhile across the pond in the USA, another dramatic saga was unravelling.

Around 8th October 1988, seven BCCI officers were arrested in Tampa, Florida on drug-trafficking and money-laundering charges. Later in 1990, BCCI was indicted and entered a guilty-plea agreement with the US authorities under the country's law of vicarious liability whereby the institution is held responsible and liable for the behaviour of individual employees. Not being a legal professional myself, the United States is one of the very few countries I have come across who use this vicarious liability law and it baffles me. It's like me running a chip shop and one of my part-time employees at the till slaps one of the customers with a hot fish across the face, knees him in the mid-section and then I get prosecuted for grievous bodily harm because my employee committed assault. I wasn't even there in that scenario! Baffling.

So let's take a look at the Tampa indictment in more detail to see what actually happened so we can put things into context and make it a lot clearer. During the seventies and eighties, BCCI was on an international rampage for acquisitions of banks in overseas territories in order to expand its global network. The takeovers were probably not as reckless and expeditious as we have found RBS's acquisitions to be under the leadership of Fred Goodwin or 'Fred the Shred' (eg. ABN Amro etc). Part of BCCI's plan was to offer services to Third World countries and nations where risk was also equally high and coincidentally where relations were not so amicable with the USA. BCCI found numerous opportunities to offer legitimate banking facilities and enhance profitability in such nations and two of the most controversial ones were Panama and Colombia. When Abedi expressed an interest in a particular Colombian bank located in Bogota, he sent Mr. John Hillbery to explore the opportunities and the environment in the area. Mr. Hillbery upon return was not too convinced that the acquisition was such a great idea due to the politically volatile and violent nature of the region, however he was informed that the management board would still approve the acquisition.

Not only was Bogota ridden with violence and gang warfare at the time but it was also a Colombian drug gang stronghold for cocaine smuggling. BCCI however maintained that it upheld a strict anti-money-laundering policy with focus on legitimate and sound practices throughout the group. Due to business being extremely successful in the Panama and South American region, BCCI attracted many high-profile customers and PEPs (politically exposed persons) such as the General Manuel Antonio Noriega Moreno who became a client of the Luxembourg branch of BCCI. This relationship, however, started when he was an acclaimed friend of the US Government and received substantial funds from the US Government, some of which may have been deposited in BCCI and some, I am sure were deposited in many other banks. Manuel Noriega didn't only use BCCI as his bank of choice, he of course had many others.

However when the relationship turned sour between the US government and Noriega of Panama, they began to take an active and deeper interest in his financial affairs linked to drugs money laundering. They started to probe into his accounts and transactions network in order to capture and prosecute him. Part of the US authorities' plan was to investigate BCCI further when they found out that Noriega used the bank to deposit his cash. It is intriguing to wonder why the authorities did not peruse the financial affairs and links of Noriega with the numerous other banks in which he held deposits. It is strange how BCCI was singled out by the authorities for their investigations linked to Noriega to further their cause.

As it happened the US authorities launched an undercover sting operation in order to entrap the bank code-named 'Operation C-chase' after an apartment complex called Calibre Chase which was the home base for the project. In May 1986 the undercover operation was led by one Robert Mazur who was trained by the FBI and said that he stumbled across BCCI randomly while driving along the streets of Tampa, Florida. This projection of coincidentally stumbling across this international bank with a high number of Asian employees is also quite questionable. However let us assume that he was telling the truth for the sake of objectivity. Robert Mazur used his alter ego and fake name of Robert Musella and infiltrated the mafia gangs and drug cartels across Colombia and Mexico that ran the largest cocaine-trafficking business.

He and other undercover agents interposed themselves as middle-men to collect valuable cocaine-sales proceeds from Columbia in hard cash from American streets and then facilitated the remittance of these proceeds to the Columbian traffickers themselves. By documenting and recording all their dealings with the drug traffickers, dealers and bank officers used to exercise the deals, they managed to hold enough evidence that would incriminate all those involved in the US courts of law by any level-minded jury.

In short, one fine evening, Robert Mazur dropped into a BCCI representative office in Tampa, Florida and introduced himself to a junior officer called Aftab Hussain and boasted himself as a wealthy financier with varied business interests. He forged a relationship with numerous BCCI employees of Pakistani origin who all believed him to be a legitimate and very successful businessman. After having earnt their trust and friendship while enticing them with potential deposits in their bank of around $5-$10 million per month, he dropped hints in various recorded conversations that some of his clients had received proceeds from illegitimate means.

Naturally when given enough bait and enticed with enough money with minimal fear of being caught some of the junior officers of the bank thought that this was their big break and saw an opportunity of potentially millions of dollars of deposits in their branch. In their mindset, although wrong and immoral by all means, they saw a way of propping up their region in terms of deposits and being shining stars as employees. Little did they know at the time that they were being set up most deceptively by the man who they thought was their friend and client. Hence it is recorded that a BCCI account in Florida was used for holding cash before its transfer to another account in Panama. Once the junior officers were convinced of Robert Mazur's authenticity, they saw further opportunity to create more business for the bank by introducing him to colleagues in London and elsewhere and suggested more sophisticated ways to facilitate the laundering of these funds. Mazur and his associates got excited as they had already entrapped one senior employee by the name of Amjad Awan who was taped saying to Mazur "I am not responsible for the morals of your clients" when he had hinted that some of his clients were involved in criminal activity. Following Awan, they became ambitious and wanted to entrap some senior figures in London, Paris and Geneva. Switzerland's authorities however did not allow Mazur to record conversations in their country due to the strict secrecy laws. The UK and French authorities however did not object.

It is to be noted that post the treasury losses that were incurred by the bank in 1985 due to the shipping industry, the management had sent memos instructing a global drive for deposits for the group. This meant that the main priority for all regions was to capitalize on all *legitimate* opportunities that were available to them via the BCCI connections and network. *Nowhere have I found in my investigations and in any of the documentation where any member of senior management has instructed any other employee to attain deposits from illegal or questionable means.* It was well documented that the bank had strict rules pertaining to anti-money laundering and corruption as well as bribery, however one cannot police the motives and intentions of each and every employee working in such a large global organisation. Perhaps, the US Customs knowingly targeted the bank because they were already aware of the enormous drive for deposits that was being encouraged in the bank globally. One can only speculate.

It is also worth mentioning that due diligence was performed in Tampa by BCCI officers when Robert Mazur first approached the bank as part of his sting operation as he was asked for the necessary documentation to verify his identity and source of income. To this, the undercover agent produced a certified letter from the local Florida National Bank (FNB) which endorsed Robert Mazur as a legitimate and well respected, long-standing customer of Florida National bank with the utmost credibility signed by a senior official of the bank. Now to me this would seem as an official and sufficient evidence of the legitimacy of Mazur and his business interests, however I am sure further verification checks could and should have been made before the BCCI officers proceeded. My point is however, that is to be noted that an American bank here has produced and certified forged and fake documentation in order to facilitate an undercover operation used to deceive otherwise innocent people. Had Mazur not been able to produce real identification that was original, then I would doubt that he would have been able to dupe the officers like he did for such an amount of time. Later on, however the officers themselves colluded with Mazur to launder the so called 'drugs' proceeds to the tune of $14 million which actually in fact turned out to be customs' money.

Once the cat was out the bag, some say that the officers had the intention or tried to alert the authorities of the suspicious transactions, however before they could do any such thing the US customs decided to move in on their suspects and arrest them after inviting them to a 'fake staged' bachelor party for the fake wedding of Robert Mazur. If they hadn't moved so fast, perhaps their efforts of the last two years would have been fruitless as if the officers had alerted the authorities then they probably could not have had enough grounds to prosecute. When the bankers arrived to the wedding party of their esteemed 'client', they were welcomed by armed FBI and US customs agents who arrested them on charges of money laundering and drugs trafficking.

Following the arrests on 10th October, 1988 there was sensational and substantial publicity of the events in the UK and USA. In fact the entire international media outlets set camp outside BCCI's Tampa and New York offices to keep the spotlight on the bank which was surprising in itself. The bank retaliated and released statements via the head of communications Mr. John Hilbery who categorically denied any wrongdoing on behalf of the bank and suggested that they were a victim of a set-up and singled out based on prejudice. This prejudice perhaps could have been deep rooted due to the success and fast growth of the bank, maybe because of a lack of a natural home or official lender of last resort or central bank or perhaps even for political reasons in the lead up to US presidential election. The latter reason seemed the most plausible at the time, given the interest that small-time Senator John Kerry was showing in the narcotics and drugs trafficking investigations. It was apparent that the folks on Capitol Hill were fishing for a big catch in the run up to the elections and the big catch could be in the form of BCCI as it was an easy target with easily-lured employees of Pakistani origin that could be used as a scapegoat.

Further down the line it was increasingly apparent that senior management of the bank had no role in the Tampa operation and they were all genuinely shocked at what had happened. So much so that a full internal inquiry was launched to investigate the controls and procedures of all operations to find out how this had happened. Major steps were taken by Mr. Swaleh Naqvi, the new CEO, who ensured that anti-money-laundering controls, training and compliance procedures were strengthened. Furthermore, special attention to compliance and regulatory measures were undertaken by Mr. Naqvi to ensure that no such lapses of judgement could take place and nor could unscrupulous elements be able to tarnish the name of the bank through undercover operations again. *These tightened compliance and AML procedures were acknowledged and praised by the late Lord Justice Bingham* in his later investigations and subsequent report as he gave them due credit. It is to be further noted that the bank co-operated fully with the authorities during their investigations and liaised with them while adhering to all the updated rules and regulations with regards to compliance and money laundering or counter-terrorist financing (CTF). The overall result was that post the Tampa Sting operation, BCCI's compliance and AML controls along with regulatory reporting procedures were exemplary.

Immediately after the arrests of the BCCI officers in Tampa, the bank employed the services of Clark Clifford and Robert Altman to act as their defense lawyers in the US money-laundering case. The bank had suffered huge deposit losses of up to $2 billion in the weeks following the arrests and was set to bleed more, thanks mainly to the negative press coverage surrounding the scandal which prompted customers to withdraw their cash from branches. Sources say that the very existence of the bank was at stake if deposits were to continue dropping at the rate they were at the time.

A 'run on a bank' threatens the liquidity and existence of any financial institution as the main backbone is deposits and people's trust. The trust factor was being dreadfully affected by the continuous headlines and front page reports damaging BCCI's reputation further week after week. Clifford and Altman called an emergency meeting with Naqvi where they strongly suggested and recommended to the board of senior management of the bank to plead guilty to the charges of money laundering brought against them. This is almost an unthinkable line of action for a credible and innocent institution whose senior management had no knowledge of any wrongdoing. Furthermore members of the board were sceptical of this approach as by pleading guilty to the charges, they would effectively admit fault and this may open a new chapter of allegations and reputation damaging cases. On the other hand, Clifford and Altman argued that given their extensive knowledge and experience of US corporate law and the fact that BCCI was being charged under the law of *vicarious liability*, it would be unlikely that the bank would win this case and pleading guilty would avoid a long battle in the courts, which would further damage the bank's reputation and cause a liquidity crisis.

Hence on the persuasion and strong recommendations by Clifford and Altman, the board agreed to enter negotiations for a plea agreement under vicarious liability, which for Mr. Naqvi was supposed to be in the best interests of the bank. His main aim and intention as CEO was to save the bank at all costs and safeguard depositors and employees and shareholders. Whether this decision was correct and whether Abedi would have done such a thing, is a matter of speculation and many opposed the move. However under the circumstances, Mr. Naqvi acted under recommendations from the bank's lawyers with noble intentions.

For those of you who do not quite follow US Corporate law like myself, the law of vicarious liability means that the organisation is held liable and responsible for the wrongdoing of the individual employees. While reading the intricacies of this case and not being a legal professional myself, I found it baffling how the United States could use this law of vicarious liability to charge and indict an entire organisation the size of BCCI (14,000+ employees) for the malpractice of a handful of employees. This is the equivalent of shutting down Harrods if an employee in the Men's underwear department is caught stealing cash from the till which is equally ridiculous. The law is more complicated for banks, however when is the last time we heard major US financial institutions being indicted for their countless number of rogue traders and phoney bogus bankers breaking the law? Insider trading is a big habit in the US and never has a bank been indicted for the insider trading activities or other rogue transactions executed by individual employees with (or without) senior management approval.

On the other side of the river, if we inspect how the laws differ in the UK or the European Union with regards to corporate prosecutions, we can clearly see that if BCCI was being stung by HM Revenue & Customs, the bank could not be prosecuted under the law of vicarious liability. This is because there are certain recommendations in place that are to be followed by legal prosecutors in the sphere of the law in order to maintain good practice in line with the public interest. If we examine some of the factors against prosecuting the company in the public's interest and hold them up against the BCCI Tampa case, we can see that the decision to indict the bank under vicarious liability was frivolous and inappropriate under the recommendations of the *Crown Prosecution Service (CPS):* A genuinely proactive approach adopted by the corporate management team when the offending is brought to their notice, involving self-reporting and remedial actions, including the compensation of victims: In applying this factor the prosecutor needs to establish whether sufficient information about the operation of the company in its entirety has been supplied in order to assess whether the company has been proactively compliant. This will include making witnesses available and disclosure of the details of any internal investigation.

In BCCI's case, this factor was addressed and satisfied as Mr. Swaleh Naqvi and his team adopted a very proactive approach in dealing with the investigations once the Tampa case was brought to their notice. To confirm this if we refer to paragraph 2.119 on page 62 (Chapter 2) of the Lord Justice Bingham report of 1992, he confirms the above factor was met by stating: "BCCI for its part reacted to the arrests by strengthening and reviewing its compliance procedures in the UK, the US and elsewhere. In the UK the review was conducted by independent lawyers and suspect accounts were reported to the National Drugs Intelligence Unit. Similar due diligence reviews were conducted in the US....Whatever the management's motivation, the evidence strongly suggests that in the aftermath of Tampa the group made a genuine and determined effort to ensure future compliance with rules intended to prevent money laundering."

a. *A lack of a history of similar conduct involving prior criminal, civil and regulatory enforcement actions against the company: contact should be made with the relevant regulatory departments to ascertain whether investigations are being conducted in relation to the due diligence of the company; – At the time of the Tampa case in 1988, BCCI was not being investigated for any money laundering or criminal offences neither were there any criminal, civil or regulatory actions being taken against the bank. Hence this constituted a lack of history of similar conduct and the bank satisfied this factor to avoid prosecution without having to plea guilty under vicarious liability.*

b. *The existence of a genuinely proactive and effective corporate compliance programme. Again if we refer to point '(a)' above we see that this factor was satisfied under the able leadership of Mr. Swaleh Naqvi and his team.*

c. *The availability of civil or regulatory remedies that are likely to be effective and more proportionate: Appropriate alternatives to prosecution may include civil recovery orders combined with a range of agreed regulatory measures. It is evidently apparent that a number of measures could have been taken so that BCCI would not be prosecuted in the US as this was an isolated incident involving a small number of officers and an undercover sting operation to result in entrapment. One action could have been a stern warning and a fine without the need to enter a plea agreement as this would have given the bank the benefit of doubt, held its reputation intact and safeguarded deposits.*

d. *The offending represents isolated actions by individuals, for example by a rogue director. It is clear in the Tampa case that only individuals were acting independently in an isolated case instigated by US Customs authorities to entrap officers who may not have committed the offence in normal circumstances. Even, if they were regular offenders and did so with full knowledge of the law, the incident was isolated and carried out without instruction, approval and knowledge of the senior management of BCCI.*

Hence from the above, it is clear that had the case been administered in the UK, the bank most likely would not have faced such stern and relatively unfair prosecution.

It is also clear that many of the other banks whose employees have undertaken gross misconduct with criminal intent and colluding with senior management with approval from the very top, have been able to emerge from such cases without having faced any such legal penalization.

The fact remains, that the decision to plead guilty to all charges of money laundering was one that is hugely contested by many still to this day. However given the circumstances, Mr. Swaleh Naqvi acted with the sole intention to save the bank from potential collapse due to the plummeting deposits after the negative publicity and he had very little choice at the time. He acted under recommendations from the bank's lawyers who knew their field diligently.

Many criticize Naqvi's decision as they say that by pleading guilty, the bank was admitting fault for something it wasn't really wholly responsible for. It has always put BCCI apologists and sympathizers on the back foot. Furthermore little did Naqvi know that later on the same authorities who accepted the plea agreement would come back with stronger force to shut the bank down anyway. Hence in hindsight, the bank was closed anyway and the stamp of money laundering had also been engraved in its reputation.

In today's world many employers, especially those operating under a limited company framework, may mistakenly take the view that if everything goes wrong, limited liability will protect the directors. Given the changes in the legal, political and social climate, this may prove to be a costly mistake and not just financially.

Employers need to be aware of criminal liability and the concept of vicarious liability (where an employer can be held responsible for the actions of an employee even in some circumstances where the employer did not countenance the employee's actions or was perhaps even unaware of them). The risks are especially acute in those employers in regulated professions such as banking. BCCI did everything it could to correct lapses and lack of diligence where it was needed. Yet in an organisation of its size, it is a gigantic task of knowing what each employee is up to 100% of the time.

Finally I do not wish to indulge in the intricate ins and outs of the actual Tampa sting operation more than necessary as that is not the focus of my analysis, however it is to be noted that the main perpetrator who likes to be addressed as the 'infiltrator' in popular culture, made a statement in court where he seemingly 'randomly' came across a BCCI branch while driving in downtown Florida. This maybe a case of sheer coincidence, but given the facts outlined above, in addition to the interest shown by the USA in the financial dealings of Manuel Noriega and the fact that an election was around the corner – I leave the reader to decide whether maintaining the stance of 'coincidence' rather than singling out and targeting BCCI, was a plausible one.

The same Robert Mazur whose book *'The Infiltrator'* is now a blockbuster Hollywood movie starring *Breaking Bad* actor Bryan Cranston, has recently come out in interviews saying how he feels awful and ashamed of his government who has let the 'people' and 'system' down. He has gone further to say that he feels sad that they went to such an effort for a massive undercover sting operation that played a role in bringing down an international bank but they have not continued the same efforts in the wake of other major banking scandals. While reading his interviews I can only gather that Robert Mazur now feels a sense of guilt that his sinister undercover operation which conned innocent hard-working bankers had ruined their lives and indeed that of their families. He cosied up to the likes of BCCI's Amjad Awan and Akbar Bilgrami in Tampa and mingled with their families. They trusted him and he betrayed that trust to the core. For what, in the end? – Did his entrapment operation set a precedent for the others? Nope.

But my main question is, how many other banking and financial institutions did the US authorities go after via undercover sting operations to catch them out? Answer: None. This is why Mazur (if that is his real name even) has suddenly become morally conscious of the immoral deeds he carried out over two decades ago, as he sees banks blatantly abusing the law and committing much worse today without being reprimanded or 'entrapped'.

It is also a baffling scenario whereby I fail to understand how the society of the day or the lawyers even did not try and counter the case on the basis that it was indeed merely 'entrapment'. Entrapment should be illegal all over the place and entrapment evidence cannot, quite frankly, be taken as serious incriminating evidence in a court of law. In US Criminal law even, it is discouraged practice to use entrapment and in many jurisdictions this itself is used as a defence against criminal liability for the actions committed. I rest my case.

Chapter Six

Regulatory Supervision Mayhem

In May 1987, a year before the Tampa case, Price Waterhouse (PW) were appointed as BCCI's overall group auditors. Prior to PW's appointment, the bank's audit was split between the firm Ernst & Whinney (E&W) and PW. E&W were responsible for auditing the consolidated accounts for the group and audited BCCI S.A., whereas PW audited BCCI Overseas, ICIC Overseas and the BCCI Emirates. It is fitting to state in all of PW's audits of the BCCI Group, never had it unsurfaced any malpractice or spotted any irregularities in BCCI's operations or accounting practices. Was this a result of negligence, poor audit practice or simple and plain inefficiency? That is not for me to answer, neither is it my line of inquiry, however due thought must be given as to why and for how long was PW complacent in this lack of diligence.

Following the Tampa sting operation and subsequent negative world-wide press coverage, BCCI had lost almost $2 billion in deposits and the bank had a real threat of a liquidity crisis. However even at this point, it has been revealed that Sheikh Zayed had in fact set aside a separate fund totalling approximately US $8 billion on an 'as and when needed' basis for the specific use of the bank.

This special fund was set aside by the Sheikh in 1985 after acknowledgement of the bank suffering huge Central Treasury losses between 1984 and 1986 which amounted to approximately $500 million and to some critics represented a huge chunk of BCCI's capital base at the time. The central treasury losses were attributed primarily to market forces and mismanagement in the Central Treasury. In addition losses were incurred in the shipping industry with which the bank had substantial ties and also maintained huge loans which were thought to be unpayable at one point due to a decade-long recession in that industry. Price Waterhouse (PW) the bank's auditors had said that BCCI was also making huge losses on option contracts as a result of inexperience in a highly complex and sophisticated market.

Abedi and Naqvi had to make good the losses in order to stay afloat as BCCI did not have the luxury of other banks where their central bank would step in to inject emergency funds. Furthermore the bank was regularly prone to negative press reports in the media (for reasons perhaps emerging from complaints from disgruntled customers or competitor banks who harboured considerable resentment towards a successful ethnic newcomer in their banking market) and so it was decided by the senior management to manage the losses temporarily for one or two years until they found a more permanent solution. This decision was taken as even a small loss or mistake at BCCI would always be blown up out of proportion and exaggerated by the media.

Abedi and Naqvi decided to use creative accounting techniques to plug the losses by a) injecting capital and cash contributions of $150 million from a Cayman entity called the ICIC Staff Benefit Fund; b) restructuring of shares and capital along with transferring additional funds from other entities to be shown as 'loans'; and c) injecting cash from the ruler of Abu Dhabi's fund.

It is to be noted here that even though BCCI had no central bank of any one country behind it acting as a lender of last resort officially on paper, however it is recorded and confirmed that Sheikh Zayed of Abu Dhabi and other shareholders always had the bank's back as it were and were supporting it at all times. These practices are by no means 'going by the rule book' as per say however these were the type of measures adopted by senior management in order to safeguard the bank and its depositors as they acted in their best interests. In hindsight I am not aware of the other options available to them at the time, however when we see that the overall financial position of the bank was 'fair and healthy' despite the huge losses, due to the sound backing of the ruler of Abu Dhabi at all times, it seems that the individual actions of the senior management in 'cooking the books' should have been dealt with, rather than attacking the entire institution which I will come onto later.

However looking at the scenario as an outsider and having interviewed Mr. Swaleh Naqvi personally on more than one occasion, the reasons he gave for not adhering to the technicalities of traditional accounting norms in order to conceal the 1985 losses were inexcusable by all accounts as an accountancy professional. However what struck me was that the intentions behind the decision to cook the books were understandable given the situation he was faced with. He revealed to me that he was faced with a catch twenty-two situation where if he were to declare the losses (attributed largely to the mismanagement by a certain handful of individuals) he would be opening up possibilities of a real 'collapse' again due to negative press which ultimately would undermine confidence on the bank and tarnish its reputation further.

The second route, which he chose, was to manage the losses *temporarily* with the intention of safeguarding the depositors, shareholders and staff. In any case, he had declared all the losses, accounting malpractices and the reasons for this during the restructuring of the group which was to take place later. More of that in the next chapter.

Hence now we can see that from 1988 onwards the bank was possibly in the line-up to facing three lines of enquiry and investigations as a result of disproportionately-biased media coverage:

1. FAB/FGB takeover accusations in the USA
2. Sting operation in Tampa for Money Laundering
3. Fears of poor liquidity as a result of Treasury losses and post Tampa 'run on bank'.

In the backdrop of all the media attacks on BCCI, the Bank of England was always wary and uncertain about BCCI due to the lack of one supervisory body or one single regulator. Hence after many meetings between the Bank of England, the IML (Institute Monetaire du Luxembourg) and senior management of BCCI, it was decided that a college of supervisory bodies would be created who would be responsible in overlooking and regulating BCCI's global operations. The college of supervisors would meet regularly to discuss issues relating to the bank and also to get an update from senior management on regulatory affairs.

Let us take a more in-depth look at the series of events surrounding the supervision of the BCCI Group that took place between 1984 and 1991.

Let me start off by describing what in my opinion was the regulatory and supervisory state of affairs in the United Kingdom in the seventies and eighties. It was pretty shoddy to say the very least.

Today we have a plethora of regulatory bodies, supervisory committees, advisory panels and federations – but two decades ago these campaigns were in their infancy and very much a work-in-progress. Firstly we have the Basel committee which started as the Bank of International Settlements (BIS) that was established in 1930 in the town of Basel, Switzerland. Basel is a beautiful town where the world's elite like to mingle, wine and dine with other like-minded megalomaniacs. Much like Davos but quieter I must admit after visiting last year to deliver a talk. The role of the Basel committee is primarily to supervise the liquidity and capital ratios of financial institutions and achieve global agreement on good practice. This basically means it sets the standards of how healthy a bank should be to avoid the risk of collapse.

Then we had the Labour party's initiative of the 'The 1976 White Paper', followed by The Banking Co-ordination Directive of 1977, the Banking Act of 1979 and 1987. The Banking Act was significant because it incorporated the preceding directive along with the intention to create a new system of supervision which was designed to *safeguard depositors specifically*. This is a crucial element to my argument regarding whether this act was actually implemented in the true sense which we will discover a bit later.

In essence the main UK Supervisor responsible for oversight of Banking operations within the UK was the Bank of England. This responsibility later diluted and branched out between the Bank and the Financial Services Authority in December 2001. The FSA regulated the financial services industry in the UK until 2013 when it was abolished and its place two new bodies were created which are active till today: the Financial Conduct Authority (FCA) and the Prudential Regulatory Authority (PRA). The FCA is now responsible for overseeing the integrity of the financial industry with a particular focus on the conduct of financial institutions. The PRA is more involved in prudential regulation and supervision of the individual firms.

In July 1972 Agha Hasan Abedi approached the Bank of England and asked permission to open the first branch of BCCI in London. The green–light go–ahead was given cautiously yet a full banking status was never approved and one must explore the reasons for such a suspicious welcome in the UK from the very outset. Abedi and his entourage came with the backing of the Bank of America that held a 25% shareholding in the new bank and his own personal reputation, at the time, was that of an amicable and successful banker.

However regardless of these facts, much later in 1979 the Bank of England in consultation with the Luxembourg Banking Commission (LBC) decided to refuse a full banking licence to BCCI but instead granted it the status of a 'Licenced Deposit Taker' (LDT). Many pro–BCCI lobbyists believe that no legitimate or plausible explanation existed for the Bank of England to not grant them a full banking licence and restrict it to the status of merely a 'Licenced Deposit-taker'.

Let us explore the reasons given by the Bank Of England for this refusal when Abedi complained against the decision in 1979:

1. The structure of the BCCI group (split between BCCI S.A., BCCI Holdings and BCCI Overseas) caused the Bank of England grave concern due to the lack of a single supervisor or regulating authority. Even though LBC was the main regulator for BCCI S.A. (Societe Anonyme), it accepted the fact that it was unable to efficiently supervise the entire group globally from the tiny duchy of Luxembourg.

2. Ultimate Beneficial Ownership (UBO) issues. Nobody was clear as to who owned or actually controlled the group from a legal perspective. Abedi was in charge obviously, but the ownership structure was cloudy. A company was set up in the Cayman Islands called ICIC Overseas, which was owned by ICIC Holdings (also incorporated in the Caymans)!

3. BCCI apparently lacked a 'lender of last resort', which was later to be proven untrue, since this was the Abu-Dhabi Government/Central bank of UAE, who also became the majority shareholders.

4. The group was practically homeless. Ideologically born as the brainchild of a Pakistani with predominantly Pakistani senior management, majority ownership by Arabs and Luxembourg/Cayman incorporation. What a colourful mix though don't you think?

5. Regions where the group operated were considered 'murky' where regulatory supervision was either lacking or scarce.

6. The rapid expansion of the group worldwide along with forty-five UK branches in merely seven years was frowned upon by onlookers and competitors alike. The Banking industry was generally prudent and not prone to such rapid growth by any single entity or group.

7. Large exposures to the Gokals/Gulf group reported by the US authorities to be almost twice the capital of the bank in 1978.

8. The uncertainty of the group if Abedi fell 'under a bus' as he single-handedly steered the bank yet whom the Bank of England looked upon with unease and could not trust

9. BCCI had antagonised and angered the American authorities over the First American case.

Now some of the above reasons may seem plausible however nobody from the Bank of England probed to ascertain or document the question of where the principal place of business was for BCCI. This was a question from a legal perspective and not from the physical aspect. Some would have said that it would have been whichever country Abedi would be in at any given time! However had this question been investigated and I believe it should have been done, then one would discover that the principal place of business was indeed London from as early as 1974! Bearing this in mind, the push for incorporating a UK entity of BCCI should have begun from a very early stage but this never took place unfortunately.

The refusal to grant a full banking licence by the Bank of England was not taken lightly by BCCI by any means as Abedi was even willing to make structural changes to the group if needed. Diplomatic efforts were also made on behalf of BCCI by various channels including Dr. Ghaith Pharaon who was also a customer and stakeholder as well as a representative of the bank. These complaints of course landed on deaf ears but the bank was consoled on the basis that they would be eligible for re-application soon, however they never exercised this option.

The 1979 BCCI accounts caused some concern at the Bank of England due to certain UK loans for which provisions had been made under S.A. and accounted for yet it prompted them to ask Ernst & Whinney (E&W) (now known as Ernst & Young (EY)) to have a closer look at S.A.'s loan portfolio which they did and provided a reassuring report. These concerns however were still apparent up to 1982 even though the 1981 consultation gave BCCI a very strong financial outlook with improved relations in the industry amongst its peers. For the BofE, supervision was at the forefront so in 1982 Brian Gent who was deputy-in-charge of Banking Supervision wrote a detailed paper formally calling for a single supervisor for the group and possible structural changes based upon the principle place of business. Finally the inquiry into this topic was made when a team from the BofE visited the BCCI

HQ at 100 Leadenhall Street in the city afterwhich they had no doubt in their minds that the bank was effectively being run from London and that Luxembourg had virtually no role in the day-to-day affairs of the bank.

Gent then revised his paper twice and finally forwarded to the Governors and his boss Peter Cooke (Head of Supervision) in January 1984. As Gent affirmed the Institute Monetaire du Luxembourg's (IML) admission that they could not effectively supervise BCCI on their own, he came up with two possible solutions in his conclusions:

1. Revocation of BCCI's UK licence
2. Proper Consolidated supervision by the Bank of England

The first option was not practical or viable at the time given both the opportunity and option of consolidation was available to them.

Hence Gent concluded that due to the IML's limited resources and BCCI's tiny presence in Luxembourg it was no longer practical or logical for them to supervise the group's worldwide activities. The IML was also not eager to hold onto this gruelling responsibility and therefore the suggestion to incorporate the holding company to the UK was raised in order to fulfil a consolidated global supervision of the group. This could only be done following a thorough analysis and review of the BCCI group operations globally by one of the 'Big Four' accountancy firms which would be paid for by BCCI itself. The IML and BofE Governors agreed to this plan but BCCI did not.

Cooke approached Abedi in April 1984 to tell him of the BofE's plan to initiate a UK corporation for S.A. and undertake this comprehensive review of BCCI's worldwide business so that consolidated supervision could be accomplished if S.A. and Overseas were merged. Abedi was unusually pugnacious at this meeting and resisted the idea of merging S.A. and overseas as he had planned to take Overseas into the USA after taking over a US bank. Cooke then reassured Abedi by stating the BofE's willingness to incorporate the group into the UK with an appropriate licence however this recognition could not happen without their conditions fulfilled.

Abedi did not comply with Cooke's request on that occasion and this could be due to the fact during the 1981–1984 period BCCI was experiencing some of the most profitable and successful years ever and Abedi was indeed flying high on this triumphant vibe and therefore did not deem it necessary to bow down to the BofE's demands coupled with the fact that lack of recognition was not such a cause of concern anymore. In hindsight this was probably a poor decision as he unfortunately did not realise that lack of supervision would cause him and the bank considerable damage in the future. Furthermore the BofE also were at fault for not exercising their own authority in order to compel Abedi to be compliant in this regard. Abedi's initial refusal was enough deterrent for them not to pursue this route which could have seen them execute legal powers and would have saved much headache later on.

In June 1985, following expressive remarks by Pierre Jaans of the IML that he could no longer supervise Overseas, Abedi held a meeting where he informed the BofE of tentative alternative schemes to solve the issue whereby there would be three banks: one in the UK (S.A.), Caymans (Overseas) and the USA. Meanwhile there was strong persuasion within the BofE that a UK subsidiary should be incorporated to solve the problem which would encapsulate the Central Treasury also based in London. This idea also faced some criticism from within the BofE, as some of the officials were unhappy with the increased workload this task would bring and the question of whether they were equipped for such a gigantic move.

On 22nd November 1985, Rodney Galpin (Exec Director of Banking Supervision) wrote to Abedi confirming the need for a UK subsidiary and gave the go ahead on the condition they were satisfied following visits to the Central Treasury in London and discussions with the UAE counterparts, since talks of moving the treasury to Abu Dhabi were also taking place. BCCI acted swiftly in response to the letter and made arrangements to allow the UK subsidiary to be established quickly. E&W accountants were assigned to review all the controls and procedures for the operations in the UK as well as an independent banker who checked the UK's loan portfolio. Both reported back positively in December 1986 with no major concerns.

The plan for a UK subsidiary was quite paramount for two reasons:

Firstly it would help the BofE more effectively manage the supervision of BCCI in the UK directly and secondly provide some comfort for UK depositors in the form of protection against any disasters. In hindsight this was a complete mess unfortunately as we will discover soon.

Another spanner in the works as it were was the fact that the BofE suddenly had a change of heart about consolidated supervision of the BCCI group even though it was approved and backed by the stakeholders. Surely this would have been a more appropriate move had they pressed Abedi hard enough but perhaps the Johnson Matthey Bankers scandal scared them off?

Johnson Matthey Bankers Ltd (JMB) started in 1965 and collapsed in 1984 following irrecoverable loans due to shockingly-large exposures. The key in the JMB case was that the parent company was unable to support, prop up or bail-out its subsidiary. There was also major deception from JMB to the BofE and they were not forthcoming about their exposures to major borrowers, neither were they maintaining effective systems, controls and procedures for risk management or operations.

The JMB scandal had resulted in the 'Leigh-Pemberton report' of June 1985 and then followed by the Banking Act of 1987 to incorporate further changes to prevent such events happening again. But they both obviously did not help!

During the same period the news of BCCI's Central Treasury losses began to unfold and make the rounds of the city. In February

1986, Abedi himself informed the group auditors E&W about the extent of the losses before the BofE found out. PriceWaterhouse (PW) (now known as PriceWaterhouseCoopers (PWC)) were earlier commissioned to review these losses and suspected them to be much lower. The BofE learnt of the full amount of these losses in May 1986 and apparently it came as somewhat of a surprise even though they had been dealing with PW for many months on this issue. The extent of the losses were not fully known at the time but was said to be around $400–$500m and was naturally a cause of concern for the BofE and IML who were considering incorporation into the UK, but this new development made them feel uncomfortable about the whole idea.

A month later in June 1986, Brian Quinn (Head of Banking Supervision at BofE) met with his team to discuss the question of revoking BCCI S.A.'s UK licence before even the consideration of the incorporation of a UK bank. The fact that such a meeting even took place is puzzling to me because the matter was not even that serious to cause such drastic action. The meeting however concluded that the licence should not be revoked because S.A. did not pose any short-term or long-term threat to UK depositors as the losses had been made good and were also under review by the auditors who gave the bank a clean bill of health year after year.

It is surprising to me that the talk of closure of the bank in the UK was being considered as early as June 1986! There were literally no grounds for such banter based on the facts and figures we have today – also they decided against the move because the closure of forty-five UK retail branches of BCCI would cause havoc apparently, both diplomatically and politically. All this commotion seems highly unnecessary at the time.

The primary aim of the BofE was to protect UK depositors and they failed miserably in this task. Had they wanted to they could have pressed ahead with conditions and sought the earlier plan for incorporation to the UK and therefore paved the way for consolidated worldwide supervision. Instead, they were deterred by the Treasury losses as they felt they could not trust the senior management of BCCI due to the late reporting. This, in my opinion, is not a justified reason for thwarting efforts to supervise BCCI globally with local incorporation. Had this been done in June 1986, then we would be writing a different story today and the UK depositors would be protected.

What happened next is extremely interesting.

In March 1987, Abedi formally requested the BofE to consider consolidated supervision and was willing to accept all conditions that they would put forward. The BofE refused this request.

Simultaneously, Pierre Jaans of the IML was adamant and now also formally requested the BofE to relieve him (and Luxembourg) of the near-impossible task of supervising the entire group. I appreciate that it was considered unreasonable and impractical for the IML to supervise BCCI globally bearing in mind that BCCI's presence in Luxembourg was merely as its statutory head office. Indeed the real head office was in London, where the Central Treasury was and so the onus definitely fell upon the BofE to take on the responsibility of global consolidated supervision but it did not live up to its responsibility. It would have been the most tiresome yet most effective solution but they avoided it like the plague.

PW were appointed by BCCI in May 1987 to become the group's overall auditors as it was advised by the BofE that a single accounting firm should be in charge of the consolidated audit. Previously, the audit was split between E&W and PW. It is fitting to mention here that neither accounting firm had detected or raised any suspicion of fraud and malpractice during their tenure until the very end. Surprising to say the very least at how international accounting firms from the 'Big Four' could be so negligent year after year for such a prolonged period of time. I digress.

Despite repeated calls by Jaans at the IML for the BofE to take responsibility and incorporate a UK subsidiary and then to offer consolidated supervision, they continued to resist and Galpin (BofE) refused to discuss this option further. He did accept however the alternate option, which was to form an international college of supervisors, who would meet together twice a year with an update on BCCI's financial health. The original college consisted of the BofE, IML, PW (auditors), BCCI management along with the supervisors of Switzerland and Spain. This was somewhat odd since BCCI did not have a massive presence in either Switzerland or Spain and considering a large amount of business was conducted in the Middle East, Africa, and Far East (Hong Kong, for example), none of their national supervisors were invited to attend the meetings.

The meetings began in 1988 and funnily enough were unable to address the main problem of the BCCI group and ironically the purpose for the exercise: its structure!

The bank then experienced two tragedies one after the other which proved 1988 to be the worst year for the entire group. Firstly, Abedi's heart attack in February and then the US undercover Tampa Sting Operation which resulted in the bank being entrapped for money laundering with seven officers arrested.

The BofE at this point looked upon BCCI's predicament sympathetically as there was (and never has been) any evidence to suggest that senior management had any hand in drugs trafficking or money laundering. Mr. Swaleh Naqvi who acted as CEO following Abedi's heart attack was also fully compliant with all authorities world-wide and continued to insist on consolidated supervision of the group but his repeated requests fell on deaf ears.

The main concern for the BofE in the immediate aftermath of the Tampa sting was whether the adverse media (which was unprecedented) would lead to a run on the bank ultimately causing a liquidity crisis for the UK and its depositers. This prompted the BofE to make arrangements with BCCI to get daily liquidity reports and hold weekly meetings for review and analysis of deposits and cash positions. It is to be noted that all requests were honoured by

BCCI and all enquiries were satisfied especially in terms of the strengthening of systems, controls and procedures.

The group's problems improved nearer to the end of the year after a couple of months as they acted quickly and efficiently to address the issues.

The second college meeting of international supervisors took place on 29 November 1988 where Naqvi was questioned on the effects of the Tampa Sting on profits and the major unsecured loans to customers exceeding 10% of the group's capital. He responded with predicted profit figures including damage done by the Tampa affair and confirmed that the unsecured loans were historical but no more lending would be sanctioned by the group to those customers going forward.

PW signed off BCCI's 1988 accounts and produced their audit report on 11th April 1989. This showed a loss of $49 million which was explained to be due to the effect of the Tampa indictment, the need for increased loan loss provisions which was raised to $145 million and higher lending to the owners of the CCAH shares (investors of First American Bank).

However after a cash injection in the same month, PW confirmed in their audit report that BCCI's *risk-asset ratio was still much over 1% of the minimum level set by the Basel Committee!*

The third meeting of the International College of Supervisors took place on 6th July 1989 and welcomed the arrival of the Hong Kong and Caymans counterparts.

The main subjects of discussion were as usual the large exposures and now the question of restructuring of the Central Treasury. There were nineteen people at this meeting including Swaleh Naqvi, who as the new CEO of BCCI answered all of the fierce questions fired at him by the chair of the meeting Roger Barnes (Head of Banking supervision BofE).

Naqvi gave detailed and lengthy answers to all questions relating to the large exposures and confirmed that the loans were to be phased out completely and no new accounts had been opened. PW agreed and confirmed that Naqvi was working very closely with them to figure out a plan on how to execute this. Furthermore PW also commended the group's management on their enhanced due diligence procedures and reviews of systems and controls following the Tampa scandal.

The conclusion at the meeting was that there was a need to restructure the Central Treasury which had physically moved location to Abu Dhabi post the 1985 losses (three years earlier) and the bank also had no reservations for this. There was also commendation for the bank in its UK operations as all forty-five retail branches were running smoothly with no signs of suspicious behaviour. The running of the entire UK region in fact never raised a cause for concern as we will discover in more detail later with evidence.

The second meeting that year took place in December 1989 which was the most instrumental thus far. The former British Prime Minister Lord James Callaghan had made many attempts on BCCI's behalf to convince the Bank Of England to accommodate them within the UK from a structural and supervisory point of view. Hence the BofE began to consider a temporary arrangement for two UK subsidiaries of BCCI and also a permanent solution of group incorporation in the UK with consolidated supervision.

However, unfortunately the BofE rejected both Lord Callaghan's request and proposal for BCCI's incorporation into the UK.

James Callaghan was a man of honour who enjoyed huge respect both within the UK and abroad as former Head of State. He was well regarded by peers and by the establishment itself. Yet he was still somehow drawn to Abedi's charisma and vision which in turn developed into a more meaningful and personal friendship. A similar situation developed between Abedi and many other world leaders including Jimmy Carter, Sheikh Zayed and countless others. A pattern can be seen here where one can easily spot that the men

Abedi was befriending around the global glitterati were seemingly men who simply 'cannot be bought or purchased' with the lure of money (or power) as they themselves wielded more money, power and fame than most could only dream of. This is an important point to be noted as these men were drawn to a *higher moral purpose* which Abedi helped focus their attention to.

Lord Callaghan by this time had become very close friends with Abedi and since the heart attack had even acted as a de facto advisor to the group. Abedi would even convey messages and share his personal thoughts with Callaghan during his days of illness.

The Governor of the BofE heard Callaghan's requests but rejected them outright based on the following reasons (and I shall comment on all of them one by one):

1. Uncertainty about the identity and nature of the shareholders;
   This was not valid because the shareholders and directors of the BCCI group were all well documented and established.

2. The dominant position of Abedi with no clear successor:
   This was also very clear. Swaleh Naqvi took over as CEO and spearheaded the group post Abedi's illness. Nobody, not even Naqvi could replace the charismatic leadership and authority that Abedi commanded but nevertheless his position was clear.

3. BofE was unable to understand BCCI's management culture:
   This is a tragedy and many will be unable to understand the essence of 'real management'. Abedi had instilled the culture of humility and giving into each employee. This was nothing suspicious or unorthodox, rather a very noble outlook.

4. Absence of trust with the supervisor;
   I cannot see any reason how or why this reason was applicable as to my knowledge and research the group were transparent about operations and complied with all BofE instructions.

5. The need for a new style of supervision;
   Well this is exactly what Callaghan was prompting for!

6. Complaints received about BCCI's business practices:

There should have been an independent inquiry to verify this. So far it was all suspicion without any evidence and no evidence was ever brought forward.

Overall it was clear that the BofE was unwilling to take further responsibilities towards BCCI, but they should be thinking of saving UK depositors. That is one of their most important roles at the end of the day.

Following the refusal of Callaghan's request, John Beverly (another deputy leader of supervision at BofE) wrote to Barnes that he believed that no other option except consolidated supervision of the group was desirable. Barnes on the other hand preferred two UK subsidiaries at the time, one for the central treasury and the other for the UK regional business.

Finally a paper was published on 1 November 1989 by the Banking Supervision Division that favoured Barne's suggestion of two UK subsidiaries but for a temporary interim period only so that the BofE would be pressed for future consolidated supervision. This was an improvement from the conclusions drawn from a paper a couple of years earlier.

A month later the fourth supervisory college meeting was held on 1 December 1989 where Clark Clifford and Robert Altman gave a very smooth presentation of facts with regards to the Tampa Sting Operation. They also indicated their intent of pleading guilty to charges under vicarious liability laws in the US in order to draw a line under the whole saga. They also emphasised the most important steps taken by BCCI in order to prevent such an event happening again which was reassuring to the meeting. Naqvi also gave his go ahead for the incorporation of two UK subsidiaries and the BofE was eager to move forward on this in order to assumingly 'safeguard UK depositors'!

As we learnt in the previous chapter, on 16th January 1990 BCCI signed a plea-bargain agreement with the US authorities on the accusations in the Tampa sting operation. This bearing in mind it was found that the senior management of BCCI had no involvement whatsoever in the isolated money-laundering scheme.

Lord Bingham stated in his report:

> *"It was believed, in my view quite correctly, that BCCI had made genuine efforts to ensure compliance with international guidelines for the prevention of money laundering... it has never (to my knowledge) been suggested that the directors or controllers of S.A. were party to the money-laundering conspiracy. Nor there is evidence known to me that senior managers were implicated."*

Powerful statement. These words in itself nullify the argument that the bank had a criminal culture or was the money-laundering bank of the world. If senior management were never privy to any activity related to money laundering then how can they be accused of condoning such behaviour?

Nevertheless around this time PW were still finalising their audit of the 1989 accounts which was causing them a considerable headache. They were also being fed certain inside information by a so-called 'informant' whose revelations were casting doubt in the minds of the PW auditors about the information being provided to them by BCCI management.

Believe it or not, instead of observing client confidentiality and duty of care to client obligations, Tim Hoult and Chris Cowan of PW went straight to the BofE to disclose the information the so called 'BCCI insider' had given them. This was supposedly information on CCAH shareholders and their loans. This was early February 1990 when the meeting between PW and Barnes took place at the BofE in strict privacy. So private in fact that they entered at different times and in secret so that BCCI may not get a whiff of what they were up to. Of course this type of double dealing would be unacceptable in the eye of the client when their own auditors were seemingly plotting against them.

Chapter Seven

Road to doomsday

Between February and April 1990 these 'secret meetings' between PW and BofE continued where PW would be updating them on their ongoing investigations into certain areas of BCCI audits which gave them concern. This was also based upon suspicious 'rumours' pointed out to them by the so-called informant. PW began to confront Naqvi and Naqvi was as honest and frank as he could be with regards to the somewhat poor financial state of the bank that he had inherited as CEO. It was made plain by Naqvi in a meeting held on 6th April 1990 with the audit committee that the group needed more provisions and possibly an injection of funds.

On 11th April 1990 PW went to see Barnes again at the BofE and updated him on the situation. At this stage they expected that approximately $2 billion in capital was needed with shareholder support. The same day Barnes asked Hoult and Tim Charge of PW whether BCCI was insolvent. Hoult answered that it was probably not.

Price Waterhouse report: 8th April 1990

PW created a report which included issues that needed to be addressed/rectified before they could sign off on the accounts and final audit. They outlined that the group needed $1.8bn and provisions for unsecured loans up to $400 million. In addition they raised questions about the large exposures related to the Gulf Gokal shipping loans which were historically problematic. The total exposure was now near to $700 million. A further $200 million was needed for the CCAH securities and $50 million to cover the 'fishy' Cayman entries.

It was now clear that BCCI needed help. Naqvi was CEO and

in absence of Agha Hasan Abedi who was bedridden in Pakistan and unable to speak, he had to take unprecedented action and fast.

He flew to Abu Dhabi and pleaded to the Abu Dhabi Shareholders to rescue the bank. There present also listening to Naqvi's plea was HE Ghanim Faris Al Mazrui who was a close advisor to Sheikh Zayed and headed the Abu Dhabi Investment Authority (known today as ADIA). Mazrui had become the representative of the Abu Dhabi shareholders on various boards of companies and Government offices. He had been the on the board of BCCI since 1981 but was not proactive in its dealings.

Naqvi summarized the losses to the shareholders which were claimed to be due to standard market forces and bad banking rather than fraud, malpractice or deceit. He did however reveal and admit to the utilization of the ruling family's portfolio to plug losses earlier (as a temporary solution) but these were also accounted for.

In summary here is what Naqvi disclosed at the meeting which was handwritten in a three page statement and were a rough estimate:

	Cause of Loss	Principal	Interest
Treasury loss	630	580	1210
Gulf Gokal Shipping group	600	730	1330
Adjustment of non-performing loans	350	150	500
Carrying cost of nominee shareoldings and maintaining portfolio profitability	125	75	200
Total	1705	1535	3240

(Source: Bingham report, 1992)

Naqvi was extremely forthcoming with the shareholders and explained that the Gulf Shipping exposures had continued to spiral out of control for many years. The group had made substantial losses attributing to more than just the Gokal lending but fundamentally the bank was a good and sound institution.

Naqvi however conceded that he did not enjoy the personal friendship and relationship with the ruler of Abu Dhabi that Abedi was privy to. Indeed he was unable to plead to the ruler in the same way that Abedi could with his added charm. Hence in a dramatic effort to save his bank, Abedi in his frail condition boarded BCCI's private Boeing jet in his wheelchair – still unable to speak properly – and set off for Abu Dhabi with Naqvi to meet HH Sheikh Zayed.

The friendship of the Sheikh and Abedi was displayed for all to see in this sincere episode where Abedi in his wheelchair called upon the court of the Sheikh at his palace and pleaded with him to save his bank. Sheikh Zayed and Abedi spoke with their eyes and their friendship had lasted the test of time. His Highness was deeply moved by Abedi's honest plea for help and he had also asked for the Sheikh's forgiveness for the various problems surrounding BCCI including the mismanagement.

HH Sheikh Zayed is reported to have told his friend Abedi: "You go and look after your health, I'll look after your bank." He then instructed one of his aides to do whatever is necessary to sort out the problems.

HH Sheikh Zayed agreed to rescue the bank in the form of a financial package that would cover all losses and provisions in addition to propping up the capital base of the group.

A formal memorandum and letter was written and signed by HE Habroush Al Suwaidi (Chairman of the Abu Dhabi Finance department) which was duly read out by HE Mazrui at a meeting held in Luxembourg on 20th April 1990 in the presence of BCCI management, PW, the IML and the BofE. The new entrant for the first time at meetings of this level was Mr. Zafar Iqbal who along with being Managing Director of BCCI (Emirates) was also a close aide to the Sheikhs of Abu Dhabi after being placed there by Abedi.

In the meeting it was also conveyed that immediate action would be taken in the form of issuing new shares as the Abu Dhabi Government would now become 77% majority shareholders by subscribing $400 million in cash. The capital was injected immediately as was the extra 20% shareholding actioned.

The next board meeting in Luxembourg was held on 30th April 1990 where the 1989 accounts were signed off by PW with the usual official audit opinion including the new increased interest of Abu Dhabi shareholders and injection of capital.

Everybody, including the BofE took a breath of assurance that finally they could visibily and physically see a 'lender of last resort' or some central financial authority who would undertake responsibility for BCCI at a time of financial distress. It was a sigh of relief for BCCI management too of course that their efforts to keep the bank afloat had paid off. Naqvi had been honest about his presumed shortcomings but that left PW deeply sceptical about his ability to co-operate with them further. It seems PW developed a deep mistrust of Naqvi following their earlier meetings of April 1990. Maybe it was the fact that PW as auditors of BCCI were not able to unearth what Naqvi had told them (or what he told the Abu Dhabi shareholders later) themselves. One can only wonder I suppose.

Nevertheless PW were not comfortable with Naqvi being a signatory on a representation letter to be signed by the board and BCCI management. So Iqbal signed it instead and this led the way for PW's intent on having Naqvi sidelined.

Restructuring and June 1990 UK redundancies

As a result of majority control by the Abu Dhabi shareholders, the BofE and supervisory board began to think that the natural home of the bank would now become Abu Dhabi. However they were sceptical about the Central Bank of UAE's ability to handle such a complex consolidated supervision of the group (similar doubts they had about the IML).

The first move was to implement a thorough restructuring plan of the group and streamline operations to make it leaner both in terms of costs and size. This included decreasing the size of the UK business as rationalization of the region was a priority for the shareholders. Inevitably this meant branch closures in the UK along with some unwanted redundancies for employees.

Telling someone that they are about to be sacked is always an unpleasant conversation but it had to be done. The true family culture within the BCCI family was about to be shaken up and face some stark realities. A father may have to tell a son not to come to work tomorrow or vice versa. Workers who stay at branches till late daily would be asked to leave. It is never easy no matter how you put it.

So that June, one early morning Swaleh Naqvi set out to inform some of the UK branch managers personally about the task which they were about to undertake. One such manager was Mr. Qaiser Malik who was in charge of the Swiss Cottage branch. Naqvi stopped by there first as it was the nearest to him on the way to Central London from his North London residence in Hendon. Malik was shocked that he had to sack some of his hardworking staff but understood the pressure that Naqvi was under at the time. Soon throughout the UK news spread like wildfire that BCCI was making redundancies and a lot of staff were laid off. Many of these ex-employees who were made redundant in June 1990 still hold a grudge against the management of the group as they feel they were unfairly dismissed and were not compensated to the extent to which they expected under the 'BCCI family ethos'. Many of them got three months' statutory pay for their redundancy package which is the norm for most companies but they felt BCCI would offer them more in return for their many long hard years of service and late hours. Some were jealous of others due to the 'golden handshakes' given to more senior employees earlier on before the main liquidity squeeze started.

It is during this rather difficult time for the employees of the group, that the management of BCCI faced a further blow. On 19th June 1990, the supervisory college met again and PW this time insisted that Naqvi should not attend based on their apparent mistrust of him which as auditors is a very strange intervention. Iqbal attended instead and at this meeting the IML gave the group an ultimatum to leave Luxembourg within twelve months. Similarly the Cayman supervisor also demanded that BCCI (S.A.) exit the Caymans within the same time period. This naturally caused a big problem for the BofE as now they faced a confusing situation, whereby BCCI were being forced out of Luxembourg and apparently were not able to fully move to Abu Dhabi due to the UAE central bank inexperience at the time. The BofE were still in favour of a UK subsidiary for the region and overall consolidated supervision. At the same meeting, BCCI was given steps to undertake before the next meeting which was due in October 1990. These steps included a new CEO (Iqbal), a clearer legal structure and shareholding with list of new directors and restructuring. Iqbal had already laid out plans for reduction in global operations including pulling out from the higher risk regions like Columbia and other Latin American countries (similar to what HSBC has done post their 2012 massive money laundering and terrorist financing ordeal).

What is startling for me and probably for many other informed readers is the fact that having acknowledged the fact that the Abu Dhabi ruling family have taken a majority controlling in the group, the college of supervisors or more importantly the BofE made no effort in making any sort of direct personal contact with the shareholders!

It is documented that HE Habroush had invited Miss Helen Jones and John Beverly of the BofE to visit Abu Dhabi in April 1990 immediately after the HH Sheikh Zayed had agreed to inject cash into BCCI. Habroush wanted to make sure that the BofE and others were happy and content with the arrangements put into place. Also for the added security for the BofE and to ensure they were satisfied that the requirements put forward to BCCI would be met within the year – and now more specifically with regards to the twelve month IML deadline. I found it immensely surprising that the BofE and counterparties did not make any effort to meet with the shareholders personally when invited. The travel arrangements were already booked by Habroush for them to visit but they declined. Why did they decline?

Surely meeting the shareholders would have given them added assurance and a personal touch or interaction with them would have made them more aware of what they were doing for the bank in order to save it? Wouldn't progress on the required urgent matters to save the bank have sped up if they had a face-to-face meeting? Maybe the BofE did not want to meet them for other reasons? Perhaps they had other things in mind whilst talking to PW behind BCCI and the shareholders' backs.

Even when Iqbal went to see the BofE on 2nd August 1990 to provide updates on progress, BofE refused to goto Abu Dhabi on the basis of 'presentational issues'. This is laughable. The Abu Dhabi leadership were at the same time now engulfed fully in the political crisis of the Gulf War as Iraq had just attacked Kuwait so their attention was also diverted. But I feel it was necessary for the BofE to have met *as no meeting had taken place before the ultimate closure of the bank*. This is truly extremely disappointing and unfortunate on so many levels that I cannot even comprehend the logical rationale behind this decision.

PW on the other hand were very cosy with the Abu Dhabi representatives and met regularly until the end. This also highlights the apparent 'double-dealing' going on here.

Many meetings continued to take place between PW, Iqbal (who had now become the acting CEO replacing Naqvi), and the Abu Dhabi representatives (namely HE Habroush, HE Juan Al Dhaheri

Salem and Mazrui). This all culminated with a report issued by PW on 3rd October 1990 telling the financial state of affairs of the BCCI group and what was needed to rectify the problems.

The PW 3rd Oct report is summarized as follows:

1. Projected loss for 1990 was known to be $311 million (excluding provisions)
2. Financial support needed of approx. $1.5 billion
3. Major loan accounts had increased borrowing significantly to $4.2 billion

At the next college meeting on 5th October 1991, Mazrui produced a letter to the IML signed by the Department of Finance of the Abu Dhabi Government stating that they will support the group to the level of financial aid required as per PW's October 5th report.

Following the meeting the need for new directors and managers was urgent. Hence a former head of Lloyds Banking group was proposed as the new Chairman of BCCI in the UK along with many other senior management reshuffles as the restructuring of the group was also being finalized. The restructuring was proposed by Iqbal to be in the form of three individual subsidiaries in London, Abu Dhabi and Hong Kong for Europe, MENA and AsiaPac regions respectively. These three subsidiaries were to be incorporated as freestanding bank entities and not under any holding company as consolidated supervision was still proving to be difficult. We can see that the USA operations were to be closed down as a result of this three-bank proposal which the BofE started to consider seriously as the only solution moving forward. The IML's deadline was also half-way approaching for the group to leave Luxembourg and Pierre Jaans along with Schlaus of the IML were showing no signs of extending the date.

US Authorities

On the other side of the pond, as we learnt in the earlier chapters, another investigation was being undertaken in the background by the District Attorney of New York Robert Morgenthau and his assistant John Moscow. The US authorities had already been antagonized by BCCI's supposed takeover of First American via nominee shareholdings and then since the Tampa Sting they were looking for blood.

Moscow was adamant in demanding to see the October 3rd PW report as were the Fed and Iqbal finally showed it to them in December 1990. After reviewing the report they ordered a fresh investigation into the CCAH loans and lending to the 'BCCI shareholders' secured on CCAH shares. The US authorities felt that they were double crossed on the issue of CCAH and First American. As a result the formal investigation into CCAH/First American began in February 1991 when two American lawyers namely Richard Small (Washington Fed) and Thomas Baxter (NYC Fed) arrived in London. Simultaneously BCCI had been issued subpoenas in New York whilst a grand jury investigation was underway. This of course went alongside massive US press coverage giving damaging accusations on BCCI painting a dim picture for the future of its business and profits. The *Wall Street Journal* (*WSJ*) in particular was on a war front criticizing the BofE as well as BCCI for all the issues surrounding CCAH, capital shortfall and other problems.

Even further across the continent there were thorough internal investigations going on in Abu Dhabi along with the taskforce that was set up to weed out all the problems. Naqvi was being interviewed in detail by PW and the first interview was held on 19th January 1991 where Naqvi disclosed everything to PW partners at length. He spoke about various transactions, movements of funds, nominee shareholders, Gulf group lending since the seventies and ICIC used as a parallel bank to fund BCCI. PW were aware that whatever

Naqvi was saying had depth and substance as it correlated in tune with what Iqbal was telling them and Naqvi had no reason to make such damaging revelations without it being the truth.

The surprising thing here is that PW, having now known all the facts from Naqvi and Iqbal along with BCCI's own internal taskforce at hand discovering the details, they still did not disclose these details to the BofE in January 1991. It seems at times they were colluding with the BofE and then genuinely retaining important information they received from BCCI thus hiding it from the BofE! This was extremely confusing and no sense of direction can be found in these dealings.

Majority Shareholders Support and Final Financial package

At 9am (GMT) on Monday 4th March 1991 (12pm UAE time) the BofE learnt that the financial package as proposed by PW estimated at approx. $5.6 billion had full support of the Abu Dhabi Government and that the documents would be signed as soon as possible. We must bear in mind that all the ruling family and government officials were still very much preoccupied with the Gulf War crisis so bailing BCCI out and signing papers was not on the priority list in those crucial months.

PW Section 41 report commissioned

Lo and behold on the very same day that the BofE received formal notification of the shareholders supporting the group (4th March 1991), they (Barnes) commissioned a report under section 41 of the Banking act to investigate all the matters of apparent 'malpractice' as per Naqvi's earlier revelations. Barnes appointed PW, BCCI's own auditors, to draft the report and informed Iqbal and the firm Allen & Overy the same day. The majority shareholders and Mazrui only learnt about PW's appointment for the report on 27th May 1991 (two months later) which caused considerable anger from their side.

They seemed to have valid reasons for displeasure for the following reasons:

a. *They were not informed about this appointment on the same day as everybody else. This is true however Iqbal was informed and as de facto CEO he should have in fact informed the shareholders.*

b. *They believe the BofE acted in duplicity as they were keen to have a financial support package signed by the Abu Dhabi government but in actual fact they were planning to use the section 41 report to shut the bank down in any case.*

c. *PW should not have accepted the appointment as they have a duty of care and confidence to the BCCI group as auditors and this arises a serious conflict of interest along with their inability to have a fair and objective judgment.*

Meanwhile Booz Allen Hamilton had been appointed as management consultants to help with the new strategic direction for the group's business. The UAE central bank's Mr. Khalid Kalban also held talks with the BofE, along with HE Khalifa Nasser, who was overseeing the restructuring.

The directors of BCCI namely Mr. Yves Lamarche, Dr. Alfred Hartmann and Mr. JD Van Oenen were furious at PW that as directors of the company they were not being kept informed about the group's finances and restructuring plans.

A lot of people seemed to be getting their knickers in a twist at this time and venting their anger towards PW. This included the New York D.A., who put immense pressure on PW and even threatened to indict them for false accounting whilst their 'World firm' had been given subpoenas.

The Kerry Factor

John Kerry, former unsuccessful runner for US President against George W.Bush (how difficult could that be!?) and current US Secretary of State was at the time of the BCCI investigations a mere senator. A *very ambitious* senator I must add. As mentioned previously, he seemed to be hell-bent on singling out BCCI as the only bank to be handling the proceeds of narcotics drug trafficking in the USA! It is surprising that he viewed BCCI as the only culprit (which it was not of course) bearing in mind that the Tampa indictment was due to entrapment from an undercover sting operation and a one-off event! Yet he was adamant on pursuing the bank for further unfounded criminal investigations.

So on 12 April 1991 he wrote a letter to Alan Greenspan who was the then chairman of the Federal Reserve saying in very clear terms that they should not, under any circumstances, approve any transferring of assets of BCCI or the CCAH company until all entities were under the umbrella of a single consolidated supervisor.

As Lord Bingham quoted in his report also (para 2.372): *"this letter was plainly intended to thwart BCCI's proposed restructuring plan."* He knew that the three bank structure was viable and plans were underway but he wanted to exert pressure onto the Fed in order to throw a spanner into the works. In other words, Kerry did not want BCCI to restructure, he wanted the bank shut down at all costs.

Chapter Eight

The Shutdown

Robin Leigh-Pemberton, the Governor of the Bank Of England (one of the most important positions in World Finance) was attending the Basel Committee meeting in April 1991 where he met Alan Greenspan and Gerald Corrigan from the New York Fed. Both men took the Governor to one side and gossiped about an upcoming prosecution against BCCI in NYC for a variety of different breaches of law.

John Bartlett from the BofE happened to be in NYC at the time and held a meeting with the New York Fed on 15th April 1991 at the instruction of the Governor to discuss the BCCI prosecution in detail and to ascertain the effect on the UK operations. This meeting was followed by Barnes (BofE) visiting both NYC and Washington to meet the Fed on 29th April 1991.

The message in these meetings with the BofE was clear: Washington, New York Fed and John Moscow the Assistant New York District Attorney made it plain that they wanted BCCI out of the USA and that they would press ahead with the prosecution very fast and with full force in the coming weeks following their investigations.

Gerald Corrigan came across as unusually more resentful and fiercely 'anti-BCCI' for reasons we cannot understand. The main gist that Barnes received for the reasons of the overall US prejudice against BCCI was the whole 'deception' over the FGB/First American/ CCAH takeover. Corrigan went so far as to tell Barnes that there would be possible *'serious consequences'* for the BofE as a result of BCCI 'blowing up' as it were. He described BCCI as *'all bad'* and a *'cesspool'* of wrongdoing threatening the BofE that the effect on them would be "as bad as Johnson Matthey" from the eighties.

Therefore, he urged the BofE to not allow any form of restructuring of the group until the prosecution was completed. Wow! To think the Americans would have such an effect or opinion that would hold any weight with the Bank of England is truly remarkable. Strong and harsh words right? Surprised me too that the prejudice and anti-BCCI rhetoric in the United States was that bad. But what surprises me further is that the BofE would take heed of any such advice from a foreign body over their own interests and more importantly, the interests of UK depositers, whom they vow to protect. Fortunately though, the BofE did not halt restructuring process immediately at the behest of the Americans, although they were under considerable pressure to do so.

A month later again at a Basel meeting in Switzerland on 13th May 1991, Corrigan applied pressure on Leigh-Pemberton and Quinn to halt the restructuring and stated that the upcoming negative US media press coverage assault on the BCCI could very well bring it down for good. At this point, the Governor and Quinn both knew that the grounds for a US prosecution on the basis of the First American/CCAH could be somewhat convincing, however, all the other issues like fraud, money-laundering and terrorist financing were quite weak without any solid evidence. However, the BofE realized that the US media assault would bring about non-proven allegations upon BCCI and would have far reaching political implications as a result.

Back in London and Luxembourg, talks were going ahead with the restructuring and the finalisation of the financial rescue package all to be completed by a deadline of 30th June 1991, including the UK authorisation to incorporate a BCCI UK bank.

Final Financial rescue package

PW's original figure given earlier of the amount of funds needed to rescue the bank had changed once more, pending investigation of the 'ICIC' entity which caused much confusion for all involved as to who actually owned it. By 20th May 1991 the group's liquidity was in a much healthier position as $400 million had now been injected by the majority shareholders.

Finally on 22nd May 1991 following an erstwhile period the good news that the BofE, PW and the supervisory college were anxiously waiting for had arrived. The final signature on the financial rescue package for BCCI had been obtained and a letter was acknowledged stating the Abu Dhabi government's full support of the BCCI group covering all losses and shortfalls necessary to save the bank.

The full support package which in fact was a considerably detailed and heavy document is outlined as follows:

i.   Promissory notes $3.061 billion
ii.   Guarantee $750 million
iii. New shares subscription $650 million
iv.   Unrecorded deposits cover $600 million

The package totalled about $5.1 billion.

HE Mazrui was now assigned as the main communicator between Abu Dhabi and the UK authorities on all matters pertaining to the restructuring and BCCI since HE Salem and HE Habroush were increasingly busy on other assignments. The shareholders were also increasingly getting agitated by PW hence Mazrui would now be the bridge.

Quinn and Barnes (BofE) met the New York Fed again on 23rd June 1991 where the Fed's threatening rhetoric continued and they reapplied emphasis on the damaging effects on the BofE as supervisors/regulators especially since John Kerry was gearing up for criminal proceedings against BCCI which may include the $600 unrecorded deposits issue to be released to the media. They also met the D.A. of New York Robert Morgenthau and his deputy John Moscow again. Moscow disclosed that he had 'overwhelming

97

evidence that senior management of BCCI knew of widespread drug money-laundering activities in the group'. – This has never been proven and no overwhelming evidence has ever come to light to suggest this. It was also confirmed following formal investigations in the Bingham report (1992) that senior management of BCCI had no knowledge or were ever complacent in any money–laundering related activity. As a result no evidence of money-laundering was found in BCCI's UK operations ever.

Final Restructuring and UK subsidiary

Booz Allen consultants were busy restructuring the BCCI group along with BCCI management. Mazrui had informed the BofE earlier on 28th May 1991 that the majority shareholders had decided to remove **ALL** current senior management and so the three new banks would have a new structure and three new CEOs. This was in essence an effort on behalf of the shareholders to 'make do with the old and bring in the new' style of operations. This would also help satisfy any reservations by external parties (including US authorities) about suspicions of senior management who may have been involved in so called 'wrongdoing' in the past.

The BofE received the application for BCCI's new UK bank on the 28th May 1991 along with a presentation by Booz Allen, PW, BCCI and a representative of the shareholders. The new BCCI (UK) would be renamed and begin operations in October with a new British CEO Mr. Leonard Kingshott (former Lloyds banker) and new management. The new BCCI (UK) bank would be a more streamlined and leaner bank.

Before signing off the 1990 accounts, on 24th June 1991 PW wrote a letter to HE Habroush to outline ongoing uncertainties about the financial position of BCCI and to ensure the majority shareholders support. In hindsight this must be incredibly frustrating for all the majority shareholders to time and time again be given different accounts and figures. Every time PW asked for support, the shareholders had always obliged and continued to do so. The real reason appears to be the fact that PW and the BofE were still awaiting the last tranche of $650 million of support from Abu Dhabi. The shareholders had already lost any remaining confidence in PW and had privately informed the BofE that they would seek new auditors at the Annual General Meeting that was to be held four days later on 28th June 1991.

PW's Secret Draft Section 41 report

On the night of 22nd June 1991, Tim Charge of PW delivered the secret draft section 41 report to the BofE (which was sanctioned earlier) and handed it to the security guard addressed for Bartlett. The report when one examines it in detail was clearly just a draft! It was not even fully completed at the time of delivery! PW even expressed in their report the fact that *further verification was needed* since most of the information had been received very recently! The report outlined the following 'misfeasance' in BCCI :

a. *Creative accounting to plug losses*
b. *Use of nominee shareholders (CCAH) to buy American banks*
c. *Use of Ruling family's portfolio to plug losses*
d. *Creation of seventy entities to plug, help and fuel Gulf Gokal group loans*
e. *Central Treasury loss*
f. *ICIC entity and Staff benefit fund question mark*

It is fairly obvious just by looking at the above, that the BofE and PW were well aware of all these problems already. Naqvi himself disclosed the majority of these findings back in 1990 when he was pleading to Abu Dhabi to rescue the bank!

On Monday 24th June 1991, Chris Cowan of PW himself said

there was nothing very new in the report when he called the BofE to discuss it that afternoon!

If we bear this fact in mind, then the joint reactions of Quinn, Bartlett, Eddie George (deputy Governor) and Leigh-Pemberton et al from BofE upon reading the PW report is flabbergasting. All of them seemed to have read the report with horror and awe as if a bombshell had been dropped in the lap and they could not believe what their eyes were witnessing. As if a catastrophic avalanche of fraud and deceit had knocked on their door and was smiling at them with taunts. However with careful reading of the report, we find hardly anything new or significant enough that would warrant such a reaction considering what they already knew in terms of 'fraud'. Yet the BofE decided that they could no longer continue with the restructuring of BCCI after reading the PW report.

An emergency meeting was called by the Governor of the BofE Leigh-Pemberton on the beginning of the new week Monday 1st July and it was meant to be extremely hush-hush only to be attended by Board of Banking Supervision where the course of action was meant to be discussed. They not only decided that the restructuring could not continue, but also agreed on closing down BCCI for good worldwide. Somebody in the meeting suggested an orderly winding down of the group with shareholder support so that depositors were protected but this was ruled out by the Bank of England. A 'sharp, quick and lethal supervisory action' was meant to be taken according to the Board of supervision's member Mr. Nigel Robson without informing the shareholders.

Here there could have been two courses of action:

a. *To visit Abu Dhabi at once and inform the majority shareholders of the PW report, their 'new findings' (not really new) and tell them about the future plans and the halting of the restructuring. By doing this they would ensure the safeguard of UK depositors at the very least.*

b. *Shut the bank down using joint supervisory action by keeping everything 'hush hush' and act behind everybody's back whilst risking or squandering the chance of saving the depositors.*

On Tuesday 2nd July and Wednesday 3rd July they met PW along with the college of supervisors from different countries including Hong Kong to co-ordinate what was to come after. I must give credit to certain members of PW and also Mr. Alan Hardcastle (of the board of Banking Supervision) who at these meetings strongly advised the Bank of England (namely Quinn, Eddie George, Bartlett and Leigh-Pemberton) to inform the ruling family of Abu Dhabi. The BofE refused. Quinn said that this would prompt the ruling family to withdraw their funds and discontinue to support the group financially.

This shocking revelation displays a clear motive and incentive to not inform the ruling family of Abu Dhabi of their imminent action to shut BCCI globally as then they would not receive the funds that were expected. As we already know they were expecting the final tranche of $650 million which was to be received any minute. They were afraid that had they informed Abu Dhabi of their decision, then this money would be lost. Naturally, who would invest a further billion or so into a deal that was going to crash anyway? Considering the majority shareholders had already injected over $6 billion into BCCI in recent months and a total of $7 billion was readily available, it was always clear to the BofE and PW that they were ready to save the bank at all costs. They had been given both written and oral assurances by the Abu Dhabi Government that they would financially support the group to the core, provided the Bank would be able to stay alive. Again, who would invest so much capital if they knew already that the ship would sink?

The majority shareholders had been given assurances by PW and the BofE by signing the financial restructuring and rescue package just a few weeks earlier that BCCI would be kept alive and the three bank scheme would come into effect. On that basis more capital was made readily available.

On the morning of Thursday 4th July 1991 the section 41 draft PW report had been leaked to the United States. It was on the table of the Office of the District Attorney of New York. How did this happen and who executed the leak? We will never know. Mr. Alan Hardcastle of the Board of Banking Supervision described it as a "nightmare scenario". The NY D.A. Robert Morgenthau was already thirsty for blood and now he apparently had some concrete evidence of BCCI's criminality on paper provided by their own auditors. Yet when asked by the BofE about the status and credibility of the report, PW were unable to qualify it or confirm anything in the draft report because it was a draft!

On the same day (4th July 1991) PW said that they "could not fully support the detailed information in the draft report, or confirm its completeness". Wow! This still didn't shake any heads in the boardroom at the BofE and they still went ahead with their plan of action.

According to the *Financial Times*, the timing of the shutdown was dictated by the supervisors' *'keenness to avoid disrupting the dollar markets (as BCCI was a dollar-based bank).'* Gerald Corrigan of the New York Fed made a secret trip to London around this time to check and confirm arrangements.

The plan as decided by the BofE was to merely inform the majority shareholder's representative HE Mazrui about the action they were about to take at the meeting scheduled for the next day (5th July) in Luxembourg. No prior warning or intimation about what was coming. Mazrui was meant to come to this meeting intending to discuss outstanding issues with regards to restructuring and the financial support package. Little did he know about the deception, deceit and duplicity that was about to be detonated in front of him.

Friday 5th July 1991

Fridays are religious holidays for most of the Arab and Muslim World. One can draw similarities with the Sabbath or Sundays in the west where no work is done and traditionally all banks are closed. It is therefore not a working day for many in the Middle East. Friday is even more significant as the weekly compulsory 'Friday prayer' otherwise known as the 'Jummah' prayer is held at midday noon time which must be offered in congregation. Many who do not offer the mandatory five prayers daily still consider it dutiful to at least make an effort to make it to the Friday prayer. Hence this day, the 5th of July 1991 was also a Friday when people sleep till midday and go to pray at the mosque. They are mostly unaware of what is unravelling at the offices elsewhere or generally at their workspace. This also sparks interest in the decision for the BofE to ignite such a mighty flame on such a day.

Let us have a detailed look at the events of the day:

8am (GMT) – Notification acknowledged that $650 million had been wire transferred by the Abu Dhabi Investment Authority (ADIA) via the National Bank of Abu Dhabi to BCCI (S.A.) – the tranche of funds that the BofE and other authorities were waiting anxiously for before taking any drastic action.

9am (GMT) – Mazrui arrives at IML head office in Luxembourg to meet the BofE and IML for what he thought was a discussion and update regarding restructuring and outstanding issues like finalisation of 1990 accounts. He had brought with him proposals for the three new banks to be registered, as was agreed.

10am (GMT) – Quinn along with Pierre Jaans of the IML started to paint the picture for Mazrui and explained to him how they were no longer able to continue with the proposed restructuring of BCCI as was previously agreed and signed upon. They cited reasons of new findings in a PW report which indicated widespread fraud over a number of years along with PW not being able to sign off the year-end accounts. Mazrui was perplexed to register what they were saying as these 'findings' were already known to the BofE and other parties involved and indeed an internal taskforce was set up to investigate further.

Quinn further began to relay the events that were to unfold next which included the freezing of all assets of the BCCI group (with an immediate freeze on UK assets and liabilities) and then an orderly winding down of the entire bank with collusion of several global regulators. Jaans then added that on that basis Luxembourg could not renew BCCI's licence to operate. The bank was to be liquidated.

Mazrui was flabbergasted and unable to digest what he was being told. It came as an utter and devastating shock to him naturally since he was there to finalise arrangements for the new banks that were to be established under a scheme which was approved and given the green light just days before!

11am GMT – Mazrui stepped out during the break of the meeting and frantically tried to call Abu Dhabi and get hold of the Crown Prince's office so that he may prevent further damage and stop the wire transfer of $650 million. However the funds had already left Abu Dhabi and had been received by BCCI and were now in the hands of the provisional liquidators.

Mazrui was rightly furious at Quinn and Jaans as to why they had not informed him or the majority shareholders in advance of their decision to close the bank. He complained how they had deliberately misled Abu Dhabi into injecting cash into BCCI when they had already decided to shut it down. He bargained for time to report to his Government and to discuss a possible solution to thwart their intended action, but his request was refused point blank. Swift and immediate action was to be taken without delay.

12pm GMT – PW entered the room to join the meeting. At that very moment Mazrui stood up and shook hands with Quinn and Jaans and marched out the room without even acknowledging PW's presence.

Jaans left the office to frantically obtain the Luxembourg court order from a judge on the premise of the so called 'insolvency' in the 1990 accounts of BCCI, though we now know it was never insolvent with the backing of the Abu Dhabi Government. Jaans returned with the liquidation court order and then began telephoning other supervisors, regulators and central banks around the world in a co-ordinated effort globally to shut the doors on BCCI. Quinn updated PW and arranged for a UK court application to appoint provisional liquidators.

1pm GMT – By order of the Bank Of England, the UK High Court appointed three senior partners of the Touche Ross firm (now known as Deloitte) to act as joint liquidators of BCCI S.A. Similar actions were then undertaken by other regulators in other jurisdictions that were convinced by the UK's actions. However others refused to follow instructions from the IML and BofE and US authorities as we will see in the next chapter.

As soon as the clock struck 13:00 GMT in London, armed personnel marched into all of the UK branches of BCCI and ordered staff to pack up their things and leave the building immediately. No prior notice, no warning and no pleasantries.

Mr. Basheer Chowdry, UK General Manager of BCCI sent a telex to all staff at the 100 Leadenhall Street Head Office to comply with the enforcers as employees were stunned with mouths wide open in utter disbelief. It was like a scene from a Hollywood movie is how many ex-BCCI employees describe it.

It was a testimony to how *well-planned and skillfully* executed the global shutdown was with *military precision and timing.*

Chapter Nine

The Aftermath

So what was the real effect in the aftermath to the July 5th forceful closure of the fourth largest private bank in the world? One would expect an impending global financial crisis that would send markets tumbling into a free fall and havoc on the financial system? Not quite.

You see the timing of the closure was also planned skillfully and deliberately as to cause as minimal disruption to the markets as possible. The fact that BCCI's closure had little damaging effect on the international system as a whole is another testimony to the planning and execution of the move.

The days following the closure saw frantic correspondence between regulators and central banks in all of the seventy-six countries that BCCI had a presence in. Some complied with the requests of the NY Fed and BofE/IML almost immediately and froze assets, however other countries such as China, Pakistan, UAE, Zimbabwe and others did not see the need to bow down to the request of the (in their opinion) 'aggressive' western regulators. I can see their point, if being a sovereign state with a stable economy they would wish to judge the operations of the BCCI entity in their own country based on its performance and conduct in that jurisdiction. Similarly in the UK, there was never any solid evidence of malpractice such as money-laundering or fraud within the UK operations yet UK depositors and employees still suffered. The disease should be treated where it is found and not torture the rest of the body.

Let us examine who was affected.

The CEO Mr. Swaleh Naqvi and other Senior Executives

Under pressure from the United States, the Abu Dhabi government kept approximately eighteen senior management of BCCI in confinement at the heavily-guarded police officers club near the airport. At first they were reluctant to release Naqvi but then extradited him after a deal was signed with the Americans to hand him over in exchange for dropping all charges against the ruling family in the bank's ordeal. This was also a very testing time in the diplomatic relations between the United States and the United Arab Emirates. However the UAE spent a lot of time, effort and resources in trying to clear its name from the now tainted name of the bank they helped to start.

Naqvi was handed over to US authorities, tried and then sentenced to eleven years imprisonment. During his trial he remained silent most of the time and when he spoke he almost always stated that as CEO he was 'responsible for everything that happened in the bank' and therefore took full responsibility for all that was allegedly committed. He did this out of moral purpose that was inbuilt in his personality after spending over three decades with Agha Hasan Abedi, his mentor. He took it all onto himself and bore the brunt of the punishment on behalf of the entire group.

Swaleh Naqvi's total sentence was for eleven years. Of these the three years spent in Abu Dhabi were adjusted. Two years were further reduced in lieu of co-operation. In all Naqvi was there for about five years in a minimum security facility in Pennsylvania called Ellen Wood.

Naqvi says: "We lived in barracks which contained cubicles that housed two to three people. The barracks were locked. They were opened for breakfast. After that some work or the other was assigned that we went out to do. After that we were locked up in the barracks again, which were next opened at lunch time, and after that at dinner time. After dinner we had another two to three hours of freedom. It was fairly relaxed, being a minimum security facility. There was a library and television. There were a fair number of black Muslims and arrangements were in place for Namaaz (prayers). These were eight years of the prime of my professional life during which I should really have risen to the pinnacle of my career. They were all gone. I was separated from my family, with just one daughter in the US who visited me once a month."

Then there was the time spent researching current affairs in the library, and the writing of memos to his court appointed lawyer. "That caused for considerable frustration and anguish. To see how other institutions were being allowed to get away with committing huge crimes with no more than a token slap on the wrist. I was perhaps too engrossed in my personal situation, and not being able to step back and view the big picture. That the BCCI and its staff were really prisoners of war, and not ordinary white collar criminals." ★(Credit: Mr. Adil Ahmad)

The US still was hungry for Abedi, but Pakistan refused to extradite him plus he was by this time too fragile and unwell to move.

Employees

Some 14,000+ employees in seventy-six countries were made redundant and told not to come into work the next day without formal prior notification. How are these employees, their families and children meant to come to terms with what has just happened to them due to no direct fault of their own?

Let me take the UK as a main example in my analysis as it was the region with the most branches.

Approximately 2000 employees suddenly became unemployed in the UK. Sounds like a nightmare for the Government of the day right? These poor individuals did not receive any three months' statutory severance pay or any other compensation.

Imagine if this happened to you. Just for a minute, imagine if you were to lose your job tomorrow morning when you went to work after dropping your kids off to school and kissing your spouse goodbye. Imagine you then going home on the tube just after the lunch break with a cardboard box in your hand full of your office items. Imagine the conversation you will have to have with your family about finances and paying bills. How will you pay your rent or your mortgage? How will you buy food and clothes for your family or pay for their school fees? What are you going to do when you cannot even access your own bank account because it is frozen? No more salaries, no more bill payments even. Sounds like a nightmare scenario doesn't it? Well imagine that this happened to 14,000 innocent employees worldwide not just in the UK. And it did.

It all happened. Marriages broke, divorce settlements, kids were taken out of school, families moved abroad and some people had nowhere to live or any food to eat. I am sure that John Major, the Prime Minister of the day, would have envisaged scores of queues at the job centres lining up for unemployment benefit (now known as Job Seekers' Allowance). However that did not prevent him from giving Norman Lamont and Leigh-Pemberton the nod to go ahead with the bank's closure. Some Members of Parliament did have a conscience though, like Keith Vaz for instance, Labour MP for Leicester.

Keith helped numerous former employees of BCCI and gave them a voice in the UK Parliament so that they could be heard. He spoke up for them in the House of Commons and tried to fight for their rights. He campaigned with them on the streets and outside public buildings. Many of the 2500 UK staff of BCCI had outstanding loans with the bank including mortgages which they could now not pay off even. Hence a group of former employees formed the BCCI Campaign Committee, headed by Mohammad Qayyum and with senior active members Qaiser Malik and (late) Rehan Mahmud who worked tirelessly day and night to fight for compensation for all former UK staff. They did a formidable job and won many court cases for a plethora of employees.

The single biggest problem for former BCCI employees became the issue of being stigmatized by the entire BCCI saga. The media had slung so much mud at the group (both pre and post closure) that anybody who had any connection with BCCI was looked upon as a crook or plain 'dodgy'. Therefore this stigma was causing immense difficulty for any former employee to find new employment elsewhere. As a result a ground-breaking case in British Legal history and in case law took place when Qaiser Malik fought his case against the bank. The case known as '*Malik vs BCCI*' made a vital change in UK Employment Law whereby the employer must give mention to 'mutual trust and confidence' as a reputable employer in the contractual agreement. The House of Lords unanimously held that the term of mutual trust and confidence would be implied into the contract as a necessary incident of the employment relation.

Keith Vaz to this day does not understand why the UK operations were not 'ring fenced' and why efforts were not made to save the bank when one of the richest men in the world, Sheikh Zayed, offered to and actually injected money into the bank. Vaz's puzzlement deepens when he discovered that the UK operations had a high liquidity ratio and none of the branches were ever tainted with any form of bad banking or malpractice.

Let us quote the Diane Abbott Parliamentary Treasury Select Committee from 1991 when the Bank of England were summoned to answer questions from Members of Parliament. At this Select Committee Robin Leigh-Pemberton et al were grilled and it was a highly charged event.

When asked by the chair of the committee Mr. Terence L. Higgins and by Mr. Giles Radice about the state of the UK operations and branches of BCCI, the governor of the BofE Leigh-Pemberton replied: "*The branches in this country have not worked badly, indeed we think they are possibly asset surplus so that it did not occur to us (earlier) that closing down here in the United Kingdom was a good course of action."*

Then Mr. Radice pressed for more details about possibilities that overseas operations were extracting profits from the UK. The Governor responded: *"It could not be said the international group was milking the UK branches."*

Depositors / Creditors

The next set of victims were undoubtedly the creditors or those who kept their hard-earned money in BCCI with trust. Again due to no fault of their own, they were left with no access to their bank accounts. Simple grocery shopping would have been impossible if your bank card wouldn't work and you could not withdraw cash from your local ATM!

However in the UK in particular BCCI had many corporate and official clients who held accounts entrusting their funds with them. According to the *FT*, a total of seventy-eight million pounds was kept with the bank by local authorities and councils. The Western Isles Council had about twenty-three million pounds in the bank.

The Chinese government invested $400m and many diplomatic salaries were paid via the bank.

However we must address the most popular question and allegation that BCCI was insolvent and had a huge financial hole in the middle. That it had no money to pay back to depositors even after Abu Dhabi bailing it out.

Almost every political-financial pundit and analyst from Wall Street to Hong Kong was yacking on about the fact how $20 billion or so had vanished into thin air. The *Financial Times* along with the group liquidators said they would be lucky if they could salvage the assets and return a maximum of up to 30–40% of deposits to creditors.

What a joke!

Let us examine the total figures we have from the Global Recovery Report issued by the liquidators in 2012:

Figures stated in the final liquidators report show:

Total Value of claims paid: $6,895m
This amount equates to 90.185% dividend paid by liquidators

Total value of fees and other costs: $1,709m
This amount equates to an additional 22% dividend on the value of claims paid.

Wow!

Evidently as we can see by the liquidators report, following twenty-five years of liquidation, they have managed to 'salvage' and recover almost every penny. Where was the $20 billion hole?

According to the report, all BCCI creditors have been paid a minimum dividend of 90.185 % back to creditors totalling a whopping $6.9 billion! Additional 22% on the original claim following the liquidation costs!

In other countries where operations were ring fenced efficiently (which should have been done in the UK) creditors were paid back 100% like in Hong Kong for example!! Therefore hardly anything was 'lost' or 'stolen' except for what the liquidators took: a colossal $1.7 billion in fees!

Liquidators: Touche Ross (now Deloitte)

So after years of salvaging BCCI the joint liquidators ran up costs in excess of $1.7 billion!

That is 1 billion GB Pounds Sterling!

Considering BCCI was apparently 'insolvent' as per the auditors PW, the Bank of England and the liquidators Deloitte, they did a pretty damn good job of squeezing over 90% back to creditors and extracting $1.7bn for themselves!

There has been a great deal of outrage and uproar from former employees and creditors of BCCI at the unreasonable excess of expenditure incurred by the liquidators. They believe had the liquidation costs not been so high, then they would have received over 100% of their deposits back in full (the figures above confirm that this would be the case).

The anger was fuelled during the nineties when liquidators were seemingly conducting the project in an extremely luxurious and ostentatious manner booking first or business class flights and staying in five star hotels.

In their defense they state that the unusual high costs were associated with the immense complexity of BCCI's affairs along with workload of cases spread across the world in many different jurisdictions.

Abu Dhabi Ruling family

In my opinion, without a doubt the biggest victims of the entire saga were the ruling family of Abu Dhabi and the majority shareholders. They were led down a long track of injecting more and more never-ending cash into the BCCI group after been given verbal and written assurances that the funds would be used for restructuring. Even the threat of closing down the bank was never given by the BofE or PW to the majority shareholders.

Naturally one can sympathise with the royal family on the money that was lost which eventually was used up by the liquidators. Furthermore the worst damage came to them in the form of negative publicity worldwide as their good name was maligned across front page newspapers along with ruthless exaggerated stories about BCCI.

The negative media did not stop at newspapers and television, but about five different books have been authored and published about BCCI since its closure, even a Hollywood film was made.

Branches and Assets of BCCI group

Apart from the USA and UK, as stated earlier many countries and their central bank regulators decided to ring fence the BCCI operations. This then enabled them to both protect depositors in those countries and also sell off the BCCI business to other financial institutions.

In the majority of countries we can see BCCI still operating to this very day but trading as different names. It was a potential goldmine for many other banks who jumped at the chance to take over BCCI's regional business along with their customer base and goodwill.

One such example in Pakistan is Bank AlFalah (owned by the Dhabi group headed by Sheikh Nahyan) which took over BCCI branches in the country and re-branded. The iconic BCCI glass building on I.I. Chundrigar road is now the Bank AlFalah head office in Karachi. The former CEO of Bank Alfalah is also an ex-BCCI banker Mr. Sirajuddin Aziz (now heading Habib Metropolitan Bank).

In the UAE, the BCCI (Emirates) branches were kept open for some time until they were converted into United National Bank (UNB) offices.

In numerous other countries from Hong Kong to Beijing and from Zimbabwe to Cairo, we still see BCCI flourishing and doing incredible good business, but without the BCCI logo.

We see reminders of the institution everywhere from the iconic buildings they erected, like the current Metro bank building in the heart of Chelsea, London was built by BCCI. Now Metro Bank is also one of the fastest expanding financial groups in the UK with a large retail network similar to BCCI's growth, but it is an American bank.

Bank of England case

Touche Ross Tohmatsu issued a writ to the Bank Of England to sue them over the BCCI saga on behalf of creditors and were hoping that the bank would pay up. After more than a decade, the liquidators launched a scathing attack on the Bank Of England which bought the case to courts which was set to become the longest serving case in history in the UK (and the most expensive).

The liquidators were claiming the Bank of England had not only made a series of breath-taking errors and omissions in its supervision of BCCI, it had done so knowing full well that depositors' life savings might be in peril. It was the first time the Bank of England was being sued in its 300-year history but luckily for them they *are protected by law and enjoy immunity from being penalized or prosecuted for dishonesty.*

On 2nd November 2005, the liquidators dropped the case against the bank after the chancellor of the high court said it was no longer in the best interests of creditors for the litigation to carry on.

The Bank of England breathed a sigh of relief and prepared for a counter attack involving a $100m lawsuit to claim for damages.

The Bingham Report 1992

Shortly after the forced closure of BCCI, the UK Government ordered an independent inquiry into the regulatory supervision of BCCI and to comprehend in effect whether the Bank of England conducted their job properly.

Lord Tom Bingham was a proper classic English gentleman. Very few match his calibre these days. During the inquiry, which I must say was conducted most thoroughly, he interviewed hundreds of people around the world and analysed thousands of documents, memos and correspondence with a fine comb. He was also one of the most notable and respectable judges in England making him the best man for the job since he was a man of respect, honour and integrity.

John Hilbery, former director of Bank of America and later head of communications at BCCI was also interviewed by Lord Bingham in 1991 for three hours. Hilbery described Bingham as a compassionate gent who was hard-working and had no interest in personal wealth. Much like how people describe the likes of Clark Clifford and Agha Hasan Abedi. "Lord Bingham was the most outstanding Law Lord of his era and equal to no other. In its purest form, quality is universal. But it is rarely, if ever, totally pure. The mind of an English gent is honed over time into Englishness. The mind of an outstanding Muslim gent has a different quality. The two might meet, but never fully except, perhaps, in the world of mathematics." Hilbery said.

"I did my best to explain BCCI and Agha Hasan Abedi to Lord Bingham. But he could never quite get it. It takes years of honing to understand where an Asian entrepreneur is coming from, even when he is the best of his kind. The Americans will never get it at all. They have a young mind and it's honed solely to American values," he added.

When one reads the Bingham report carefully which was published on 22nd October 1992 just over a year after the bank's closure, then you clearly feel that between the lines Bingham felt that the worst course of action inevitably taken by the Bank of England could have been avoided in order to safeguard UK depositors. Furthermore he felt the Bank of England, the IML and PW should have informed the Abu Dhabi shareholders in advance of shutting the bank down and understood the validity of their anger. As a matter of courtesy or on the very basis of honour and integrity he felt that the majority shareholders should have been notified beforehand especially as they had committed such large sums of money to saving the bank. He felt that Abu Dhabi were justified in their dismay and anger causing diplomatic rifts between the two countries which enjoyed a mutual understanding of trust. They felt naturally wounded as they acted in good faith to save the bank (which they had no obligation to do) and injected funds on the request of PW, the BofE and BCCI.

Global Reactions

It is difficult to ascertain what the world general opinion on the closure of BCCI was overall but the global media did a pretty decent job of swinging opinions against the bank as we have seen based on inaccurate reporting.

It is to be noted though that following the closure and throughout Agha Hasan Abedi's illness, his close friend and confidante former US President Jimmy Carter telephoned him regularly to check up on his wellbeing. He even said to him once "I do not believe for a second anything that is being reported about you or your bank in the media".

People like Jimmy Carter and James Callaghan saw Abedi for who he really was. They were lucky enough to spend copious amounts of time with him and his family and tour the world with him during his philanthropic efforts which struck a chord with them. Hence as a result when they spent time with Abedi, they spent time with BCCI and saw the true nature of their ethos and culture which was of 'Giving' and joint vision which encompasses morality and humility. At an interview given shortly before his passing, Abedi described the closure of his bank as a grave tragedy and that the truth will one day prevail. "They misunderstood us, God knows best".

Chapter Ten

The Big Fish and LIBOR

Since the forced closure of BCCI in 1991, we have suffered many setbacks in the financial industry and the road has not been smooth by all means. But we must analyse what we learnt from the BCCI shutdown. Did the regulators want to give a clear and stark message to all banks and financial institutions that if you commit or are seen to commit a financial crime, then you will also face the fate of BCCI? Are all banks 'clean' and free from wrongdoing and how many have been forcefully closed in the past twenty-five years?

No doubt the headlines of the last ten years alone have raised many questions about the state of the financial system following the global financial crisis in 2008 with the real collapse of Lehman Brothers. But now we have learnt that almost every bank or financial instutuion that we can name has committed a crime or has at least seen to be facilitating a crime. So what punishment have the regulators imposed on them. Let us look at those in more detail over the next few chapters and compare them with the punishment meted out to BCCI.

Let me take you on little ride around the theme park of financial frauds and scandals undertaken and proven by some of the largest and well-known financial institutions of our time. I will endeavor to outline their respective punishments wherever possible so that one may assess the severity of the fraud, align it with the penalty and then compare it with the capital punishment unleashed on BCCI over twenty years ago.

If the BCCI shutdown and forced closure was meant to make a statement or set a precedent or to give a warning to other banks that this is what will happen to them if they commit the same crimes BCCI was accused of doing, then it certainly didn't achieve that or anything close to it.

Indeed, the recent scandals and frauds of the banking giants of late make the BCCI saga look like a parking violation.

LIBOR

"This dwarfs by order of magnitude any financial scam in the history of markets" — Andrew Lo, professor of Finance, Massachusetts Institute of Technology (MIT)

LIBOR is a concept that began in the mid–1980s when new products were introduced to the financial sector, including interest rate swaps, foreign currency options, and forward rate agreements. Seeing the opportunity and risks, the BBA (British Banker's Association) partnered with organisations, including the Bank of England, to establish various working groups dedicated to develop measurement standards for the new product offerings thereby creating a clearinghouse for competitors to list their daily rates. The culmination of the London banking industry's efforts is the LIBOR.

Scratching your head? Still doesn't make sense does it? Let me break it down even further for you.

Libor (London interbank offered rate) is one of the key European benchmarks for the interest rate that banks charge each other to lend money. It is calculated by averaging borrowing costs between banks. It is the average interest rate set every day and submitted at 11am, that London's biggest banks would charge another big bank. LIBOR is released for overnight, one day, one week, one month, two months etc periods of time.

All other financial institutions (smaller banks, credit card companies, mortgage lenders, currency traders) base their interest rate slightly higher than LIBOR. Even the Swiss National Bank uses the LIBOR as a reference for their monetary policies. So it provides a benchmark for interest rates practically globally and not limited to Europe.

The first allegation is that these banks colluded to manipulate the LIBOR rate, and each tried to net huge profits. Banks can estimate what the LIBOR rate will be and the team that calculates this rate is kept away from the rest of the bank. However, some traders at Barclays began to influence the LIBOR rate by either early access or by asking the team to manipulate the numbers. Allegedly, some traders had insider access to information about LIBOR hours before it was released, and even knowing the movements by 0.01 percentage points could result in gains of millions of dollars. It is also suggested that since many banks did this, the net result would've been the banks canceling out each other's profits.

A BBC report discovered that as early as 2005 there was substantial evidence Barclays had tried to manipulate dollar Libor and Euribor (the Eurozone's equivalent of Libor) rates at the request of its derivatives traders and other banks.

Misconduct was widespread, involving staff in New York, London and Tokyo as well as external international parties and traders.

Between January 2005 and June 2009, Barclays derivatives traders made a total of 257 requests to fix Libor and Euribor rates, according to a report by the FSA.

According to an article by Bloomberg in the USA, Barclays former chief operating officer, Jerry Del Missier said that the Bank of England encouraged the lender to suppress Libor submissions. In October 2008, days before RBS and Lloyds looked for bailouts, the Bank of England asked Barclays to lower its rates because they were concerned about the bank's stability, Del Missier told a panel of British lawmakers on July 16. Tucker, the deputy in charge of the central bank, in turn denied allegations of any such comments or orders.

On 17 July 2012, US Federal Reserve Chairman Ben Bernanke told a Senate committee that the Libor system was "structurally flawed" and said that he still did not have full confidence in the system.

Earlier, the former governor of the Bank of England, Sir Mervyn King, told the Treasury Committee that UK authorities had been worried about senior management at Barclays, even before the recent Libor scandal broke. Sir Mervyn said Barclays had sailed *"close to the wind"* too often.

The second allegation against Barclays is that it manipulated LIBOR so that Barclays would seem less risky and also to show that it was healthier. Several banks, and it is alleged the Bank of England too were involved, submitted lower LIBOR rates to make it seem that the banks were doing better than they actually were.

This is basically the equivalent of you and me lying about our salary on a loan application form.

Here we are talking about a potential fraud where a whole bunch of international banks were colluding together frauds to a tune of $800 trillion.

Libor is the most widely used interest rate in the world. Estimates of how much is tied to Libor vary from $350 trillion to $800 trillion. To give you a rough estimate, $350 trillion *would pay for all USA government spending for the next century*. Some banks including Barclays artificially inflated or deflated their rates, depending on what would benefit them the most. Some may have deflated their rates to give the impression that they were more creditworthy than they actually were. This is deceit to depositors, investors and the general public on an unprecedented scale. According to my research BCCI never lied to its customers and fulfilled all of its financial commitments until the very end of its existence nor did it manipulate LIBOR.

In June 2012, Barclays *admitted to misconduct* and the UK's FSA imposed a £59.5m ($92.7 million) penalty, which gave the bank the biggest fine it had ever imposed in its history.

The US Department of Justice and the Commodity Futures Trading Commission (CFTC) imposed fines worth £102m and £128m respectively, forcing Barclays to pay a total of around £290m.

Two days later, chief executive Bob Diamond said he would attend a Commons Treasury Select Committee and that the bank would co-operate with authorities. However, *he insisted he would not resign*.

The same day, Bank of England governor Sir Mervyn King called for a "cultural change", *but ruled out a Leveson-style inquiry into the banks*. Very strange, why though? Sounds very flaky to me. Had this been BCCI, it would've been a different story.

At the Libor investigation hearing with the parliamentary select committee, John Mann MP fairly stumped Diamond when he asked: "Can you remind me the three founding principles of the Quakers who founded Barclays?" As Diamond sat stoney-faced, Mann told him what they are:-

"Honesty. Integrity. Plain dealing. That's the ethos of the bank you've just spent two hours telling us is doing so well – in fact so well that I wonder why you've not received an extra bonus rather than the sack." [Diamond, even though he did not know the principles claims to have abided by them].

"You're the man in charge. But you're accepting all the good things and the bonuses [and] the people working for you are fiddling the system, potentially going to prison... give me a suggestion of how you're going to show contrition to those staff and customers who are wondering whether to take their money out of this rotten, thieving bank?"

Priceless!!

Matt Taibbi from the *Rolling Stone* magazine in the USA, who regularly and quite flamboyantly reports the financial corruption cases said: "This is the world's biggest banks stealing money that would otherwise have gone to textbooks, housing and medicine for ordinary Americans and turning cash into sports cars for the already very rich. It's the equivalent of robbing a church fund or charity to pay for lapdances."

All this being said, the fact remains Bob Diamond, Jerry Del Missier and other senior management of Barclays were never indicted or faced any criminal charges relating to the LIBOR scandal which happened under their noses during their time in office. They were in positions of responsibility and should have taken the full responsibility along with the consequences as Mr. Swaleh Naqvi did at BCCI even though he wasn't solely responsible for any wrongdoing at the bank.

Barclays Bank PLC

The pride and joy of Britain. The spurious Former Chief Executive Bob Diamond seemed to think it was a beacon of virtue and success. However I would like to remind Bob of some of the bamboozling activities of the old British institution in recent times which was outlined by financial journalist Ian Fraser:

Below is an extensive but not exhaustive list of recent scandals involving Barclays alone, however I shall detail only a selection afterwards.

1. The swindling of retail customers by selling them largely redundant PPI (total compensation >£1bn)
2. The Project Brontos tax scam, which will see the criminal trial of four executives of Barclays Italian arm. Unicredit was also involved (penalties unclear)
3. The infamous tax avoidance factory led by Roger Jenkins, of which Brontos formed a part (deemed "highly abusive", Barclays forced to pay £500m in a "clawback" settlement with HMRC)
4. The £12.3bn Protium deal, a deceptive ploy designed to shift vast amounts of toxic assets off the Barclays balance sheet, which rewarded executives at shareholders' expense (penalties unclear)
5. The £7bn deal with Middle Eastern investors that was hugely detrimental to the interests of ordinary shareholders (penalties unclear)

6. The betrayal of corporate customers like Del Monte (settlement to Del Monte shareholders $90 million)

7. The wholesale doctoring of documentation to hide the movement of funds into the US from Iran, Cuba and other prohibited countries (US settlement $298m)

8. The mis-selling of income funds (FSA fine £7.7m) The 'serious weaknesses' in providing data on trades to the City regulator (FSA fine £2.45m)

9. The industrial-scale mis-selling of interest rate swaps to SMEs, which is crippling tens of thousands of smaller firms across the UK.

10. The commingling of customers and proprietary assets (FSA fine £1.1m)

11. The abuse of IFRS to double its own profitability and massively inflate executives' bonuses (source: PIRC)

12. Barclays – QATAR scandal (see below for further detail)

13. The systemic faking of its Libor (interbank borrowing) numbers (FSA/CFTC/DoJ fine $453 million)

(Source: Ian Fraser)

Now the first question that comes to my mind is was the accountancy firm responsible for Barclays sleeping and drinking cheap Ukrainian lager during their yearly audits? They must've been sniffing something! It is difficult to understand how SO many suspicious activities can continue undetected by the auditors.

In March 2009, Barclays was accused of violating international anti-money-laundering laws. According to the NGO Global Witness, the Paris branch of Barclays held the account of Equatorial Guinean President Teodoro Obiang's son even after evidence that Obiang had siphoned oil revenues from government funds emerged in 2004. According to Global Witness, Obiang purchased a Ferrari and maintains a mansion in Malibu with the funds from this account.

A 2010 report by the *Wall Street Journal* described how Barclays and other banks were involved in helping the Alavi Foundation,

Bank Melli, the Iranian government, and/or others circumvent US laws banning financial transactions with certain states. They did this by 'stripping' information out of wire transfers, thereby concealing the source of funds. Barclays settled with the government for US $298 million. – ("Probe Circles Globe to Find Dirty Money", Carrick Mollenkamp, *Wall Street Journal*, 3 September 2010)

So what punishment was given to the Banks global management in the light of these Money-laundering allegations? What Media coverage was there in the USA or Europe? During BCCI's Tampa case, there were hundreds of journalists and TV crews outside the Bank's head office which in itself was detrimental to the Bank's operational activities and credibility in the eyes of depositors.

Even the fake wedding of Robert Mazur during the BCCI Customs undercover Tampa Sting was filmed by TV channels hence validating the notion of pre-emptive action.

Tax avoidance

According to the *Guardian* and other sources, in March 2009, Barclays obtained an injunction against the *Guardian* to remove from its website confidential leaked documents describing how SCM, Barclays' structured capital markets division, planned to use more than £11bn of loans to create hundreds of millions of pounds of tax benefits, via "an elaborate circuit of Cayman Islands companies, US partnerships and Luxembourg subsidiaries". In an editorial on the issue, The *Guardian* pointed out that, due to the mismatch of resources, tax-collectors (HMRC) have now to rely on websites such as WikiLeaks to obtain such documents, and indeed the documents in question have now appeared on WikiLeaks. Separately, another Barclays whistleblower revealed several days later that the SCM transactions had produced between £900m and £1bn in tax avoidance in one year, adding that "The deals start with tax and then commercial purpose is added to them."

In February 2012 Barclays was forced to pay back £500 million in tax which it had tried to avoid. Barclays was accused by HMRC of designing two schemes that were intended to avoid substantial amounts of tax. Tax rules forced the bank to tell the UK authorities about its plans.

David Gauke, Exchequer Secretary to the Treasury, said that "We do not take today's action lightly, but the potential tax loss from this scheme and the history of previous abuse in this area mean that this is a circumstance where the decision to change the law with full retrospective effect is justified."

One tax scheme involved Barclays claiming it should not have to pay corporation tax on profits made when buying back its own IOUs. The second tax avoidance scheme, also designed by Barclays, involved investment funds claiming that non-taxable income entitled the funds to tax credits that could be reclaimed from HMRC. The treasury described this as "an attempt to secure 'repayment' from the Exchequer of tax that has not been paid". BCCI on the other hand, according to all auditors and the Bingham report of 1992 adhered strictly to all its Tax commitments specifically in the UK to HMRC and also globally.

Barclays / Qatar Scandal

The Barclays/Qatari scandal prompted Antony Jenkins, the CEO of Barclays to forfeit his annual bonus for 2012 which was estimated at 75.2 million pounds.

The timing of the Qatari scandal was the worst for the bank. "Barclays Group is a cripple and a swamp of financial scandals; but the scandal of "Barclays–Qatar" won't completely destroy the group; it will remain a big brand in banking world, rather; it will weaken it a lot", David Thomas, banking expert said.

"Banking system depends on trust and credibility; but Barclays' credibility eroded recently; eager to make more profits, Barclays has violated the ethical and moral norms of the British financial institutions. This will be reflected on the trust of customers and the profit rate in the future",

A leading financial expert John Arthur said: "The matter goes back to 2008; at the height of the world financial crises, the big knives of Barclays Group wanted to avoid the interference of the British government, through emphasizing the success the group is achieving and the trust of the international investors in the financial performance of Barclays".

Arthur added: "To do that, Barclays Group had to launch campaigns to raise money from international investors. Qatar Holding Co. has invested 3.5 million Pounds (4.8 US Dollars) in June and October of 2008, to help the bank to not ask for bailout; on the contrary of its top competitors; Lloyd Group and the Royal Bank of Scotland"

Hence on 26th November 2015 the FCA in the UK fined Barclays £72,069,400 (72 million GBP) for failing to minimise the risk that it may be used to facilitate financial crime.

In a press release the FCA stated "The failings relate to a £1.88 billion pound transaction (Transaction) that Barclays arranged and executed in 2011 and 2012 for a number of ultra-high net worth clients. The clients involved were politically exposed persons (PEPs) and should therefore have been subject to enhanced levels of due diligence and monitoring by Barclays.

Barclays went to unacceptable lengths to accommodate the clients. Specifically, Barclays did not obtain information that it was required to obtain from the clients to comply with financial crime requirements. Barclays did not do so because it did not wish to inconvenience the clients. Barclays agreed to keep details of the Transaction strictly confidential, even within the firm, and agreed to indemnify the clients up to £37.7 million in the event that it failed to comply with these confidentiality restrictions."

Mark Steward, director of enforcement and market oversight at the FCA said:

"Barclays ignored its own process designed to safeguard against the risk of financial crime and overlooked obvious red flags to win new business and generate significant revenue. This is wholly unacceptable.

"Firms will be held to account if they fail to minimise financial crime risks appropriately and for this reason the FCA has required Barclays to disgorge its revenue from the Transaction."

This is nothing new. BCCI was held to account by being shut down but nobody seems to remember this anymore.

The one British bank that did fail and collapse in the real sense as a result of fraud was Barings Bank. Barings, one of Britain's oldest, collapsed in 1995 after Nick Leeson, the original rogue trader, lost £860 million while betting on the future of the Tokyo stock market.

Agha Hasan Abedi aged 4 years old.

Abedi with US President Jimmy Carter.

HH Sheikh Mohammad of Dubai (then Crown prince) being introduced to Yahya Khan of Pakistan by Abedi.

Abedi with HH Sheikh Zayed (left) and Pakistani President Yahya Khan (right). HH Dr Saeed Al Otaiba can be seen at the back.

HH Sheikh Khalifa of UA
(then Crown Prince) with
Agha Hasan Abedi.

HH Sheikh Zayed with President
Ayub Khan of Pakistan. Abedi is
behind the Sheikh to his right.

Agha Hasan Abedi
greeting the President
of Zimbabwe Robert
Mugabe to inaugurate t
Zimbabwe branch
of BCCI.

Abedi with wife and daughter Maha
at a BCCI reception.

Outside the BCCI Karachi
main branch (now Bank Al
Falah HQ.)

(left to right) Agha Hasan Abedi, Michael Manely (Prime Minister of Jamaica), Former
British Prime Minister James Callaghan, Shrideth Ramphal (Secretary General of
Commonwealth) and Olaf Palme (former Prime Minister of Sweden) at the Inaugural
Third World Prize Ceremony hosted by BCCI in London, 1979.

Jimmy Carter being introduced to
Pakistani Prime Minister Nawaz
Sharif (then Chief Minister Punjab.)

Charles, HRH the Prince of Wales
greeting BCCI's Basharat Malik
and his wife at a reception
held at Kensington Palace,
London in 1990.

King Khalid of Saudi Arabia
shares a light moment
with Abedi.

President Yahya Khan escorting the late HH Sheikh
Rashid of Dubai. Abedi and Sheikh
Mohammad can be seen behind.

Ashraf Nawabi (BCC Emirates, Dubai), HH Sheikh Humaid bin Rashid Al-
Nuaimi (Ruler of the Emirate of Ajman) and Agha Hasan Abedi sitting in
Sheikh's court.

Swaleh Naqvi , CEO of
BCCI and Abedi's loyal
right hand man.

BCCI head office in Abu Dhabi
Corniche UAE
(now Union National Bank.)

US President Jimmy Carter with wife Rosalyn
Carter on tour in Africa. Abedi to the right.

Abedi meeting the Pope John Paul II in 1986.

Inside the magnificent foyer and
entrance hall of the BCCI Karachi
branch on I.I. Chundrigar road.

BCCI Senior Management with representatives of the Prince's Youth Business
Trust and other senior British Officials.

Dildar Rizvi BCCI AsiaPac (far left.)
HE Sir Angus Ogilvy, husband of Princess Alexandria of Kent (3rd from left.)
Swaleh Naqvi CEO of BCCI (Centre, 4th from right/left.)
Lord Thomas Boardman, Chairman of NatWest Bank (3rd from right.)
Basharat A. Malik, BCCI UK (Far right.)

The elegant marble reception of BCCI Cannon Street branch, London.

BCCI Far East Manager Dildar Rizvi receivin
Agha Hasan Abedi in Hong Kong.

Agha Hasan Abedi with Ibne Hasan
Burney (Early pic
before BCCI days.)

Agha Hasan Abedi & colleagues
onboard the BCCI private Boeing jet.

Swaleh Naqvi, CEO of BCCI with the
author M.B. Malik at Infaq (former
BCCI Foundation) offices in
Karachi, Pakistan 2015.

Chapter Eleven

Holy Grails – Global International Banks

Standard Chartered Bank

"The bank operated as a rogue institution"
  -Former prosecutor, Benjamin Lawsky of the New York State
  Department of Financial Services (DFS)

On August 6th 2012 it was reported worldwide that New York's top financial regulator was about to crack down on US operations of the British bank Standard Chartered and threatened to revoke its NY State licence therefore seemingly posing a potentially lethal threat to its very existence in the USA.

Why was this threat posed?

Reuters reported on the same day that Benjamin Lawsky of the DFS who was leading the investigation into Standard Chartered, believed that the bank had concealed a whopping **$250 billion** of transactions that were linked with Iran and consequently violating US law on a colossal scale.

Lawsky added that Standard Chartered 'schemed' with the Iranian government and were conceited in their actions by deliberately withholding information from authorities. This included up to 60,000 secret and hidden transactions that were carried out to conjure up hundreds of millions of dollars' worth of fees over a decade.

The DFS further said that these activities 'inevitably exposed the US banking system to terrorists, drug traffickers and corrupt states.'

The bank also became an expert in the game of 'wire stripping' which meant that they removed codes on money transfers and altered message fields, inserting phrases such as "NO NAME GIVEN" to conceal the origin and nature of the transactions. This is a widely-used method by a number of banks apparently who try and circumvent anti-money-laundering laws and this practice of wire stripping was never practised or proved to be practised at BCCI.

In reply to these accusations at the time Standard Chartered simply issued a statement saying that it "does not believe the order issued by the DFS presents a full and accurate picture of the facts."

Firstly they contested their position as to the actual amount of Iranian transactions that took place. According to the bank, the figure was under $14 million and that they had shared documentation with the DFS to prove this. My argument isn't the amount, whether its $14 million or $250 billion, it is the question of why were they violating the law in the first place which is the worrying factor and then being let off. In their opinion it seems even $14 million worth of Iranian transactions seemed to be 'ok' as it were. Wait a minute… wasn't $14 million the amount BCCI was stung with in the fake money-laundering sting? $14 million seemed a lot to the authorities back then in 1988, why isn't it such a big deal for Standard Chartered and their illegal Iranian transactions two decades later?

The appointment to bring in an external consultant (Deloitte) was requested by the New York regulators much earlier in 2004 so that they could investigate the problem transactions in detail. Therefore this was evidently an ongoing long-term investigation which only came to the frontline newspapers recently, allowing Standard Chartered to continue these illegal transactions for a decade.

It was further highlighted by Jonathan Stempel and Carrick Mollenkamp from Reuters that during the Deloitte probe 'at one point, Standard Chartered asked Deloitte to "delete" references to certain improper Iranian transactions, according to the New York order.'

In a subsequent email, a Deloitte partner said the firm had "agreed" to the request because it was "too politically sensitive for both (Standard Chartered) and Deloitte. That is why I drafted the watered-down version," they added.

This was working perfectly for Standard Chartered then, as it seemed to have Deloitte on their side after a couple of negotiations it seems. The resulting report that was submitted in 2007 by Deloitte to the New York regulators made sure that it portrayed as if Standard Chartered had demonstrated clear effort in tidying up its act with regards to adhering to the anti-money-laundering laws that were in place.

In the following weeks, after much media kerfuffle the British bank's chief executive Peter Sands went to New York in order to negotiate a settlement with the regulators so that they could keep their US licence.

Again Peter Sands admitted that some of their transactions broke US sanctions, but said that the amount was just $14m, as mentioned above. He maintained his stance, however the statement released on 14th August 2012 by Lawsky and the DFS read: "The parties have agreed that the conduct at issue involved transactions of at least $250bn."

On the other hand a short statement from Standard Chartered simply confirmed a settlement of $340 million had been reached.

Wow! So this technically means, that if I was to launder $250 billion somehow, I would only pay a maximum penalty of $300-odd million for it, get to keep all the proceeds and not spend a day in jail! Sounds ludicrous! But this is what happened here. Nobody went to jail and nobody was bought to account for these transactions. As CEO, Peter Sands should have resigned at the very least and taken responsibility for the actions of his subordinates. CEO of BCCI Naqvi however faced the brunt of the adverse media and the authorities and spent time in prison for the actions of others because he was the CEO of the bank and took full responsibility.

The most prominent activity was the "U-Turn" transactions, which involved money that was shifted for Iranian clients within banks in Britain and the Middle East and cleared through Standard Chartered's New York branch, but neither of which began or ended in Iran. These 'U-turn' transactions, however were legal until November 2008, when the US Treasury Department made them illegal after suspecting they could be used to evade sanctions, and also that Iran was using banks to fund their nuclear and so called missile development programmes.

The DFS prosecutor described how Standard Chartered transferred vast amounts of money through its New York branch on behalf of Iranian customers, which included the main Central Bank of Iran and state-owned Bank Saderat and Bank Melli that were both under strict US sanctions.

All being said and done the $340 million fine slapped onto Standard Chartered was no big worry for the bank that was said to be in a 'strong' financial position by the *New York Times*. All other US agencies like the FBI, the Federal Reserve, Justice department and Treasury who were simultaneously conducting their own investigations into the bank were surprised and taken aback by the swiftness and speed of the settlement, which has practically brushed off any chances of criminal proceedings against the bank. The double standards adopted by the authorities here in contrast to BCCI is astonishing. $340 million money-laundering fine for Standard Chartered and is allowed to continue in US, but $14 million fine for BCCI after planted sting operation and they were shut down.

HSBC

> *"They (HSBC) violated every goddamn law in the book… they took every imaginable form of illegal and illicit business."*
> — *Jack Blum, an attorney and former Senate investigator.*

It is needless to say sometimes I am at loss for words on my reaction to the HSBC scandal and the resulting treatment it received. It is still one of my favourite banks though and the people who work there are equally lovely.

The closest feeling of my reaction to the scandal I can relate to is when I got scammed by a bloke sitting in Nigeria who wanted to buy my car online from *Autotrader* and did the old postal cheque and Western Union scam. I was gullible enough to fall for it and then gutted when the cheque bounced. Fortunately my already-battered German car was still sitting pretty on my driveway and I hadn't shipped it away to some dodgy handler who was going to come and pick it up that evening! Or even worse the time I discovered that everything my ex-girlfriend ever told me was a blatant lie.

The London-based bank was being used as a conduit for "drug kingpins and rogue nations" as described by the 300+ page report drawn up for the US Senate Committee that was investigating HSBC.

> *"We have apologised unreservedly to all our stakeholders and have paid huge penalties both in monetary cost and reputational damage. And I take this opportunity to apologise again in person"*
> – *Douglas Flint, HSBC chairman.*

Let's analyse in some detail what HSBC has been doing for the past twenty years. I will do this by referring periodically to the excellent article by Matt Taibbi called 'Gangster Bankers: Too big to jail' which was published in the Rolling Stone Magazine in February 2013. He has demonstrated and proved that the US government and authorities have been lenient towards HSBC and shown complacency where in the normal world if anybody else was to be guilty of those crimes, then they would be serving life imprisonment. He has also highlighted and identified the 'arrestable class and the un-arrestable class'. The arrestable class which is plain for all to see was the management of BCCI and the un-arrestable class was obviously the super-corrupt criminal management of the other banks.

Matt Taibbi, surprisingly however, omitted any mention of BCCI in article. I believe that mention of BCCI in his article would have added extra weight to his argument that the US Justice system and Federal Reserve didn't indict HSBC on grounds that it was 'too big to fail', but could be more politically motivated than we think. Although he was coming from a different angle, in that he argued brilliantly that banks were too powerful to prosecute and that criminal proceedings should have taken place, given the findings of the whistleblower named Everett Stern, he didn't make the correlation or reference to the powerful international bank with Middle Eastern roots that had already been shut down in the past for crimes which now seem like a walk in the park and miniscule compared to the HSBC scandal. Indeed, to give him due credit, Matt did mention that the Obama administration seemed to be in favour of letting HSBC off the hook, similar to the Bush administration who was also favourable to HSBC unlike previous administrations who were not as lenient to the likes of Richard Nixon, Pablo Escobar or Al Capone. He seemed to be convinced that the current US Government is almost too afraid to prosecute these big banks on criminality due to the 'effects' that the criminal proceedings would have on the World Economy. They are forgetting however, that in comparison, the global shutdown of BCCI had a minor impact on the world financial markets and the only ones that suffered were the employees, shareholders and customers of the bank.

HSBC Money laundering and Mexican Drug cartel links

HSBC, which officially stands for the 'Hong Kong and Shanghai Banking Corporation' started in China in 1865 and was a product post the First and Second Opium War. In Mexico it operated a contumelious network of branches where people could walk directly into any random Mexico branch and easily open up US dollar accounts using the 'Cayman Islands' branch of HSBC Mexico. The legal requirement was that all accounts in that vicinity had to be opened in pesos. This was hardly adhered to and the haphazard non-existent controls meant that little customer information was submitted or verified at the time of opening an account and even less to document the original source of their vast deposits.

Matt Taibbi described this operation as a 'pure shell company, run by Mexicans in Mexican bank branches'. He further made an analogy of the HSBC Mexico operation with a 'drive-through heart transplant clinic or a fully-stocked minibar in the cockpit of every plane'! Hilarious analogy but very serious. Bearing in mind, this network of branches held 50,000 customers and $2.1 billion in assets, following an audit in 2002, 41% of the reviewed accounts were revealed to have had incomplete and inadequate client data. 15% of customers there didn't even have a file on them, which shows the complete lack of systems and controls for basic KYC (Know Your Customer). Despite HSBC Mexico (HSMX) operating in a country "under siege from drug crime, violence and money laundering" it had inadequate money-laundering controls.

Between 2007–8, for example, HBMX shipped $7bn to HSBC's US operation, more than any other HSBC affiliate. Also the best bit is yet to come: Between 2006 and 2009, a mind blowing and scurrilous $200 trillion transactions were wire-transferred (from

countries like Mexico and others). Taibbi also revealed that HSBC
failed to comply with rules or apply any checks on a whopping $9
billion cash purchase from Mexico and also subsequently mastered
the black market peso exchange that enabled Medellin drug cartels
in Columbia and Mexico to convert US dollars from drug proceeds
into pesos to be utilized at home. In an even more shocking
revelation, he had described how drug dealers in Mexico were so
accustomed and knowledgeable about HSBC's lack of scrutiny
and poor compliance procedures that they built special cash boxes
that would fit perfectly within the measurements of HSBC cashier
windows. Completely mind-blowing how this was never caught on
camera by the authorities!

Mexican and US authorities expressed huge concern that drug
traffickers were able to circumvent the anti-money-laundering
controls at US banks by transporting US dollars to Mexico, and
then using HBMX to transfer it to the US, but nothing was ever
done about it.

In addition a report to the Senate committee also detailed that
HSBC in USA (HBUS) nevertheless classed Mexico as a low-risk
country and as a direct result, failed to properly monitor its transfers
and other dealings with it.

Another bloke worth mentioning here who spoke out against
HSBC was former federal prosecutor Neil Barofsky, who Taibbi said
was instrumental in many foreign money-laundering indictments.
Barofsky said that HSBC wasn't dealing with your average drug
dealer on the street or the leader of the gangs even, they were
actually doing business with the likes of Columbia's Norte del Valle
and Mexico's Sinaloa cartels and he termed them as the 'worst
trafficking organisations imaginable'. He further added that these
are groups that not only commit mass murder on a global scale but
torture their enemies, film them and then chop their heads off. All
this criminal and atrocious activity is funded by drugs and laundered
by the big banks. Barofsky also said that a guy called Pablo Trujillo
who he caught was sentenced for ten years for dealing with a cartel

that HSBC was dealing with, and yet HSBC was doing it on a much larger scale than Pablo was and got away with it.

The OCC examined HSBC on a regular basis and kept giving it 'cease and desist orders' for various crimes. Taibbi mentions: "Russians identifying themselves as used-car salesmen were at one point depositing $500,000 a day into HSBC, mainly through a bent traveller's-cheques operation in Japan. The company's special banking programme for foreign embassies was so completely f★★★★d that it had suspicious-activity alerts backed up by the thousands. There is also strong evidence that the bank was allowing clients in Sudan, Cuba, Burma and North Korea to evade sanctions."

In hindsight, even the undercover-sting operation undertaken for BCCI which duped the officers in Florida wasn't using such clichéd, open and blatant methods as this Mexican affair. US undercover investigator and agent Robert Mazur was astute enough to drop 'subtle hints' to officers apparently that the deal being brokered was slightly suspicious, but it was nothing close to what was discovered at HSBC Mexico with these containers of cash being fitted through the teller or cashier windows! Where is Robert Mazur and his team now? Why aren't they carrying out sting operations at these larger banks or random routine checks even? Where is the consistency in the US Customs agents' activities and undercover covert operations? Why has their agenda and focus changed?

These are all relevant and pertinent questions which we should all be asking the regulatory authorities.

HSBC violations of US sanctions and Iran dealings

US laws prevent banks doing business with 'sanctioned countries' with whom they do not have a fruitful relationship.

The BBC reported that HSBC frequently circumvented the rules designed to prevent dealings with Iran, Burma, North Korea and other listed countries.

The report given to the senate committee also mentioned that actions taken to get around these safeguards in the system "may have facilitated transactions on half of terrorists, drug traffickers or other wrongdoers".

This included 28,000 undisclosed sensitive transactions that took place at HSBC between 2001 and 2007 which were found by an internal audit commissioned by the bank. The vast majority of those transactions worth $19.7bn were tied to Iran and/or Iranian clients.

The bank altered transaction information to take out any reference to Iran through the popular wire stripping method. This method was obviously used to prevent red flags in the system triggering an individual review of an accepted transaction, slowing it down.

Taibbi disclosed leaked emails from HSBC employees and management detailing their plans for Iran: "... In one memo from HSBC's Middle East subsidiary, HBME, the bank notes that it could make a lot of money with Iran, provided it dealt with what it termed "difficulties" – you know, those pesky laws.

"It is anticipated that Iran will become a source of increasing income for the group going forward," the memo says, "and if we are to achieve this goal we must adopt a positive stance when encountering difficulties."

HSBC links to terrorist financing

HSBC did a substantial amount of business with Saudi Arabia's biggest financial institution, Al Rajhi Bank. *The Senate committee report* claims that after the 9/11 terrorist attacks, evidence emerged that Al Rajhi and some of its owners were suspected to have links to banned organisations.

Thereafter HSBC Middle East was one of a number of affiliates which continued to work with the bank.

HBUS in the USA at first closed the accounts it provided to Al Rajhi and partially severed links with them, before resuming some ties with them in 2006.

HSBC got around the issue by closing accounts relating to Al Rajhi banking but continued a strengthened business relationship with Al Rajhi Trading Company which is related to its banking arm. According to Taibbi, in March 2005, Alan Ketley, a compliance officer for HSBC's American subsidiary, HBUS, gleefully told Paul Plesser, head of his bank's Global Foreign Exchange Department, that it was cool to do business with Al Rajhi Trading. "Looks like you're fine to continue dealing with Al Rajhi," he wrote. "You'd better be making lots of money!"

Then soon after George Bush and the OCC removed the cease and desist order from 2003 in 2006, HSBC sent Al Rajhi $1 billion US dollars as part of their special 'relationship'.

The senate report, however claimed that HSBUS had restored the Al Rajhi relationship after pressure from HSBC, after Al Rajhi threatened to withdraw all of its business from HSBC globally.

So what was the punishment and were any warnings given or was HSBC shut down suddenly in USA and Mexico?

Ample warnings were given to HSBC continuously over a number of years! And no they were not shut down anywhere, but just given fines which are peanuts compared to their profits which I will explain later. The final major non–jail term financial settlement which HSBC secured with the authorities was its THIRD official strike. Now I don't know about criminal law in that much detail, however I'm pretty certain that if I was to nick a Lion Bar three times from Waitrose, on three different occasions with cautions and warnings given each time, then I would definitely be serving some sort of punishment as a result. My point is that even *the relatively minor crime* has consequences in the courts of justice and that is why we adhere to rules of social order to keep living in a civil society. If we didn't adhere to these rules, then there would be havoc and chaos everywhere. What would differentiate us from animals?

This is the holy grail of holy grails. *Monty Python* would be bemused even I'm sure!

On 11th December 2012, HSBC boss Stuart Gulliver confirmed in a statement that the bank had agreed to pay a \$1.9bn (£1.2bn) fine as a settlement over the largest drugs and terrorism money-laundering case in history. This \$1.9 billion fine was literally peanuts for HSBC as it constituted only five weeks' earnings with pre-tax profits of \$21.9bn the previous year. But more importantly, by negotiating a settlement the bank agreed to deferred prosecution, hence avoiding any criminal charges which would have inevitably meant a death sentence for the bank.

Why was HSBC not indicted on mass money laundering and terrorist funding charges?

The decision not to indict the bank was made by the US Justice Department. The reasons given openly was the fear that the indictment would shake the World Economy and further dismantle the stability of the financial system and plunge the world into a deeper recession.

In his own words the Assistant Attorney General Lanny Breuer said:

> *"Had the US authorities, decided to press criminal charges, HSBC would almost certainly lose its banking licence in the US, the future of the institution would have been under threat and the entire banking system would have been destabilized."*

I literally thought 'they are having a laugh and a giggle' when I saw this press conference while boarding a plane from Aramco's headquarters near Dhahran. Then when I heard Lanny Breuer speak I spilt my coffee over my favourite tie due to the chronic double standards my ears were being subjected to.

Deferred prosecution for systemic money laundering? The same identical Manhattan District Attorney's office that indicted BCCI for a fraction of what this scandal is.

There are others though who defend the deferred prosecution agreement. They say that it is too tiresome and difficult for the government to find the money-laundering culprits individually due to the nature of the crime. The government basically want to display to the public and voters that they are cracking down on crime in banks. Since it is difficult to press formal charges on people and individuals, deferred prosecution with a fine, on the other hand, let the government signal a victory and get favourable headlines without having to deal with the complications and risks of a full-blown prosecution.

Jesse Singal, a journalist for *NewsWeek* outlined this point in an article he wrote online. He mentioned the comments of Annmarie McAvoy, an adjunct law professor at Fordham University who worked in the US Attorney's office, Citigroup, and Morgan Stanley. "It's a slam-dunk for the government, because the bank doesn't really have much in a way of a defence," said McAvoy, who pointed out that the government has won hundreds of millions in deferred-prosecution fines from banks like JPMorgan, Goldman Sachs, and Citigroup in recent years in cases reflecting various forms of malfeasance.

Juan Zarate, a senior national-security advisor at the Center for Strategic and International Studies and an assistant National Security Advisor to George W. Bush's administration added that individual prosecutions might not deal with the core problems.

"For the anti-money-laundering system to work, you need the

major banks to set the standard, not to be the major violators of the law," Zarate said. I agree with his point here, however none of the banks are setting the standard unfortunately in the current financial climate. And when you start having selective treatment for one set of people and a totally different one for another, it sends a confusing and worrying message of unfairness and prejudice.

Good news is that HSBC has taken considerable steps to change the game around. They have strengthened their financial crime controls and since the DPA their priority has been to protect themselves and their customers from the increasing threat of Financial crime.

They have invested heavily into their compliance structure and training of staff globally so that they are using a risk-based approach at all times whilst applying their global standards consistently. Credit must be given to the change in culture that we have seen in HSBC and Stuart Gulliver who has steered the ship under immense pressure following recent media scandals. He and Douglas Flint apologised and were horrified at what was discovered at their bank.

Media reaction to HSBC scandal

The HSBC affair has also raised a number of other issues in the media which I noticed. I realized that even a scandal of such magnitude was swept under the carpet in the mainstream press merely a few days later. I remember trying to find updates of the scandal in the British papers and struggled to find any columns in the front pages. It was all 'old news' already and hardly any attention was given to it after the first week of the news breaking. The HSBC branches were operating as normal, the staff were cheery with no threat to their job security. The customers seemed to be happy with no long queues of people across the world outside HSBC branches asking for their money back. There were not even signs or instances of rumours of a 'bank run'. Even after such a high-profile senate committee report of massive wrongdoing and then a hearing in court with utter humiliation of the bank, it was still business as usual at HSBC. This was partly due to its apparent strong financial position in terms of assets and profits. And also due to the fact mentioned above that the world media didn't report the story in a way which would panic the customers of HSBC.

On the contrary there was a media circus outside the court where BCCI was indicted and there was headline news on every paper in the world about BCCI's financial troubles. Any negative publicity would undoubtedly undermine any bank and after BCCI was shutdown, the news went on forever. The negativity never stopped, the drama took more than decade to unveil itself and still people never knew the full story.

David Bagley was the head of compliance at HSBC during 2002–2012, which is when the bulk of the criminal transactions took place. He did the right thing and resigned when this scandal broke out however the fact that no charges were brought against him nor was he held accountable is strange.

It would also be interesting to hear from Lord Green on the HSBC front as he was CEO of HSBC from 2003 to 2006 and then executive chairman to 2010. He would be well placed about how money-laundering controls at the bank were so basic while he was in charge. He had stepped down as CEO after being asked to become Minister for Trade in the UK and was also an adviser to the Conservative Chancellor of the Exchequer George Osborne on banking!

There was an editorial on the scandal in the *NY Times* also on 11th December 2012 titled "Too big to indict". The editor wrote: "They also have not charged any top HSBC banker in the case, though it boggles the mind that a bank could launder money as HSBC did without anyone in a position of authority making culpable decisions."

The editorial also mentioned that: "Yet government officials will argue that it is counterproductive to levy punishment so severe that a bank could be destroyed in the process. That may be true as far as it goes. But if banks operating at the center of the global economy cannot be held fully accountable, the solution is to reduce their size by breaking them up and restricting their activities — not shield them and their leaders from prosecution for illegal activities."

Also the solution suggested of breaking the bank into smaller pieces and restricting them was also what was suggested for BCCI during the joint restructuring by the Bank of England, PWC and Abu Dhabi shareholders! It is important to note here that BCCI was restricted from its very inception by not having full banking powers in the US or UK where it was merely given the powers of licenced deposit taker or agency.

Where is John Kerry?

My other fascination and intrigue is about the whereabouts of Secretary of State John Kerry while all this was happening. I mean, wasn't he the 'voice of morality and reason' when people in 'high places' were apparently trying to 'hush hush' and sideline his noise over BCCI in the late eighties. Where was he now? And why was he quiet on the bigger banks issue?

Why didn't John Kerry, Secretary of State of the United States of America, one of the most powerful (and now richest due to his wife being the heiress of the Heinz fortune) men in the world call for the indictment of the bigger banks so that they could be called to real justice, bearing in mind his passion for this subject?

His so called 'morality' which he widely used as a small-time senator back in the eighties seems to have been silenced or sidelined this time round. Being in such a prominent position, he could have foreseen the deferred prosecution agreement and asked for a much stricter ruling on HSBC given that he was hell-bent on shutting down the Bank of Credit and Commerce twenty years ago based on it being a 'rogue institution'. Had the US Justice Department or Manhattan District Attorney back in 1991 Robert Morgenthau given BCCI 'deferred prosecution' and a measly fine, would Senator John Kerry be OK with it?

Chapter Twelve

The Wall Street Warriors – American Fat Cats

Goldman Sachs

Goldman is probably championed by the USA as if not the most, but definitely one of the largest investment banking firms in the world.

Simultaneously it is near the top of my list of financial institutions with endless unscrupulous 'banking' practices which are of a questionable nature. Let's start with widespread accounting fraud, manipulation of balance sheet and moving assets.

BCCI was accused of 'massive accounting fraud' and 'account manipulation' in order to hide losses and create a 'healthier balance sheet' to make the bank seem more profitable. BCCI was subsequently shut down as a result of such apparent practices. However it seems that many banks are using some new financial vehicles called Special Purpose Entities or 'SPEs' to do essentially exactly what BCCI was accused of and much worse!

"What on earth are SPEs"? I hear you all cry. Despair not my friends. They are basically separate legal financial entities that are created by firms to carry out certain 'special purposes'. However in a recent study the law experts William Bratton and Adam Levitin disclose "they never fully coalesce as independent organisations that take actions in pursuit of business goals."

In an excellent article in *Time* magazine, Christopher Matthews describes 'SPEs as companies running on autopilot that serve one purpose: removing assets and liabilities from the parent company's balance sheet.' So this means that SPE hold assets and owe debt for the companies and carry out special 'illegal' purposes which is plain and simple accounting fraud. Shifting assets and liabilities from one place to another to make themselves look more profitable is exactly what this is.

However there is a proper legitimate use for SPEs too for example, an oil company might want to finance an expensive and risky exploration project without putting the whole firm at risk of its failure. Therefore they will set up an SPE with limited resources, put only those resources at risk in pursuance of the new project, and fully disclose the arrangement to potential investors. But as Bratton and Levitin's study and paper describes, SPEs can be and the majority of times are ingredients for catastrophe and fraud.

Goldman Sachs used SPEs to manipulate its own accounts on an unprecedented scale. Matthews of *Time* magazine further explained: "Goldman Sachs was one of the more famous users of SPEs, when it created ABACUS, a synthetic collateralized debt obligation, which like most of these collections of subprime mortgages ended up in default. Goldman was fined $550 million by the SEC for not disclosing the true nature of this collection of mortgages to the investors that eventually bought them, but the greater problem with vehicles such as ABACUS were that it enabled banks to appear to regulators and investors as if they had moved the risk of the mortgages off their books, when in reality, many banks (and ultimately the taxpayer) ended up bailing out their special purpose entities when they went under."

Goldman Sachs was not shut down as a result of this massive accounting fraud and account manipulation nor were the instigators or management bought to account for these frauds. Instead The Financial Accounting Standards Board, a non-profit organisation that is charged by the SEC with writing accounting standards, created more stringent rules recently which forced banks to bring many of their SPEs onto their own balance sheets. I very much doubt that Goldman and other banks are sticking to these so-called rules today.

Goldman Collaterised debt obligations scandal

Collaterised debt obligations known as CDOs are structured financial products that pool together cash-flow-generating assets and repackage this asset pool into discrete tranches that can be sold to investors. CDOs securities are split into different risk classes, or tranches, whereby "senior" tranches are considered the safest securities. Interest and principal payments are made in order of seniority, so that junior tranches offer higher coupon payments (and interest rates) or lower prices to compensate for additional default risk.

Subprime mortgages became increasingly popular in the US in the years before the financial crisis. They were mortgages given to borrowers at higher risk of being unable to pay the money back. These high-risk loans were repackaged by banks into more complex mortgage investments (CDOs) and sold on to other banks, causing chaos in the banking system when borrowers began to default.

Goldman sold a lot of CDOs such as mortgage-backed securities (MBSs) before the housing-market collapse. One group of "synthetic CDOs" was sold to investors. What Goldman concealed was that it was John Paulson (the American hedge-fund billionaire) whose fund had a role in picking the composition of those CDOs at the time of selling them. Goldman paid $550 million to settle charges related to it. Furthermore former Goldman mid-level trader Fabrice Tourre who is nicknamed 'Fabulous Fab' went to trial for his role in the case and a New York jury found Tourre liable for fraud in a complex mortgage deal that cost investors $1bn (£661m). He was accused by the Securities and Exchange Commission (SEC) of misleading investors about investments linked to subprime mortgages that he knew would fail.

However due to the case being civil in nature rather than criminal, he faces possible fines and a ban from the financial services industry. At the time of writing the final outcome is not yet known, however again if this was BCCI, criminal charges would have been placed against it and senior traders along with management would have been locked up in prison. Nobody has been jailed yet at Goldman for the CDO and sub-prime mortgages scam which was instrumental in the build up to the World Financial crisis starting in 2008.

Coincidentally the same hedge-fund billionaire Paulson who helped Goldman in the CDO deals made over $1 billion during the housing market collapse in the States. Coincidence or planned collaboration? You decide.

Andrew Ceresney, co-director of the SEC's enforcement division, said: "We will continue to vigorously seek to hold accountable, and bring to trial when necessary, those who commit fraud on Wall Street." In August 2013 the BBC reported that the SEC has charged 157 firms and individuals so far, including sixty-six senior executives, and has secured $2.7bn in fines and penalties.

Goldman Sachs settled its case with the SEC in 2010, paying $550m without admitting or denying any wrongdoing.

Goldman Involvement in European Sovereign Debt Crisis.

Goldman Sachs is reported to have systematically helped the Greek government mask the true facts concerning its national debt between the years 1998 and 2009.

The *New York Times* reported that just before Greece came under the world spotlight with its financial mess, a team from Goldman Sachs arrived in Athens with a very modern proposition for a government struggling to pay its bills.

The team of bankers who went on this special trip were led by Goldman director Gary D. Cohn, who offered a financing instrument in the form of a 'Credit default swap' or CDS that would have pushed debt from Greece's health care system far into the future, much as when strapped homeowners take out second mortgages to pay off their credit cards. For those still not familiar with some of the banking jargon, a credit-default swap is a form of "insurance" used specifically to insure against the risk of default on debt instruments. Such deals let Greece continue deficit spending, much like how most other European countries including Britain are doing, hence spiraling their debt-spending ratio out of control.

According to the *NY Times*, soon after Greece was admitted to Europe's monetary union in 2001, Goldman helped the Greek government secretly borrow billions of dollars. This deal was hidden from public view because it was treated as a currency trade rather than a loan and it enabled Athens to meet Europe's deficit rules while continuing to spend beyond its means and driving it to further disaster. These types of deals have always been controversial within government circles for many years. As far back as 2000, European finance ministers fiercely debated whether derivative deals used for creative accounting should be disclosed and the final outcome was always a big 'NO'.

I strongly believe that derivatives are and can prove to be extremely useful but they must be used carefully. Gustavo Piga, an economics professor who wrote a report for the Council on Foreign Relations on the Italian transaction summed up derivatives beautifully "They just become bad if they're used to window dress accounts."

Nobody from Goldman Sachs was bought to account over this serious affair.

Goldman US Government favouritism and 'revolving door' employment

BCCI was accused of bribing Government officials including USA politicians in return for 'favours' and lobbying support in Washington which again, as with the rest of the accusations were baseless and untrue.

However Goldman Sachs seems to be operating a scheme whereby top Goldman Executives move from senior banking positions to senior powerful positions in the US Government. Surprising? I think so. Doesn't this cause concern for conflicts of interests? It was reported by ABC News in 2009 that despite President Barack Obama's pledge to limit the influence of lobbyists in his administration, former Goldman CEO Paulson became Treasury Secretary and lobbyist Mark Patterson became chief of staff to Treasury Secretary Timothy Geithner. Furthermore in February 2011, the *Washington Examiner* reported that Goldman Sachs was "the company from which Obama raised the most money in 2008" and that its "CEO Lloyd Blankfein has visited the White House ten times". If this isn't buying 'influence', then I honestly do not know what is. In my research and recollection, BCCI never funded any political campaigns for running US presidents or heads of states in any country. The normal legitimate practices adopted by Mr. Abedi at BCCI were limited to 'hospitality' which was common and accepted within limits. The Western media however were quick to brand this as 'influence buying'.

Goldman 2008/2009 false financial reporting

According to the *Financial Times*, in April 2009, there was much talk that Goldman Sachs had "puffed up" its first quarter 2008 earnings by creating a December "orphan month" into which it shifted large writedowns. From Goldman's own financial statements, in its first full quarter as a bank-holding company, the firm reported a $780M net loss for the single month of December alongside Q1 net earnings of $1.81B from January–March 2009.

The Washington Post reported that the December loss also included a $850M write down on loans to bankrupt chemical maker LyondellBasell. Again nobody was taken to court regarding these financial statement irregularities. It was just shoved under the carpet like the rest.

Goldman AIG Insurance Scandal

When insurance giant AIG nearly went bust, one of the reasons it was bailed out by the US government was it was thought to be too big to fail. According to CNBC report in 2011 the only thing that was going to make them fail was the credit default swaps (CDSs) that were initially sold to Goldman Sachs in case a counterparty's credit declined. Therefore any guesses who got billions of dollars in the US taxpayers' bailout of AIG? You guessed correct my friends: Goldman Sachs.

Goldman also realized that AIG was so eager and aggressive to "cash in" on what it perceived to be a banking gold-mine that it would write-up insurance on anything – irrespective of whether its own personnel had any genuine understanding of what they were writing up.

Thus, Goldman Sachs began to take the worst of its financial rubbish to AIG, in order to get AIG to write-up CDSs on the "assets" in question and essentially using AIG as their toilet, flushing everything down there.

Many will agree now that the CDS "industry" was simply a big scam. It created fake "insurance" for these assets which was never intended to be taken seriously or used. These fake insurance contracts would then allow the Goldman Sachs to pretend they had reduced their "risk" – which would, eventually let them leverage their huge amounts of paper to even more atrocious levels.

Finally, as Goldman began to aggressively sell the various "assets" of the US housing bubble, instead of having AIG write-up CDS contracts as protection, Goldman had its housing shorts deceiving AIG to enter into these CDS contracts – for the specific purpose of making massive scale profits when those CDS contracts "blew up". And they did. How sweet!

Again nobody from Goldman was bought to account over this.

Goldman Insider Trading

What has been a notorious practice in the corridors of Wall Street for many years, the insider trading whispers, has been most prevalent in the cabins of Goldman Sachs. Insider trading can be defined as transactions in a company's securities, such as stocks or options, by corporate insiders or their associates based on information originating within the firm that would, once publicly disclosed, affect the prices of such securities. The 'Corporate insiders' could be employees with the firm or those whose privileged access to the firm's internal affairs (as large shareholders, consultants, accountants, lawyers etc) gives them valuable information. Over the years many insider traders have been caught. Their institutions have not been punished though neither have management. It has to be noted that insider trading was never a practice at BCCI, a bank which had presence all over the world and whose transactions had a considerable impact on the financial markets.

The *Fortune* Magazine and the *New York* magazine released articles outlining the cases in 1986, where Goldman's David Brown was convicted of passing inside information to Ivan Boesky on a takeover deal. Robert Freeman, a Senior Partner at Goldman, who was the Head of Risk Arbitrage and a protégé of Robert Rubin, was also convicted of insider trading, for his own account and for the firm's account.

Goldman Sachs has also been connected to the investigation of insider trading at defunct hedge fund Galleon Group on a number of occasions. *The Times* has said that to date only three Goldman Sachs employees – Korenberg, a salesman named David Loeb and a technology stock analyst named Henry King – have come under scrutiny. What is still unclear is whether other Goldman employees were also involved in the Galleon scandal.

JPMorgan Chase

JPMorgan Chase is arguably America's largest investment banking network. It is however, as suspected, riddled with scandals in recent times.

In November 2013 following a state and federal probe into its mortgage-bond sales, including a criminal inquiry, JPMorgan struck a $13 billion deal with the authorities. A $13 billion deal!

Let's look at JPMorgan's other main big scandals of late:

London Whale Scandal

In 2013, with agreements with regulators totalling $1 billion, JPMorgan settled four civil cases pending investigations into what was named the "London Whale" trading scandal and two more into the wrongful billing of credit-card customers.

In an NBC report released in May 2012, it was revealed that large trading losses occurred at JPMorgan's Chief Investment Office, based on transactions booked through its London branch in May/June 2012. The unit was run by Chief Investment Officer Ina Drew, who has since stepped down. A series of derivative translations involving credit default swaps (CDS) were entered, reportedly as part of the bank's "hedging" strategy. Trader Bruno Iksil, nicknamed the London Whale, accumulated outsized CDS positions in the market. An estimated trading loss of $2 billion was announced, with the actual loss expected to be substantially larger.

Now excuse me if I'm wrong, (which I'm not), however wasn't BCCI accused and consequently closed as a result of the same thing? BCCI suffered huge trading losses in its Central treasury in 1985, not half as much as JPMorgan and with effective management, improved controls and some clever accounting BCCI managed to pull through the 1985 troubled period.

The consequent $1 billion fine figure for JPMorgan is including

$920 million of penalties for JPMorgan's London Whale trading scandal, which Reuters reported in September 2013. The Chief Executive Jamie Dimon was also reported to have dismissed the same scandal as a "tempest in a teapot"! A tempest which finally resulted $6.2 billion in losses. The only surprising factor here was that these settlement deals included an *admission of wrongdoing and fault*, which has been very rare and almost unheard of in past settlements made by the US Securities and Exchange Commission.

Further settlements include $80 million of payments for incorrectly billing credit-card customers for identity-theft protection services that they never received. The deals, made with the US Office of the Comptroller of the Currency and the Consumer Financial Protection Bureau, came after the company issued $309 million of refunds to customers. This is an undue headache that customers do not need when they put their trust in a bank that apparently looks after their needs. JPMorgan settled a further $100 million dollar fine that was slapped by the CFTC on 16th October 2013 and the bank admitted that the "London whale" trading scandal had a manipulative effect on markets.

JPMorgan Manipulation of Power and Energy markets and obstruction of Justice

Back in late 2013 a criminal investigation was underway probing whether JPMorgan employees were involved in deliberately manipulating Energy markets. Reuters had reported that three Houston-based employees had given evidence regarding the California and Midwest deals that the bank was involved in. However the authenticity and truthfulness of the information provided has come under question recently.

The criminal probe was being conducted by the Federal Bureau of Investigation and prosecutors in Manhattan US Attorney Preet Bharara's office. It is common knowledge that deliberately withholding information from investigators or lying during interviews that are being conducted as part of an investigation is considered obstruction of justice and a serious criminal offence. We are yet to see the outcome and treatment of this affair as the investigation is ongoing, however earlier in June 2013 the bank paid a fine of $410 million penalty to settle a similar manipulation case for electricity forwarded by the Federal Energy Regulatory Commission.

JPMorgan irregularity and irresponsibility in Derivatives markets

In January 2013, the Office of the Comptroller of the Currency (OCC) issued a cease and desist order to JPMorgan and Chase that directed the bank to 'correct deficiencies' and irregularities in its derivatives trading activity.

Therefore due to non-compliance by JPMC, the OCC stated in a press release on September 19 2013 that they had issued a $300 million civil money penalty (CMP) action against JPMorgan Chase for "unsafe and unsound practices related to derivatives trading activities conducted on behalf of the bank by the Chief Investment Office (CIO)."

The statement also added that "the bank's controls failed to identify and prevent certain credit derivatives trading conducted by the CIO that resulted in substantial loss to the bank, which has exceeded $6 billion. The OCC has conducted several targeted exams which found the following deficiencies related to the credit derivatives trading practices conducted by the CIO: inadequate oversight and governance to protect the bank from material risk, inadequate risk management processes and procedures, inadequate control over pricing of trades, inadequate development and implementation of models used by the bank, and inadequate internal audit processes."

JPMorgan US Sanctions Violations

Now this is a real corker! BCCI was accused (and never found guilty) of violating US Federal laws by apparently taking over US banks using front men. And now we have the biggest bank in America violating their own government's sanctions.

Below I have extracted the text from the US treasury website from 25th August 2011 which details the violations and the penalties imposed:

"JPMorgan Chase Bank N.A. Settles Apparent Violations of Multiple Sanctions Programs:

JPMorgan Chase Bank, N.A, New York, NY ("JPMC") has agreed to remit $88,300,000 to settle potential civil liability for apparent violations of: the Cuban Assets Control Regulations ("CACR"), 31 C.F.R. part 515; the Weapons of Mass Destruction Proliferators Sanctions Regulations ("WMDPSR"), 31 C.F.R. part 544; Executive Order 13382, "Blocking Property of Weapons of Mass Destruction Proliferators and Their Supporters;" the Global Terrorism Sanctions Regulations.

This settlement covers the following apparent violations of the CACR, WMDPSR, and RPPR, which OFAC has determined were egregious:

JPMC processed 1,711 wire transfers totalling approximately $178.5 million between December 12, 2005, and March 31, 2006, involving Cuban persons in apparent violation of the CACR. In November 2005, another US financial institution alerted JPMC that JPMC might be processing wire transfers involving a Cuban national through one of its correspondent accounts. After such notification, JPMC conducted an investigation into the wire transfers it had processed through the correspondent account. The results of this investigation were reported to JPMC management and supervisory personnel, confirming that transfers of funds in which Cuba or a Cuban national had an interest were being made through the correspondent account at JPMC. Nevertheless, the bank failed to take adequate steps to prevent further *transfers. JPMC did not voluntarily self-disclose these apparent violations of the CACR to OFAC. As a result of these apparent violations, considerable economic benefit was conferred to sanctioned persons. The base penalty for this set of apparent violations was $111,215,000.*

On December 22, 2009, in apparent violation of the WMDPSR, JPMC made a trade loan valued at approximately $2.9 million to the bank issuer of a letter of credit in which the underlying transaction involved a vessel that had been identified as blocked pursuant to the WMDPSR due to its affiliation with the Islamic Republic of Iran Shipping Lines ("IRISL"). Although JPMC supervisors and managers determined that this trade loan was likely an apparent violation of the WMDPSR and, in late December 2009, decided to submit a voluntary self-disclosure to OFAC, JPMC did not mail its voluntary self-disclosure until March 2010, three days prior to the date on which JPMC received repayment for the loan without OFAC guidance or authorization. JPMC also failed to respond promptly and completely to an OFAC administrative subpoena seeking information on this transaction. OFAC determined that JPMC made a voluntary self-disclosure of this apparent violation. The base penalty for this apparent violation was $2,941,838.

In reaching its determination that the above-referenced apparent violations were egregious because of reckless acts or omissions by JPMC, OFAC considered all of the information in its possession related to these apparent violations, as well as the General Factors Affecting Administrative Action set forth in OFAC's Economic Sanctions Enforcement Guidelines. OFAC determined that JPMC is a very large, commercially sophisticated financial institution, and that JPMC managers and supervisors acted with knowledge of the conduct constituting the apparent violations and recklessly failed to exercise a minimal degree of caution or care with respect to JPMC's US sanctions obligations.

An apparent violation of the ITR consisting of a May 24, 2006 transfer of 32,000 ounces of gold bullion valued at approximately $20,560,000 to the benefit of a bank in Iran. JPMC did not voluntarily self-disclose this matter to OFAC."

– *US treasury website, 2011.*

Above we can clearly see violations of sanctions imposed by the US Government on countries like Iran. There have been dealings in transactions, transfers and letters of credit with Iran, Sudan and other countries involving millions of dollars. JPMC appears to not have disclosed any of these dealings voluntarily on its own until it was probed during an investigation by the authorities. In addition to all the above in 2009 JPMorgan's futures broker paid $300,000 to settle CFTC allegations it co-mingled accounts and created a $750m shortfall in customer funds. The shortfall was cleared up the next day, but the CFTC faulted the bank for its delay in notifying the regulator.

The FSA fined JPMorgan Securities £33.32m ($48.2m) in 2010 for failing to protect its clients' money by lumping it in with its own over a period of almost seven years.

Under the FSA's rules, firms are required to keep customers' funds in separate accounts to protect it in case the financial firm becomes insolvent. More recently, the CFTC alleged the bank mishandled Lehman Brothers' customer funds for almost two years before the broker filed for bankruptcy court protection in September 2008. The bank allegedly counted customer money when calculating how much credit it would extend to Lehman. So again the bank settled with the CFTC for $20 million with regards to Lehman. The commission also alleged JPMorgan did not return the customer funds until it was ordered to do so almost two weeks after the bankruptcy.

Also one of JPMorgan Cazenove's most senior bankers Ian Hannam resigned after the FSA announced it was fining him £450,000 for market abuse.

Last but not least, according to Reuters the bank is also facing possible criminal charges with regards to its conduct during an energy trading investigation, sales of mortgage securities in the United States and possible bribery in mainland China! Reuters reported that the bank released a disclosure on an investigation by US officials about whether its Hong Kong office hired the children of powerful heads of state-owned companies in China with the purpose of winning underwriting business and other contracts

On 25th October 2012 it was announced that JPMorgan had reached a $5.1bn (£3.2bn) settlement with the US Federal Housing Finance Agency (FHFA) over charges it misled mortgage giants Fannie Mae and Freddie Mac during the housing boom. The bank added that the agreement relates to "approximately $33.8 billion of securities purchased by Fannie Mae and Freddie Mac from JPMorgan, Bear Stearns and Washington Mutual" from 2005–2007 according to the BBC.

JPMorgan took over two firms Bear Stearns and Washington Mutual when the financial crisis was at the peak in 2008, yet since then it has continued to argue the case that it should not be held accountable or punished for 'mistakes' that were committed before that time. In my opinion this is a strange stance as then all the banks would continue to make mistakes up to a certain point and then beg the authorities for leniency due to 'xyz' circumstances and financial turmoil in the markets. JPMorgan then paid $4bn to Fannie Mae and Freddie Mac to settle claims that it violated US securities law.

It also paid an extra $1.1bn for misrepresenting the quality of single-family mortgages. On top of it all it is to be noted that the firms Fannie Mae and Freddie Mac are the biggest mortgage lenders in the US. They received $187bn in US taxpayer bailout money to help them remain in business during the credit crunch. Both of them have so far repaid $146bn of the loan.

We can also take note that BCCI did not use the cash injected by Sheikh Zayed to fight legal battles or pay settlements all the time. It was used to keep the bank solvent and liquid at all times. In hindsight there was no point because the authorities had made its decision to shut it down anyway.

Bernie Madoff Scandal

The latest fine to hit JPM was in regards to its Bernard Madoff Ponzi scheme exposure and they settled with US regulators on 7ᵗʰ January 2014 for $1.7bn (£1bn). Less well known, JPMorgan's primary relationship with Mr. Madoff in America was two large chequing accounts. Which raises the question whether, because of these chequing accounts, JPMorgan had an obligation to alert American authorities as well?

Federal prosecutors accused the bank of ignoring red flags about Madoff's crimes and the bank admittedly only reported issues to the authorities long after the world already knew about the scandal.

"It took until after the arrest of Madoff, one of the worst crooks this office has ever seen, for JPMorgan to alert authorities to what the world already knew," said George Venizelos, head of the FBI's New York office, during a press conference.

Bernard Madoff was a flamboyant financier who used JPMorgan as his primary bank for his vast fraud and arguably one of the largest Ponzi schemes in history. Madoff's account – account 703 – received deposits and transfers totalling $150bn over the period from 1986 until the fraud was unearthed in 2008, almost entirely from Madoff Securities.

Madoff who is seventy-five years old, pleaded guilty to the fraud and is currently serving a 150-year prison sentence in the US. However the real fact of the matter is that *nobody from JPMorgan has ever been prosecuted or jailed as a result of negligence* or otherwise in the Madoff case. What happened to the much celebrated new 'KYC Know your customer' procedures? This evidently failed in Madoff's case.

The settlement of $1.7 billion also includes deferred prosecution agreement that will dismiss criminal charges after two years if the bank complies with all instructions and investigations by the authorities. Hence no employee of JPMorgan was prosecuted or jailed. A further $2.5bn was added later for the Madoff scandal.

In an interview given to the BBC, Seth Berenzweig, a corporate lawyer, said that US authorities are reluctant to press criminal charges against major banks. I couldn't stop laughing at this comment, as it didn't stop them back in 1991 while bringing BCCI to its knees.

"It's very dangerous to criminally indict a commercial bank," Mr. Berenzweig said to the BBC in January 2014. "It could throw the institution into a tailspin – and the government can't afford a banking crisis with JPMorgan."

Nice! I let you figure that one out.

The problems certainly do not end here for JPM and they have set aside a total of $23bn to help the bank work through its many investigations by regulators in the US and abroad, but I have no doubt in my mind that despite multiple allegations, they will continue to operate as normal.

Bank of America + Meryl Lynch

Mortgages and foreclosure fraud

In June 2013, it was reported by Reuters that six former Bank of America Corp employees had said that the bank deliberately denied eligible home owners loan modifications and lied to them about the status of their mortgage payments and original paper documents.

In fact the bank used these tactics to force homeowners into foreclosure, as well as in-house loan modifications and changes. Both yielded the bank more profits than the government-sponsored Home Affordable Modification Programme, according to paperwork that submitted and filed as part of a lawsuit at the Massachusetts federal court.

The employees who were interviewed when the scandal broke out, who worked at various Bank of America locations across the USA, said the bank regularly encouraged and rewarded customer service staff who foreclosed on homes with cash bonuses and gift cards to large famous retail outlets and stores.

This was basically a staff incentive scheme which was far too extreme in nature and put the pressure on employees to commit wrongdoing. A typical example would include a customer service representative who placed ten or more accounts into foreclosure a month could get a $500 bonus. In the same vein, the bank penalized and punished those who did not make the numbers or objected to its sales methods with discipline, including sacking them.

Reuters further reported that Bank of America and four other banks reached a $25 billion landmark settlement with regulators in 2012, following a scandal in late 2010 when it was revealed employees "robo signed" documents without verifying them as is required by law.

However the problems did not end there by any means. Some 18,000+ homeowners have filed complaints about Bank of America with the Consumer Financial Protection Bureau, a new agency created to help protect consumers. More recently, the attorney generals of New York and Florida accused Bank of America of violating the terms of last year's settlement. Again all we see is fines, penalties and more fines.

Bank of America State Fraud and Criminal Activity across the USA

In December 2010, *The Washington Post* reported that the Bank of America paid $137.3 million to settle allegations that it defrauded schools, hospitals and dozens of other state and local government organisations. The settlement came after a long investigation into fraud in the municipal bond business that raised money for localities to pay for public services like schools and hospitals affecting millions of American citizens.

Bank of America was thus accused of depriving local

governmental groups and organisations of millions of dollars by carrying out fraud when investing the proceeds of municipal bond sales.

The *Washington Post* further reported that the bank ended up paying $107.8 million to the government organisations in compensation, $25 million to the Internal Revenue Service for abuses related to the tax-free status of municipal bonds and $4.5 million to state attorneys general for costs related to their investigation.

The funny thing was however, that the government showed Bank of America a certain amount of leniency in the above settlement due to the fact that it was the bank that had come forward with the disclosure of the irregularity and illegal activity which then prompted the full investigation. Therefore because of that, the bank paid restitution payments but did not face further penalties or any criminal proceedings, which should have been the case regardless of who approached who. The bank was further accused of taking part in a conspiracy in which it and other banks paid kickbacks to win the business of municipalities seeking to invest the proceeds of bond sales before the money is ready to be spent.

Controversy over Merrill Lynch acquisition

In August 2009, the Securities and Exchange Commission (SEC) charged Bank of America with making false statements to investors about its pending acquisition of Merrill Lynch.

Bank of America cleverly and promptly agreed to settle the SEC's charges without admitting or denying the allegations and were ready to pay a penalty of $33 million according to the *NY Times* paper in 2009. Then, however the US Judge Rakoff refused to settle on the $33 million and we all got excited that maybe some real justice would come here and people would be held to account more stringently so that such irregularity doesn't occur. However I was wrong, and Judge Rakoff reluctantly agreed to settle on $150 million dollars.

Bloomberg reported in February 2010 that Judge Rakoff criticized what he named to be "very modest punitive, compensatory, and remedial measures" in the matter.

The judge further added "An even more fundamental problem, however, is that a fine assessed against the bank, taken by itself, penalizes the shareholders for what was, in effect if not in intent, a fraud by management on the shareholders," he stated, while acknowledging that this was the main reason he rejected the earlier settlement.

It came very clear to Rakoff and others with him that the bank failed to sufficiently disclose its agreement to pay Merrill management a total of $5.8 billion or the fact that Merrill was suffering, in fact, losses of up to $15.3 billion in the fourth quarter of 2008 which was astonishing! He said the bank made a "somewhat *coy refusal to concede the materiality* of these nondisclosures."

Finally on 12th December 2013, Tess Stynes from the *WSJ* reported that "Merrill Lynch & Co. agreed to pay $131.8 million to settle Securities and Exchange Commission allegations that it made faulty disclosures regarding the collateral selection in two collateralized debt obligations that the firm structured and sold to investors. The settlement also covers accusations that Merrill maintained inaccurate books and records for a third CDO. The SEC said Merrill failed to inform investors that hedge fund Magnetar Capital LLC had a third-party role and exercised significant influence over the selection of the collateral. The agency said Magnetar's interests weren't necessarily aligned with those of other investors because it hedged its equity positions by shorting against the CDOs."

Morgan Stanley

The American bank Morgan Stanley has had less trouble it seems than the other of its contemporaries. Nevertheless here are some of its most famous fines and settlements:

1. $125 million in order to settle its portion of a $1.4 billion settlement relating to intentionally misleading research motivated by a desire to win investment banking business with the companies covered.
2. Morgan Stanley settled a sex discrimination suit brought by the Equal Employment Opportunity Commission for $54 million on July 12, 2004. In 2007, the firm agreed to pay $46 million to settle a class action lawsuit brought by eight female brokers.
3. The New York Stock Exchange imposed a $19 million fine on January 12, 2005 for alleged regulatory and supervisory lapses.
4. Howie Hubler, an employee, lost $9 billion in one CDS (Credit Default Swap) trade for Morgan Stanley which became the largest single loss in history of banking.
5. On 10ᵗʰ December 2015, Morgan Stanley agreed to settle with US regulators for $255 million over claims they sold toxic mortgage backed securities to credit unions that later failed.

Wells Fargo / Wachovia

Finally Wachovia Bank, part of Wells Fargo group, one of the largest in US, laundered $380 billion for Mexican drug traffickers in just three years between 2004 and 2007.

According to the WSJ in 2010, Wachovia Bank reached a "$160 million settlement with the Justice Department over allegations that a failure in bank controls enabled drug traffickers to launder drug money by transferring money from Mexican currency-exchange houses to the bank".

Bloomberg stated that Wachovia "admitted it didn›t do enough to spot illicit funds in handling $378.4 billion for Mexican-currency-exchange houses from 2004 to 2007. Thats the largest violation of the Bank Secrecy Act, an anti-money-laundering law, in US history -- a sum equal to one-third of Mexico's current gross domestic product."

No banker or individual was jailed, punished or brought to account over this grand scandal.

Citigroup (formerly Citibank)

Citicorp as it is now known is again one of the largest financial institutions in the world.

Here is the list of its recent fines and scandals:

1. According to the *New York Times* in 2004 and 2009 Japanese regulators suspended Citigroup operations in certain areas for stock manipulation and lack of sufficient money-laundering controls.
2. In 2005 the Financial Industry Regulatory Authority fined Citigroup $22.5 million for violation of their mutual fund sales practices.
3. In 2010 the Securities and Exchange Commission (SEC) fined Citigroup $75 million in a settlement over misleading investors over potential losses from high-risk mortgages. According to BBC News in 2007, Citigroup said their exposure to the sub-prime mortgages market was merely $13 billion when it was actually found to be over $50 billion. They agreed to pay the $75 million settlement charges for fraud.
4. In 2012 the *New York Times* reported Citigroup along with four other major mortgage providers in the USA agreed to pay $26 billion in relief to distressed homeowners and in direct payments to forty-nine states and the federal government.
5. In 2014, again the New York Times and the Independent reported that "Citigroup agreed a $7bn (£4bn) settlement to resolve civil

claims that it misled investors about the quality of its toxic mortgage-backed bonds sold before the 2008 financial crisis."

6. Bloomberg reported in July 2015 that Citigroup paid $70 million in fines to the United States Consumer Financial Protection Bureau and the OCC for "illegal practices in marketing add-on products" for consumers and was ordered to pay $700 million to customers affected.

Chapter Thirteen

The UK Government Banking Bail Outs funded by UK Taxpayers

So in the midst and high drama of the financial crisis we end up seeing most of the big UK banks up in smoke and in dire need of rescuing. They started calling for Superman and Batman and God knows who else. Then surprisingly a knight in shining armour came in the form of the Bank of England and the UK Treasury's purse which is funded of course by the UK tax-payer. They never came in to rescue BCCI, surprisingly. Of course not, don't be silly!

Possibly one of the most humiliating days for British banking came on 8th October 2008, when a pale-faced dithering British Prime Minister Gordon Brown stood alongside his nervous Chancellor of the Exchequer Alastair Darling to explain to the British public and press what was about to happen.

They announced that they were going to inject **500 BILLION GBP** Pounds Sterling of the British taxpayer's hard earned cash into the pockets of the greedy, deceitful and dishonest banks due to no fault of their own.

The BBC reported the following week that it was sheer humiliation for the British banks and would have negative long-term effects for competition amongst the high-street banks. Under the plans put forward in 2008 the UK taxpayer now owns 60% of RBS and 40% of the merged Lloyds TSB and HBOS.

This however, was only the beginning. In the weeks and months that followed, more and more money needed to be injected. The spending according to the BBC report on 8th October 2008 was as follows:

- Banks had to increase their capital by at least £25bn and could borrow from the government to do so.

- £25bn in extra capital was made available in exchange for preference shares.

- £100bn was made available in short-term loans from the Bank of England, on top of an existing loan facility worth £100bn.

- Up to £250bn in loan guarantees was made available at commercial rates to encourage banks to lend to each other.

Chancellor Alistair Darling told MPs that the rescue package contained: "essential steps in helping the people and businesses of this country and supporting the economy as a whole".

Source: BBC Website

Prime Minister Gordon Brown said the bail-out was:"unprecedented but essential for all of us", and would thaw frozen money markets. On that note, my appetite for dark chocolate, playing squash and spending money on things I don't really need is unprecedented but also essential for Bearing in mind the USA Government had issued a similar rescue package for American banks only a week before Gordon Brown's Government did.

My argument along with many others has always been that why should ordinary hardworking British citizens who already feel the squeeze on their disposable incomes, bear the brunt of the cost of these criminal banks when the banks are the ones to blame? The poor law-abiding citizens of the UK who churn out huge amounts of tax to the Government's coffers are paying for a problem in which they had no hand! The average hardworking 9–6pm family man has enough to worry about when he comes home to his family who have already suffered as a result of higher interest rates, repossessed homes, soaring inflation and unemployment.

Personally, I am not a huge spendthrift individual by nature which gives my friends the urge to call me stingy and 'tight' which is far from the truth because I spend on things that I want to like dining out at nice eateries, regular flights and nice clothes to name a few. However in the midst of September 2008 crisis even I started to shift from my local Waitrose to try out Tesco for a change. I began to skip the starters at restaurants and refused to pay for bottled drinking water. I mean let's face it, 6.85 GBP for a nice posh bottle of water when I can have it for free from the bloody tap – No thanks!

That's when I sold my three-litre petrol-engine car, resigned from my 'cushy' accountancy job at the largest telecommunications company in the world and accepted a lucrative tax-free package offer in Saudi Arabia. I digress.

It was an era of total financial chaos when the banks had literally all gone bankrupt and were insolvent to the core. But they need not have anything to worry about because of course as stated above they had the lender of last resort – the Bank of England.

It was this precise 'lender of last resort' that BCCI lacked as the bank didn't have a 'home'. Hence no single central bank could take the responsibility of 'bailing out' BCCI if needed. The only difference is, that BCCI actually was rescued in full by the Abu Dhabi Government who provided any shortfalls, which proves the very true fact that BCCI was completely solvent at all times. BCCI also never required a single penny from the UK taxpayer or any other taxpayer around the world. More of this later.

Let's look at some of the banks that were bailed out by the UK taxpayer and Bank of England while looking at their fraudulent activities too.

Lloyds Bank PLC

Lloyds bank was formally known as Lloyds TSB before the split in 2013. It is one of the largest banks in the UK and one of the four major clearing banks with 1300 branches across Britain. The UK

Government and the British taxpayer now owns 43.4% of the bank as of 2013.

Here are the main controversies:

1. Links to the arms and weapons industry –
    In December 2008 the British anti-poverty charity 'War on Want' released a report documenting the extent to which the UK high-street banks invest in, provide banking services for and lend to arms companies. The report stated that Lloyds TSB is the only high street bank whose corporate social responsibility policy does not mention the arms industry, yet is that industry's second largest shareholder among high street banks.

2. Money Laundering and Tax evasion
    In 2009, it was revealed through an undercover investigation by the BBC's *Panorama* programme that staff at Lloyds TSB's offshore office in Jersey, Channel Islands were actively advising high-net-worth wealthy customers on how to evade tax in the UK. It was found by the BBC programme that the staff were encouraging this practice and that the bank was also in breach of international money-laundering laws.
    The surprising thing is that nobody was ever bought to account from Lloyds over this issue and Lloyds got away with this dodgy activity that was caught on tape by the BBC by merely citing it *as an* 'isolated incident' for which it was deeply sorry.
    One should make the point here once again that the planting of fake 'drugs money' into BCCI branches by the CIA/FBI was also *an 'isolated incident'* and the officer that got 'stung' by the sting operation also operated in isolation to the rest of the BCCI staff worldwide who were innocent. BCCI was never proven to have any money-laundering links anywhere else in the world except for that planted sting operation which wasn't even real drugs money!

3. Payment Protection Insurance mis-selling
    Lloyds was one of the worst offenders in the ghastly PPI scandal

and made provisions totalling £8bn, with another £750m added in October 2013 to pay out following claims from customers. I will explain the PPI insurance scandal in detail in another sub-heading later in the chapter.

Lloyds began to sell their shares to the public and recently sold shares for 3.2 billion GBP in October 2013. Plus further scrutiny was ploughed over António Horta-Osório, the chief executive of Lloyds Banking Group, who was receiving a £13.4m pay package and rumoured £800,000 paid into his pension pot for the future! This was remarkable given the state of austerity and the fact that Lloyd's should be practicing prudency after being bailed out.

Northern Rock

I always roll my eyes when I hear anybody talking about Northern Rock. Here was a British Building Society who suffered hugely as a result of the financial crisis then eventually collapsed after the Lehman debacle. The reason why I get so agitated is because organisations such as Northern Rock and Lehman ACTUALLY collapsed and were insolvent. They suffered catastrophic losses and had no liquidity. With the exception of Lehman, all the other banks like Northern Rock were rescued by governments and state central banks because of fear of job losses and customer deposits or 'saving the world financial system'. However none of these forces came into play in order to save BCCI, who didn't actually need saving because it was always solvent throughout its history. It never 'collapsed', it was shut down.

Liquidity problems at Northern Rock, the country's fifth-largest mortgage lender, prompted the first run on a British bank in 150 years. A run on a bank is when depositors rush to the branches to withdraw money amidst reports of the banks financial problems reported in the media. Now BCCI was under fire since the seventies in all the western media.Yet it always stood strong in the face of adversity and negative media reporting even after the Tampa indictment of 1988, its worst ever time. Northern Rock however couldn't stand up to the severe problems it was facing because most of its sub-prime mortgage lending was underwritten by Lehman. Hence when the run on the bank occurred, Northern Rock failed. Then came Superman again in the form of HM treasury and Alastair Darling who promptly pumped in fifty-five billion GBP pounds sterling of UK Taxpayers money. Lovely jubbly!

Northern Rock was later bought by the Virgin Money group led by Sir Richard Branson and re-branded its branches.

The Co-operative bank

The former head of the Co-op bank BarryTootell was under fire from Members of the British Parliament who accused him of running the business with an extremely tight capital position, so much so that a "puff of wind" could have blown it over and made it collapse. Andrew Tyrie, chairman of the Treasury Select Committee further added that he was "sailing too close to the wind". These metaphors were continuously used to describe Tootell's irresponsible management of the bank but he denied all these accusations by maintaining he kept within the rules and regulations that were set out at the time.

At the close of 2012, regulators were in discussions with Barry Tootell over the weak liquidity of the bank and concerns over the capital position were raised repeatedly however he kept assuring them that the capital 'buffer' was adequate for the time being.

Tootell quit the bank after Moody (the rating agency) downgraded the Co-op bank to disastrously-low standards, much lower than anybody could have imagined. Even at this point, Tootell began to wither and said that he had mentally decided to quit many months earlier. Hmm really? So what was he waiting for then? Sounds flaky to me.

According to an article in the *Guardian* by Jill Treanor in October 2013, "Tootell told MPs he took responsibility for the analysis of the former building society's accounts and refused to blame an analysis by accounting firm KPMG. He said the regulators had scrutinised Britannia three months before the deal with the Co-op and concluded the building society needed up to £40m more in capital. The Co-op had conducted its own analysis and concluded there was a further £700m of potential "fair value" losses by Britannia." (Britannia Building society had merged with the Co-op bank earlier when Tootell was Finance Director).

I am slightly confused as to firstly why he was so defensive about KPMG's analysis of the accounts? Surely had KPMG spotted any discrepancies or shortfalls then they would have disclosed them? Or had they done the job properly then the supposed shortfall in capital or liquidity crisis would have been unearthed much earlier?

Secondly his statement to me sounds like a need for alarm bells ringing at the time. I am surprised he thought that the capital buffer was sufficient to rectify the bank's capital problems.

He further outlined how it was his decision to pull out from the takeover of 632 branches of the Lloyd's Banking Group, in a bid that was called 'Project verde'. However he then confused me further by stating that there was never a unanimous position by management and shareholders to go ahead with it and therefore they didn't.

In his defense to the Parliamentary Select Committee, Tootell gave two primary reasons for the apparent £1.5bn capital shortfall. Firstly he mentioned the PPI claims provisions (Payment Protection Insurance which I will discuss later in more detail). Secondly he stated non-core lending losses as a reason which was a result following the merger with Britannia back in 2009.

He said that the tight capital position wasn't realized until November 2012 and the plan he had in place for this was by cutting back on leverage and selling the insurance business. Again, he confuses me by firstly saying the capital position was fine and was under the rules and regulations and then admits to a tight position for which he then had to make an emergency plan.

Whatever the situation was, the £1.5bn capital shortfall is a reality and the Select Committee are continuing to investigate this at the time of going to press.

Now let's align this with the accusations and assumptions made upon BCCI's liquidity position and apparent 'hole' of up to $1 billion which many people were reporting back in 1990. We can clearly see that even BCCI's accused liquidity issue wasn't nearly as bad as the Co-operative Bank's capital shortfall of £1.5 billion which has been confirmed. Furthermore we have now proved via the Lord Justice Bingham report of 1992 that BCCI was fully solvent at the time of its forced closure and had no liquidity problems due to the permanent backing of the ruler of UAE Sheikh Zayed bin Nahyan Al Nahyan. BCCI didn't have to sell any insurance business, but was being restructured on a global scale to make the bank more streamlined and profitable, however this was not allowed to take place and the rest is history!

The Co-op found itself entangled in yet another mess when Paul Flowers, the former chairman of the bank, was arrested after being found dealing with large amounts of drugs. Just because the former chairman of Co-op is a drug addict and/or dealer, does this also imply that the Co-op is a dirty bank from top to bottom as BCCI was labelled to be? I think not.

The Royal Bank of Scotland Group (RBS)

RBS was once hailed as the world's largest company by assets in 2008/09 by the *FT* and other sources with assets totalling the 1.9 trillion GBP mark. Although this is dwarfed by my former employer Saudi Aramco which the *FT* and Forbes listed as the world's most valuable company with an estimated worth of about US $10 trillion.

Either way RBS used to be the world's biggest bank. What happened then? I hear you ask.

Fred Goodwin happened! – Well to be fair he was accredited with the feat of making RBS rise up the ranks to success since he became chairman in 2001. However he was also the catalyst and main reason for the bank's equally dramatic downfall in the run up to the World Financial Crisis. In February 2009, the Guardian newspaper ran a headline that RBS lost £24.1 billion, the largest annual loss in UK corporate history which would actually be a statutory loss of forty billion GBP if we disregard the ABN Amro acquisition which took place earlier! At the same time, Stephen Hester the new CEO of RBS following the public humiliation of Goodwin, stepped in to try and improve the situation at the failing ship. However Hester came under spotlight after the LIBOR rate rigging scandal broke out and RBS was fined 490 million quid whilst receiving no personal punishment to himself. In 2012 at the time of the LIBOR fine, the British taxpayer owned 82% of the bank , hence for them to then cheat the owners (taxpayers) out of money via the LIBOR rigging and then for the CEO (responsible for the bank) to not face charges or be bought to account is laughable. I mean if I stole a KitKat from Waitrose then I'd be behind bars right now! Or I would jolly well expect a good telling off at least! Even though I'm a Lion Bar man myself and if I were to nick a chocolate bar then I'd go for a dark Toblerone, Green & Blacks 90% dark to reach another level of pleasure. Dark chocolate connoisseurs will agree!

Back to old Freddie – Nicknamed *"Fred the Shred"* by numerous factions of the UK media, the CEO formerly known as 'SIR Fred Goodwin" was stripped of his knighthood as he stepped down from the top position in 2008. The honour was supposedly given to him in the first place for his 'services to banking and the financial industry". Well we definitely saw the fruits of his service and are still seeing them today.

How many of you know or remember that this very man who bought RBS down to its knees was made the head of the worldwide liquidation of BCCI in 1991 by the accountancy firm Touche Ross (now known as Deloitte). He made a huge packet then and he's made an even bigger packet now.

Fred the Shred made a number of mistakes which led him to destroy RBS, much like the unscrupulous way he milked the money out of BCCI's liquidation pot.

1. The first of Fred the Shred's problems was his insatiable appetite for aggressive acquisitions which formed part of his own penurious nature. He masterminded the RBS's £23.5bn hostile takeover of the ailing National Westminster Bank. His carnivorous bid for ABN Amro eventually accounted for 16.8 billion GBP losses out of the 24.1 billion GBP reported in 2009.

2. Fred presided over RBS's worst liquidity crisis in its history. The bank was exposed in full to the private equity loans and sub-prime mortgage crisis in a colossal manner. To further add to its problems, the bank was one of the main underwriters for the major Collaterised Debt Obligations (CDOs) which in turn increased exposure and losses in the consequent 'credit crunch'.

3. The increased growth in lending within the Global Banking and Markets division led to a reliance on external wholesale funding. Daniel Gross of *Slate* magazine outlined that the combination of this, along with the weak equity capital position, and the massive exposure to losses on CDOs as a result of RBS Greenwich Capital made RBS collapse.

I use the word 'collapse' because that is exactly what happened to banks like RBS. When there is no liquidity left in the bank and *they're reporting losses in excess of twenty billion GBP* then how are you expected to meet your financial commitments? The bank was deemed insolvent yet too big to fail, as the story goes.

The UK Government again had to bail it out injecting record amounts effectively nationalizing the bank in 2009. Part of the deal was that Goodwin must step down as CEO of RBS paving the way for Stephen Hester to take over the troubled bank. Goodwin didn't escape controversy even after accepting his £8.4 million pension packet which then infuriated the British public who were – and still are – largely unemployed and/or paying huge tax bills at the height of austerity measures imposed by the Government.

To add insult to injury, when George Osborne the Chancellor of the Exchequer said earlier that the Government may split up RBS into a 'good bank' and a 'bad bank', they went back on their word and decided not to go ahead with that plan anymore. On 1st November 2013, RBS announced that it suffered a £634 million loss for the third quarter. Can you compare that to the mere 500 million GBP loss BCCI incurred in 1985 and the world made a mountain out of a molehill? The UK Government now says that it will not split up RBS into 'good banks' and 'bad banks', but instead will ring fence the £38 billion toxic bad loans on its balance sheet! Can you imagine? £38 billion of bad loans!! And all this at the expense of the UK taxpayer who owns the bank! Then the same people called BCCI insolvent when the apparent 'unsecured lending and exposure' to Gokal Shipping and Gulf group weren't anywhere near the catastrophic toxic loans of RBS and others!

To sum it all up there was an excellent online article by Simon Mundy who argued Goodwin to be possibly the *'worst banker in the world'*. In the article he described Goodwin's rise and fall in detail and when Goodwin was asked about the RBS restructuring 'deal' as he stepped down, he replied: "You know, it's more a drive-by shooting than a negotiation." That indeed says a lot. Bearing in mind while he was head liquidator of BCCI he made preposterous amounts of money as did most of the liquidators at Touche Ross and will continue to do so through his pension pot at the expense of the British taxpayer even after ripping RBS to 'Shreds'.

I learnt a great deal by reading Ian Fraser's book named: *Shredded: The rise and fall of the Royal Bank of Scotland*. I am sure we will see more surprises and revelations to come.

The bottom line is that RBS is saved while Fred Goodwin is

a very very filthy-rich man whose banking career is in tatters, but still has faced no prosecution or been bought to account for his mistakes at the bank. His simple public apology and hiring of a very good PR person from the *HELLO!* Magazine seemed to do the trick.

The same trick didn't work for BCCI even after hiring Clifford and Altman and Hill and Knowlton. RBS was again dragged across the headlines of the news in November 2013 when the Tomlinson report was published, ordered by Liberal Democrat Business Secretary Vince Cable, which claimed that RBS was deliberately wrecking viable small businesses to make profits for the bailed out bank. Vince Cable has been a longtime critic of wreckless lending practices which almost ALL banks were doing prior to the crash in 2008. BCCI certainly wasn't the only one with poor lending and RBS continued bad practices even after 2008 and being bailed out by the taxpayer!

The most 'deeply troubling and extremely serious' allegations that were laid upon RBS as quoted by Bank Of England boss Mark Carney on 27th November 2013 are that they were deliberately targeting and wrecking small businesses for their own profits which was a 'fundamental violation' of integrity of banking relationships. I don't recollect BCCI wrecking small businesses or confiscating their properties, on the contrary they were focused on helping SMEs and small businesses grow whilst creating job opportunities for people. RBS has shown its irresponsibility of the public purse by targeting and ruining the livelihoods of those who bailed it out!

Sir Andrew Large, the former Deputy Governor of the Bank of England issued a report on RBS in reference to its lending to small businesses which was shown to the Parliamentary Select Committee handling the investigations chaired by Andrew Tyrie. Both Sir Andrew Large and Mark Carney were shocked to discover that RBS was technically bullying small firms into administration and then taking over their properties at bargain cost, adding them to its Global Restructuring Group (GRG) which sells on properties to its West Register division. There have been thousands of complaints to MPs over this issue by poor people whose businesses have been shut down because of RBS's (and other banks) intimidating behaviour.

Ian Fraser has been following the case since 2010 when he examined a Scottish businessman's appalling treatment at the hands of RBS under the global restructuring group GRG. He claimed that this was systematic and institutionalized fraud at GRG and the West Register including details of "manufactured defaults" which are when a bank trips a business borrower into breach of covenant through mechanisms including such as:

a.   *selling interest rate hedging products under false pretenses*

b.   *the removal of overdraft facilities at forty-eight hours' notice*

c.   *arbitrary changes to the terms and conditions of loan agreements, including raising interest rates, adding charges, shortening loan maturities removal*

d.   *the placing of false valuations on the customers' commercial property assets using "tame" firms of chartered surveyors including Graham & Sibbald in Edinburgh.*

In a recent interview to the BBC, Ian added that since he first exposed alleged maltreatment of business borrowers by RBS in July 2011, he has been inundated with calls by customers who have fallen victim to RBS's malicious and Machiavellian tactics.

The next step was the Serious Fraud Office to investigate the claims made by the report and angry customers of RBS. The FCA (Financial Conduct Authority) which replaced the FSA in March 2013 also needs to get involved as it is the primary regulator along with the Bank of England. This is a clear regulatory failure on a damaging scale and the fraud has been allowed to go on for years undetected by anybody, especially senior management of RBS. It is evident, however that RBS is not alone in this theft of distressed assets of SMEs as this is practised by all the major banks including HSBC and others.

Max Keiser the financial commentator called this 'financial terrorism' that is killing the British public.

We are yet to see what the outcome of this appalling case of malicious actions by RBS is but it only shows how BCCI didn't 'steal assets from distressed businesses', 'bully' or force its customers over anything at all but the outcome was very different for that bank unfortunately.

Payment Protection Insurance Fraud (PPI Scandal)

Am I the only balding idiot who also finds those disastrous and appallingly made PPI-claim adverts utterly irritating?

It's always the same bloody thing. Some bloke who thinks he looks hard stares at you through your TV screen then asks the platitudinous question "Are you a victim of PPI fraud?" Whenever these ads come on, I shout thuggish profanities at the screen. I am sure most of you even get text messages on your phone: "Urgent, you are owed £2590 for the PPI you took out, time is running out to claim"!!

They are now beginning to annoy me even more than the abominable accident insurance and claim adverts. I mean, please! Half of those companies are scam-ridden themselves, let alone trying to help others! It seems the whole insurance industry is kind of a big scam. However wherever there is a hint of a scam, then you know there is big money involved. This is precisely the case with the Payment Protection Insurance scandal too.

PPI, for those of you who don't know, (although EVERYBODY in England will probably know by now) is an extra amount you pay when you take out a loan with any high street bank in the UK as a form of insurance in the event you are unable to meet your monthly repayments (due to illness, unemployment/job loss, injury etc.)

It was later discovered around 2008–09 that banks were mis-selling PPI to their customers without the adequate procedures and 'slapping' on the PPI payments to the loan agreements without the customer's knowledge or full understanding. This is deception and fraud at its best when you are tricking your own customers into buying financial products without their knowledge or mis-selling them as something else. Isn't that nice?

The scandal escalated to headline news in 2008, after *Which?* Magazine reported that one in three customers had been sold "worthless" PPI which shocked the nation.

Suddenly there began to be a lot complaints regarding PPI and as quoted by Graeme Wearden in the *Guardian*, the Citizens Advice in the UK claimed that PPI was:

• Expensive – with premiums often adding 20% to the cost of a loan, and in many of the worst cases over 50%.

• Ineffective – structured specifically to limit the chances of a payout to someone who was genuinely ill and could make repayments.

• Mis-sold – without the customers consent and knowledge, or sold as "essential", or sold to people such as the self-employed who would never be able to claim.

• Inefficient – with claimants facing lengthy delays or complicated claims procedures to get reimbursed or compensated.

Now since the potential profits were so large from the mis-selling of PPI, naturally banks saw this as another activity to dupe its innocent customers. So the entire banking industry decided to collude and then make lots of money at the expense of the poor customer by aggressively selling PPI to everybody. They continued to do this for over a decade starting in the 1990s.

The Punishment for PPI mis-selling

After mounting complaints across the UK, the financial ombudsman – FSA made a ruling giving stricter rules for selling PPI and ordered that all banks who mis-sold PPI must pay compensation to customers.

Then a high-court ruling forced the banks to reopen thousands of claims for PPI, and also trawl through their past PPI sales to find customers who met the compensation criteria while addressing the complaints. Originally the banking industry wanted to fight the ruling citing unfair conditions for them, however they realized that they would be wasting their time and decided to pay out instead.

As a result of this benchmark ruling many banks like Lloyds, RBS and others faced a massive task ahead of them and needed to set aside huge provisions which impacted their financial reports.

Back in 2011, Deutsche Bank estimated that the total industry cost for PPI would be in the region of £8 billion. However this figure has been dwarfed since then when it is reported in November 2013 that the figure is more likely to be exceeding the £20 billion mark making this the largest mis-selling scandal of the century.

Again, no individual employees or management of any bank were held accountable for this deception and nobody was sacked even. Banks just have to keep setting aside further 'provisions' which affect their balance sheet slightly but no real damage or threat to the existence of the banks committing these deceptive and immoral practices.

Chapter Fourteen

European Underdogs

At the sophomoric age of seven, I distinctly remember the pocket money of £5 per week that my father used to give me. I would ardently wait for Saturday to arrive so that I could receive my weekly salary for simply being the hideous brat I was at the time. Having watched the traditional dose of children's morning trash television and completed my weekend homework, I would go out with my mother and spend the entire £5 on either the latest 'WWE' wrestler action figure or a bag full of confectionary.

Wait a minute! No saving? I hear you all cry! Well in those golden Thatcherite years, the youth didn't really think about saving much in the UK – not in the school years at all, but not even in their late twenties to much surprise. And why on earth would they? The UK economy was booming, unemployment was at its lowest in living memory, banks were flourishing, Eurosceptics were in power and Elton John had a full head of hair! What more could one want? The UK and Europe (now known as the European Union/ EU) was on target to take over the world.

But erm… something didn't go quite according to plan did it? We have all heard about the global financial meltdown and how greedy banks (namely in Wall Street) have destroyed the livelihoods of millions across the world and seen balding politicians on the news rabbiting endlessly on economic gibberish that sounds like Hungarian lovemaking to the average man on the street.

So what went wrong and who's to blame? Or the more intriguing question of why is a loaf of bread now more expensive than my German car?

A few years back, the German Chancellor Angela Merkel

breathed a sigh of relief after receiving a majority vote in parliament so that Germany could deliver a further bailout package for Greece's economic problems. (Just in case you've come back from a lazy holiday in Scotland – we were in the midst of what we call the 'Eurozone crisis' since the end of 2009).

What does this mean? Let me lay down the facts for you and keep it as simple as possible. Europe and neighbouring partners are in big trouble because most governments are spending more than they earn. It's as simple as that. So when they run out of money, they borrow more from lenders. However lenders need to feel assured that the countries/governments that they are lending to can pay them back in full. Yet, when this is not the case, like it is now, then the repercussions are huge. The debt increases because when countries run out of money, they ask for emergency loans.

For example to put things in perspective, Greece asked for €110 billion in May 2010. €85 billion was asked by Ireland in Nov 2010 and €78 billion was required by Portugal in May 2011. Total Greek debt is now standing at a whopping €340 billion Euros that is approximately €31,000 per person whereas the average Greek salary was €25,915 in 2008. These are worrying statistics especially for those who have just left university with amassing a mountain of student debt before even starting work.

The main problem lies at governments trying to fund their debt with taking on more debt! I find the vicious circle quite baffling as I would rather shift to a rented shared studio flat in a council estate in East Norwich than borrow more money from my friend Daniel to whom I already owe money for paying my parking tickets.

However why should we worry about Greece and their problems and who loses out if Greece can't pay its debts? Well, let's see: France, Germany, UK, USA, Italy, Japan and Spain just to name a few. The pressing issue is the immediate domino effect within the Eurozone. It is a widespread belief within the EU that if one country leaves the Euro and if Greece defaults on its debts then the others will follow like a contagious disease.

The Euro was originally set up as a single currency for the European Union members with the aim to boost trade and tourism within the EU and smooth out economies but it didn't enjoy much prosperity. The UK refused to join mainly due to sovereignty issues but is still affected by the crisis. But now we are thinking about leaving the EU altogether and will have a referendum vote in 2016.

European leaders such as banks and other institutions are under particular pressure to provide long-term stability for the Euro. A further expansion of the European Financial Stability Mechanism (EFSM) has been suggested. The issue of eurobonds, which would make the debt of each country to be guaranteed by all, has also been rebuffed. We must bear in mind that taking responsibility for other countries' debt may prove politically unpopular in countries like Germany as it was in the UK to some extent. The only other solution would be that leaders could focus on greater losses in the private sector. Meanwhile the burden has fallen on central banks who are under immense pressure to propose additional quantitative easing in the form of printing more cash to increase the amount of credit in the economy.

The economic instability is highlighted on the world financial stock markets as since July 2011 alone: London's FTSE 100 has fallen 14%, New York's Dow Jones has shed 15% and Germany's DAX has dropped more than 29%. These are uncertain times for the world's prominent 'superpowers'. Many of the citizens of the so called wealthy 'western' countries are questioning their own decision makers asking them why they are bailing out other countries when they themselves are unemployed and facing gross financial hardship domestically. There was a similar uproar in the UK when a small lobby group took to the streets over a £3.2 billion aid package that the UK gave to Ireland citing that they were their closest trade partners.

The uncertainty about economic growth has also triggered worries about the indebtedness of Eurozone states. If economies are not growing much then this causes tax receipts to fall, making it harder for governments to pay off their debts. Recently Italy became the latest Eurozone country along with Spain, Portugal, Ireland and Cyprus to have its credit worthiness downgraded by ratings agency Standard and Poor's, showing clear issues with its ability to pay its debt.

Earlier in July 2012, EU leaders agreed a second bailout deal for Greece, and also agreed more powers for the European Financial Stability Fund to help countries struggling with indebtedness as this would allow the fund to buy government debt which are essentially bonds, offer credit on favourable terms to countries in crisis and would create a special facility for recapitalising banks. The deal comprised of an initiative by private banks to swap existing Greek debt with longer-term debt paying lower interest.

In order to prevent borrowing costs increasing day by day, the European Central Bank (ECB) has been buying Italian and Spanish government bonds to try to bring down their borrowing costs. This resulted in the yield on Spanish and Italian ten-year bonds falling shortly afterwards, but these tactics by the ECB are seen as only a temporary fix for the major problems.

The stark fall in shares have frequently been led by bank shares as investors are concerned about what level of Eurozone government debt they are holding, and whether this will be repaid or not. Many banks in France are facing the crux of the pressure since they hold more than €40 billion euros (£35bn) of Greek debt, and this is roughly quadruple the amount of any country. A global trade body called the Institute of International Finance which represents big lenders, has said the Greek debt-swap deal technically means a loss for Greek lenders that equals 21% of the market value of their debts. If banks were forced to accept similar or greater losses on the debts of other countries it may potentially erupt a new banking crisis that would plunge the Global economy into deeper crisis.

To add further pessimistic injury to the situation, we recently learnt that the USA's AAA credit rating was also downgraded to only AA+ even though it did not default on its commitments. It was a jolly good piece of Sunday evening television when we saw the US President literally begging all of his cronies to agree on an aid package to save them from defaulting. It kind of reminded me of watching the *Muppet Show* or *Spitting Image* when I was younger. Anyway following those embarrassing near-defaulting times, US President Barack Obama had unveiled a $450bn (£282bn) package of tax cuts and spending plans aimed at creating jobs and boosting the economy. However, once again these ambitious plans will face huge trouble passing through the US Congress as usual.

So what is to be done? It's an interesting waiting game to see how things will unfold and whether governments are generous enough to help each other out in the formats described above. An even more startling and surprising solution was an aid offer by the least expected, China. It was heartwarming to see that China had recently suggested it would offer financial help to Europe and its western counterparts if the need arose, but obviously this wouldn't be unconditional. However it is interesting to see how the shift in economic power is moving to China so dramatically whereby it is in such powerful position to bail out other western countries who still see it with a hint of suspicion. Although I'm not sure the move would be entirely welcomed within China itself where many citizens are living on wages below $2 per day still. Maybe China may need to help its own people before stretching its financial arms.

All in all I'm not sure whether I should be gleeful or be boasting about the fact I have more certainty and stability in my Santander current account than Greece had in its Central Bank or even the fact that my pet cat has a better credit rating than the Italian Finance Minister. All I do know is that they had all better come to a mutual agreement so that we can look forward to the future with optimism.

Bearing that in mind, let me continue with my rant and let's take a closer look at the criminal kingpins of Europe.

UBS – The Swiss bank

I had believed for many years that UBS was in a league of its own with regards to scandals and circumventing international laws. But then from what you have read above, it doesn't really compare that much anymore. They are all pretty much the same fish in a big pond. UBS, who maintain their headquarters in Zurich and Basel, began operations in 1854. In 2011 it had more than $26 billion in revenue and nearly 65,000 employees worldwide. It was typically labelled too big to fail during the financial crisis, and had to be bailed out by the Swiss government after a $50 billion write-down on mortgage-backed securities.

UBS continues to commit financial crimes like all other banks and then continues paying fines or gets IMMUNITY from large scale criminal scandals like the LIBOR saga.

The US Justice department tell us its guidelines for charging a corporation with a crime: "A corporation, like a natural person, is expected to learn from its mistakes," and "a history of similar misconduct may be probative of a corporate culture that encouraged, or at least condoned, such misdeeds, regardless of any compliance programs. Criminal prosecution of a corporation may be particularly appropriate where the corporation previously had been subject to noncriminal guidance, warnings or sanctions." Now given UBS's history of crimes, we would've expected that it would be an ideal candidate to be implicated and charged in the LIBOR scandal. However it doesn't work like that.

James B. Stewart of the *NY Times* wrote an excellent article in July 2012 where he described UBS as having a strong record in averting prosecution, implying that they were basically experts in crime and knew how to get away with it!

Stewart outlined all the frauds committed by UBS in the *NY Times* article and showed how easily they averted prosecution in most cases.

He proved that increasing recidivism seems rivaled only by its ability to escape prosecution and then listed the following crimes:

1. On 20th July 2012 *The New York Times* reported: "UBS obtained a deferred prosecution agreement in 2009 for conspiring to defraud the United States of tax revenue by creating more than 17,000 secret Swiss accounts for United States taxpayers who failed to declare income and committed tax fraud. UBS bankers trolled for wealthy clients susceptible to tax evasion schemes at professional tennis matches, polo tournaments and celebrity events. One UBS banker smuggled diamonds in a toothpaste tube to accommodate a client. In return for the deferred prosecution agreement, UBS agreed to pay $780 million in fines and penalties and disclose the identities of many of its United States clients. At the same time it settled Securities and Exchange Commission charges that it acted as an unregistered broker-dealer and investment adviser to American clients and paid a $200 million fine. In October 2010 the government dropped the charges, saying UBS had fully complied with its obligations under the agreement." Dropped charges? Wow! Lucky UBS!

2. "In May 2011, UBS admitted that its employees had repeatedly conspired to rig bids in the municipal bond derivatives market over a five-year period, defrauding more than one hundred municipalities and non-profit organisations, and agreed to pay $160 million in fines and restitution. An SEC official called UBS's conduct "a 'how to' primer for bid-rigging and securities fraud." UBS landed a no-prosecution agreement for that behaviour, and the Justice Department lauded the bank's "remedial efforts" to curb anticompetitive practices."

3. "In what the SEC called at the time the largest settlement in its history, in 2008 UBS agreed to reimburse clients $22.7 billion to resolve charges that it defrauded customers who purchased auction-rate securities, which were sold by UBS as ultrasafe cash equivalents even though top UBS executives knew the market

for the securities was collapsing. Seven of UBS's top executives were said to have dumped their own holdings, totalling $21 million, even as they told the bank's brokers to "mobilize the troops" and unload the securities on unsuspecting clients. As Andrew M. Cuomo, who was New York's Attorney General then, put it: "While thousands of UBS customers received no warning about the auction-rate securities market's serious distress, David Shulman — one of the company's top executives — used insider information to take the money and run." Besides reimbursing clients and settling with the SEC, UBS paid a $150 million fine to settle consumer and securities fraud charges filed by New York and other states. It again escaped prosecution." (Source: *New York Times*).

4. Rogue trading scandal of 2011 The rogue trader scandal is cited as one of the biggest frauds in the UK where a City trader called Kweku Adoboli who lost £1.4bn ($2.2bn) of Swiss bank UBS's money was jailed for seven years after being found guilty of two counts of fraud. The UK's Southwark Crown Court heard Kweku Adoboli was "a gamble or two away from destroying Switzerland's largest bank". He lost the money in "unprotected, unhedged, incautious and reckless" trades, the jury was told. James Stewart also added in his NY Times article that not many UBS people have been jailed but another one in addition to Adoboli was called Bradley Birkenfeld, the original whistle-blower in the huge tax-evasion case. Mr. Birkenfeld pleaded guilty to conspiracy to defraud the United States and was sentenced to nearly four years in prison. Another UBS banker, Renzo Gadola, who pleaded guilty in the tax fraud case, co-operated, and was granted probation. A third man was charged but was never tried and remains a fugitive.

5. Finally UBS was also implicated in mortgage backed securities fraud, the LIBOR scandal but got leniency and immunity because it was "one of the first banks to co-operate". What a joke! The Justice Department wrote that a corporation can avoid criminal conviction and fines for antitrust crimes "by being the first to confess

participation in a criminal antitrust violation, fully co-operating with the division, and meeting other specified conditions. So when BCCI was co-operating with all the authorities on accounts of accusations and wrongdoing, along with the Abu Dhabi Ruling family co-operating with restructuring plans with Bank of England officials – Why wasn't leniency and immunity shown then? Why was BCCI shutdown suddenly without prior warning given to the shareholders who were actually co-operating and fulfilling all of the requirements of the investigating authorities?

Deutsche Bank

The German powerhouse and banking giant has not been spared from its fair share either.

1. In August 2009, the *Wall Street Journal* (*WSJ*) ran a headline report on the espionage activities of the bank which included spying on journalists and individuals who were criticizing them. This seems all too odd especially for an international financial institution who should be open to genuine criticism by customers and stakeholders alike. However the bank later admitted that their corporate security department and legal department were involved in these activities after hiring a specialist legal firm to help them uncover the truth.

2. In December 2012 the *Financial Times* reported that "Deutsche Bank failed to recognise up to $12bn of paper losses during the financial crisis, helping the bank avoid a government bail-out, after three former bank employees launched complaints to US regulators. The *FT* further added: "All three allege that if Deutsche had accounted properly for its positions – worth $130bn on a notional level – its capital would have fallen to dangerous levels during the financial crisis and it might have required a government bail-out to survive." This basically means that if we compare Deutsche and Lehmans

for example, then we see how bad things were to become for Deutsche. It seems that if Lehmans didn't have to mark its books for six months then it might have survived, however according to the figures above, if Deutsche bank marked their books for that period then they surely would have had the same fate as Lehmans. Therefore to avoid such collapse the employees who went to the authorities claim that the bank's traders, with full knowledge and permission of senior management, deliberately avoided recording "mark-to-market" losses during the extreme uncertainty and chaos in the credit markets between 2007–2009.

3. On 17th October 2013, *Reuters* reported that Deutsche bank will pay an $11 million settlement to end a probe and investigation into its involvement in funding subprime mortgage loans in Nevada, USA. The controversy was whether the lenders deliberately misled borrowers about the actual interest rates on their loans or added risky features without considering a borrower's ability to repay, and the main question if Deutsche Bank knew about such malpractices when it helped to finance those particular loans. As usual the bank neither admitted nor denied the state's allegations but agreed to review any future Nevada loans that would fall under the same category. Therefore the $11 million settlement has shut up the probe. For now anyway!

4. DB fined $2.5 Billion for rate rigging

    Reuters reported in April 2015 that U.S. regulators fined Deutsche Bank $2.12 billion and UK watchdogs imposed a $340 million penalty for its role in a scam that ran from around 2003 to 2010

    On 23rd April 2015 the FCA fined Deutsche Bank £227 million by Financial Conduct Authority for LIBOR and EURIBOR failings and for misleading the regulator.

    The FCA released a press release on the same day where Georgina Philippou, acting director of enforcement and market oversight, said: "This case stands out for the seriousness and duration of the breaches by Deutsche Bank – something reflected in the size of today's fine. One division at Deutsche Bank had a culture of generating profits without proper regard to the integrity of the market. This wasn't limited to a few individuals but, on certain desks, it appeared deeply ingrained."

"Deutsche Bank's failings were compounded by them repeatedly misleading us. The bank took far too long to produce vital documents and it moved far too slowly to fix relevant systems and controls."

"This case shows how seriously we view a failure to cooperate with our investigations and our determination to take action against firms where we see wrongdoing."

5. Deutsche Bank fined $258 Million for Violating U.S. Sanctions
On 4ᵗʰ November 2015 *the WSJ* reported that the New York regulator, the Department of Financial Services, said bank employees used "nontransparent methods and practices" to process more than $10.8 billion for financial institutions and others in Iran, Libya, Syria, Myanmar and Sudan that were subject to U.S. economic sanctions. The misconduct occurred between 1999 and 2006, the regulator said. BCCI was not let off the hook for its apparent shortcomings. But a DB spokesperson said: "We are pleased to have reached a resolution with the New York Department of Financial Services and the Federal Reserve," She added "The conduct ceased several years ago, and since then we have terminated all business with parties from the countries involved." This same scenario could very well have been applied to BCCI to and if indeed any historic fraud was unearthed from early days of the bank, then it was indeed dealt with before the restructure.

Crédit Lyonnais

Another bank that was exposed around 1994/95 was the institutionalised bank called Crédit Lyonnais. It was widely documented in the press in the early nineties for making huge losses and then fiddling the accounts to hide them. It was probably one of the largest frauds discovered in Europe after the Barings

Bank collapse. However funnily enough, surprise surprise, Crédit Lyonnais is still in existence.

Another lesser-known fact, and much more relevant in drawing a parallel with BCCI, was that Crédit Lyonnais was instrumental in illegally acquiring an insurance company and brokerage firm in the United States by circumventing the law using front nominees. It was proved later on that it deliberately hid its role in acquiring and owning the insurance firm by the name of 'Executive life' based in California. A cunning financial coup over Executive Life's junk-bond portfolio produced big profits for Crédit Lyonnais. But in winter 1998 it was discovered that Crédit Lyonnais had failed to disclose its direct involvement in taking over both the portfolio and Executive Life itself. Documents obtained by the American authorities suggested that the bank had knowingly broken the law and the authorities even at somepoint considered revoking the bank's licence. But they didn't. No surprise there yet again.

Instead as per the FBI's open website it is stated that following a long investigation, a wide array of fines and penalties were unleashed upon Crédit Lyonnais in the form of a plea agreement and settlement totalling $771.75 million (which at the time in 2003 was the largest single settlement in US financial history, but is dwarfed now by JPMorgan and others). A number of individual prosecutions were also made by the FBI and other authorities which included the chairman of Crédit Lyonnais, Jean Peyrelevade.

In addition to the plea and settlement agreements, a federal grand jury in Los Angeles indicted six French citizens, including two former chairmen of Crédit Lyonnais, on various fraud and other charges for their role in a conspiracy to illegally acquire the assets of the bankrupt Executive Life Insurance company.

In the FBI press release of 2003 it is stated by United States Attorney Debra W. Yang that: "Through a complicated series of secret agreements, Crédit Lyonnais and others concealed a web of illegal relationships and transactions between the French bank, its various subsidiaries, Artemis, MAAF and the sizable assets of the failed Executive Life... These repeated deceptions, which spanned more than a decade and involved the highest levels of Crédit Lyonnais management, defrauded the United States, California authorities and, most importantly, the approximately 350,000 policyholders of Executive Life."

The following charges were made by the FBI following the press release in 2003:

- Jean-Yves Haberer was chairman and president of Crédit Lyonnais from 1988 until November 1993, and served as chairman of Altus from 1990 until December 1993. He was charged with conspiracy to commit mail and wire fraud, mail fraud, wire fraud, conspiracy to defraud the United States and violate the Bank Holding Company Act, and criminal violation of the Bank Holding Company Act.

- Jean Peyrelevade, who replaced Haberer, served as chairman of Crédit Lyonnais from November 1993 until he resigned from Crédit Lyonnais in October 2003. He was charged with conspiracy to defraud the United States and violate the Bank Holding Company Act, criminal violation of the Bank Holding Company Act, and making false statements to the Federal Reserve, the United States Attorney's Office and the FBI during the government's investigation.

- François Gille was Crédit Lyonnais's general manager and financial director, and also served as a director of Altus, in the 1990s. He was charged with conspiracy to commit mail and wire fraud, mail fraud, wire fraud, conspiracy to defraud the United States and violate the Bank Holding Company Act, and criminal violation of the Bank Holding Company Act.

- Dominique Bazy was a member of Peyrelevade's Executive Committee and the Chairman of Altus from November 1993 until July 1995. He was charged with conspiracy to commit mail and wire fraud, mail fraud, wire fraud, conspiracy to defraud the United States and violate the Bank Holding Company Act, and criminal violation of the Bank Holding Company Act .

- Jean-François Hénin was the managing director of Altus and became an advisor to Pinault and Artemis. He was charged with conspiracy to commit mail and wire fraud, mail fraud, wire fraud, conspiracy to defraud the United States and violate the Bank Holding Company Act, and criminal violation of the Bank Holding Company Act.
- Eric Berloty was an Altus consultant in the 1990s on accounting, tax and other financial matters. He was charged with conspiracy to commit mail and wire fraud, and wire fraud.

The investigation in question took about five years (from 1998 to 2003). The total list of charges were against the top management of Crédit Lyonnais and the bank was not asked to be shut down as was the case with BCCI. On top of trading losses and account manipulation with aim to defraud and deceive the customers, stakeholders and public, the bank illegally acquired an insurance firm and still got away with it lightly. The bank is still operating as normal today after numerous attempts by the French government and French Central Bank to help clean up its act.

The funniest thing I read at the bottom of the FBI press release was the following statement by the then FBI Assistant Director-in-Charge Ronald Iden:

"One of the reasons the FBI investigates white-collar crime is to help keep the economy stable…. The investigation into the fraudulent business practices of Crédit Lyonnais and its subsidiaries demonstrates that we can and will aggressively investigate such crimes regardless of their complexity or duration. To that end, the FBI wishes to make this clear to all corporate and banking executives: even though we are dedicating substantial resources to the fight against terrorism, the FBI remains fully committed to investigating significant white-collar crime."

Given the financial crime committed in America and around the world today, the above statement has not been adhered to and perhaps the authorities have failed in their vision and mission above. They may have hit hard and gone against one or two easy targets, but failed to respond with similar action against others.

BNP Paribas

The much publicized saga involving France's biggest bank BNP Paribas evading US sanctions by dealing in transactions with Cuba, Iran and Sudan resulted in a massive fine of $8.9 billion. The largest fine so far for sanctions violations. BNP also entered into guilty plea to criminal charges of conspiracy and falsifying records and a suspension of its right to clear certain dollar transactions.

The fine was originally rumoured to be around the $20 billion mark which would have made it the largest fine ever in history beating JPMorgan even, but diplomacy took over and François Hollande the French Premier intervened and reportedly got on the phone to President Obama.

Either way the near $9bn fine was affordable for BNP as they are extremely profitable but the inability to clear the US $ transactions is another ball game altogether for which they also prepared for.

Credit Agricole

On 20th October 2015 *Bloomberg* reported that "Credit Agricole SA agreed to pay $787 million to U.S. regulators and enter into a deferred prosecution agreement with the Justice Department to resolve allegations the French bank violated sanctions aimed at Iran and Sudan."

Same story, different bank! Violating sanctions is unfortunately a problem which all banks are now facing and must strengthen their internal systems and controls to combat the problem. Again the DPA luxury was given to all these banks but not the unfortunate bank that never violated sanctions specifically but got closed by force instead.

Chapter Fifteen

I Love America, but why others don't?

"And so I think that it's been one of the mistakes that the American government has made since the Second World War – that we have been involved almost constantly in military conflicts, most recently, obviously, in Iraq and Afghanistan, and earlier than that in Bosnia. I could name fifteen different places where we've been in armed conflict. Japan has not; China has not; Brazil has not; and so forth. But the US stays in military conflict or the threat of that.

So I believe that in almost every case, the wars have been avoidable without betraying the basic moral principles and privileges and well-being of the countries involved. I think we've had unnecessary wars. The Vietnam War, I think, was an unnecessary war; the invasion of Iraq was an unnecessary war; and so forth. So I think that we need to be more reluctant to go to war, and to go there only in desperate conditions when all avenues towards peace are exhausted, including good-faith discussions, either directly with our potential adversaries or through a trusted intermediary."

– Former US president Jimmy Carter (in an interview given to Japanese magazine Chuo-Koron).

I love America. I love all things American too (with the exception of Donald Trump). This is not limited to my love for Frasier, Starbucks, Ralph Lauren, Facebook, New York City and the Kardashians. This love extends far beyond the superficial attraction I have towards the aesthetic features of Nigella Lawson and Penelope Cruz. It is a love for humanity and peace.

Before we embark on this most important and sensitive topic, I also wish to make it clear that the love and adoration I have for the

American people and their core values are unrivalled. Some of my closest friends and family are law-abiding American citizens who would, if given the opportunity, die for their country. In addition I love the freedom of speech and freedom of western values. Above all, *I love women* and the freedom of women to live however they wish, with the freedom of what to wear.

Having said this, my reasoning and intellect resonates moral disagreement with the American political ideology and ruthless foreign policy of late, which the majority of the American people are also deeply unhappy with. The basic principle of which I convey my argument is PEACE. Nobody wants war. Regardless of which religion or ideology one belongs to, the human soul and mind is created with the notion to reject violence. Why is there increasing anti-Islamic rhetoric in the world media? Why is there sectarian violence in Pakistan? Why are Muslims killing Muslims? Why is the Syrian regime seemingly killing their own people? Why is most of the Middle East a war zone? Why is Pakistan a ticking time bomb, and why do they want to kick the living daylights out of India all the time or vice versa?

The answer is all political! – Nobody truly hates anybody. Take my example in my home and place of birth in a North London suburb. My best friend is a Hindu from Delhi, India. My neighbour is a fine Jewish gentleman, my squash partner is Irish, my gardener is Portugese, my cleaner is Polish, my former boss is Saudi and we all live (for the majority of the time) in peace and harmony. Why has cultural, ethnic and religious background become such a major issue? It's all politics!

Anyway I digress. It has for many years, been my firm belief that all the negativity on the world stage at this current time, the conflicts, the massacres, the 'terrorism', the bloodshed, the sectarian violence and the hatred can be somehow traced back with a line of indirect connection to the post World War One Foreign Policy activities, both covert and open of the USA (and some of its allies). In the modern day we all are fed up of the Daesh, Taliban, Al Qaeda extremists, IS/ISIL whatever and countless other groups who spread violence and fear under the false pretence of Islam. But fifty years ago it was another story, as these lot didn't even exist.

In my modest opinion, which can be faulted at times, but do your own research by all means, the origins of more recent turmoil in the Middle-East and the surrounding area lie in the 1951 overthrowing of Mossadegh's Government in Iran. I shall explain this episode in further detail in a moment.

We need to analyse the US government actions that are dictated by their Foreign Policy, then draw conclusions from the results the actions have achieved and compare them with the original plausible motive (if any) to see whether the action was justified.

The underlying question I want to ask all readers is: Who has given the USA and its allies the unquestionable authority to take such unlawful actions and act as the world's police state? I certainly havn't, neither has Putin mind you!

In the same vein, I would like to add that I love Britain more than I could ever love America. I like to feel like the 'son of the soil' as they say. Both my parents may be of British–Pakistani origin, however I consider Britain to be home and my pride and joy. As a voter I was overjoyed at Cameron's decision not to attack Syria in 2014. He resisted American pressure, and succumbed to the will of the people via the MPs' referendum vote. Well done Dave. But oh wait I also love Jeremy Corbyn. Dave went in with the airstrikes and blew it.

In addition I would like to ask what moral, historical or intellectual fact brings to light the notion that the USA is a responsible nation bearing nuclear weapons, considering it is hell-bent on pressuring other states to sign up to the nuclear-disarmament treaty, but doesn't sign up itself (or Israel for that matter?) To top it all off, *it is the only known nation in the history of this world to have ever used nuclear weapons!* One would actually think that I am a raving lunatic and a mad-man wearing Einstein's checked pyjamas, however these are all hard facts.

The Nobel Peace Laureate from Argentina recently wrote an open letter to Barack Obama asking the same questions and maintaining that he should be more responsible and weary of his title as Nobel Peace winner by finding political solutions to conflicts in the Middle East especially Syria rather than military ones. The US has carried out over twenty-five foreign interventions in international territories since the second world war from Yugoslavia, Macedonia, Iran, Cuba, Bosnia to Iraq, Afghanistan and Syria. Plus countless DRONE attacks in Pakistan, Yemen and other nations.

You must think I'm making this all up. Trust me, when I started my own amateur research, I thought the same!

Let us go back to the start of my argument and briefly discuss why Iran is so perceived to be so radical and dangerous to the West (and Israel).

Ah… I see, even though I got a miserable B at Mathematics GCSE and then the subject caused me considerable grief at university where I studied Econometrics which was basically applied maths, I can still gather that it seems the USA has had at least FOUR military or covert intelligence operations involving Iran in the post WWII period. In comparison, I've never really heard of any sort of Iranian military intervention on American soil.

Sure, we've all heard the much publicized exaggerated speeches of Ahmadinejad, Iran's former President, but come on, his words from a personal ideological stance didn't really convert into any feasible action or threat historically.

The USA even shot down an Iranian passenger jet in 1988 killing all innocent 290 passengers onboard instantly. Yes you are reading correctly! The USA said it was an unfortunate accident but never officially apologised to the Iranian government who do not see it as a mere accident. Understandably the Iranians commemorate July 3rd 1988 annually to remember those who perished in the fatal incident but the world has long forgotten about this day and hardly any of you will even know that this ever happened. This dwarfs the tragic shooting of a Russian warplane by Turkish authorities for violating their airspace in 2015 even.

The then Vice President under Ronald Reagan's administration, George Bush (Senior) famously said on television after the incident: "I will never apologize for the United States — don't care what the facts are... I'm not an apologize-for-America kind of guy."

In the same vein, we heard Benjamin Netanyahu saying Ahmadinejad was an "Evil wolf" and the current President Rouhani is merely a 'wolf in sheep's skin'.

But in actual fact. Who is threatening whom?

Then we have the illegal invasion of Iraq. The late Lord Thomas Bingham, one of the most respected and revered British Judges and statesmen that England has produced, was asked in 2004 whether he thought the War on Iraq was a legitimate one or justified under international law. His explanation via the United Nations Security Council norms was clear. A country may go to war under the following three circumstances:

1. If a viable threat to their security is made with intent/provocation and they must defend themselves
2. If the UN Security Council unanimously agree that military action must be taken against said country.
3. To avoid a major humanitarian catastrophe.

If we examine closely the Iraq situation post 9/11, then we can clearly see none of the above three justifications were applicable.

Now we have another extremist terror 'death cult' among us called 'Daesh' who we should not dignify by calling them 'Islamic State' as there is nothing 'islamic' about them. Tony Blair himself in a recent interview in the USA has admitted that the coalition that invaded are somewhat responsible for the current rise of Daesh today. He in many ways was forced to make this admission due to the criticism he is expected to receive in the upcoming Chilcot report. I still do not understand how he thinks Jeremy Corbyn is 'dangerous' as leader of the Labour party as Corbyn only wants peace and is a supporter of the 'Stop the War Coalition'.

The Americans do not seem to be winding down or slowing their military operations abroad in the Middle East however they are now expanding the network of violence with no real intention of peace.

Now the purpose of my book is not to brand the US a dangerous State, I love the country too much for that, however I would just like to draw attention to the undeniable flaws in the Foreign Policy which inevitably backfire onto the US as a whole. My intention is to outline the habit of the US Intelligence agency CIA and the US governments of proposing or executing sinister covert operations with the aim of fulfilling their somewhat dubious self-interests under the false pretence of National Security. Its thirst or hunger for military intervention is unrivalled.

BCCI (Bank of Credit and Commerce International) may have been no exception. We will never really know.

However before you jump to conclusions and label me as a disgruntled British ex-pat or somebody with a grievance or a love for conspiracy theories, we need to examine the various secret operations the US Government, in conjunction with the CIA have been involved in. And hence all these covert exercises give due legitimacy to certain commentators giving inklings of the shutdown of BCCI to be another feather in the USA Government/CIA's cap of long list of coups and covert interventions.

Covert United States foreign regime change actions:

1893 Overthrow of the Kingdom of Hawaii
1948 Italian general election

1949 Syrian coup d'état
1953 Iranian coup d'état
1954 Guatemalan coup d'état
1959 Tibetan uprising
1961 Cuba, Bay of Pigs Invasion
1963 South Vietnamese coup
1964 Brazilian coup d'état
1967 Greek coup d'état
1970 Cambodian coup
1973 Chilean coup d'état
1976 Argentine coup d'état
1979–89 Afghanistan, Operation Cyclone
1980 Turkish coup d'état
1981–87 Nicaragua, Contras
2002 Venezuelan coup d'état attempt

Let's start with the 1953 overthrowing of Mossadegh. The coup, codenamed operation 'AJAX' was carried out by the US administration of Dwight D. Eisenhower in a covert action advocated by Secretary of State John Foster Dulles, and implemented under the supervision of his brother Allen Dulles, the Director of Central Intelligence.

This cowardly move ensured Western control of Iran's petroleum resources and prevented the Soviet Union from competing for Iranian oil. The joint efforts of the US and UK Governments installed the Shah Mohammad Reza Pahlavi as leader of Iran who then went on to rule for twenty-six years until the Islamic revolution in 1979 where he was overthrown himself after being abandoned by the USA.

This was a classic example of the USA using a regime or institution for its own benefit and interests until it no longer serves its purpose to them, only to relinquish support and then orchestrate its demise. Some people say the same could have been said of BCCI. I leave you to decide. All I will say however is that if the USA and its allies have the power and authority to mobilise people and orchestrate revolutions and revolts in foreign countries through funding and manpower, then to close down a relatively small bank is child's play for them comparable to squishing an ant.

Then another scandal with Iran was the infamous Iran–Contra Affair which they also accused BCCI for being entangled in (for which the US Government and CIA apparently channelled funds through BCCI to make payments to Iranians and to fund the Contras).

The Iran–Contra Affair of the 1980s stemmed from the Reagan Administration's foreign policies towards two seemingly unrelated countries, Nicaragua and Iran. The Administration believed that changes to these countries that occurred in the 1970s threatened US national interests.

Simultaneously the USA got their hands dirty in Nicaragua, where a socialist movement (the Sandinistas) seized power through a revolution in 1979. The Administration, fearful of the potential spread of socialism throughout Latin America, eventually backed paramilitaries (the contras) who sought to overthrow this revolutionary regime.

In 1979, power also changed hands in Iran when a radical Islamic movement overthrew the US-backed government. Because the revolutionary government was unfriendly towards the United States and potentially allied with the Soviet Union, the Administration tried to bolster moderate elements within Iran, a policy that became more complicated when Iranian-backed Lebanese terrorist groups seized American hostages.

Iran's need for weapons during the Iran–Iraq war from 1980–1990 complicated the Iranian–American relations. In the beginning of the Iran–Iraq war, the US actively engaged in an arms embargo against Iran called Operation Staunch and religious fundamentalist group Islamic Holy War took more US hostages beginning in March 1984. It was Iran's need for weapons, and the United States's desire to re-open diplomatic relations that in 1985 led Manucher

Ghorbanifar, an Iranian businessman working with the US, and Adnan Khashoggi, a Saudi Arabian arms dealer, to devise a skeleton plan for what would later become the Iran arms deal. This deal would alter Iranian–American relations and lead to the most controversial piece of the Iran-Contra scandal: the diversion of funds from the sale of weapons to Iran to supporting the Nicaraguan Contras.

We need not go through the extensive list of secret operations in order to prove the double standards that the previous US Governments uphold. This is all clear and plain for all to see and evident to those who like to seek truth.

The only other major event I would like to touch upon during this analysis is the global 'War on Terror' that was launched in the aftermath of the atrocious September 11th attacks on the World Trade Centre.

I would like to re-iterate here that 9/11 was a heinous and cowardly crime committed by individuals who were indeed barbaric criminals. They were NOT Muslims, neither did they share any beliefs or philosophy with the 1.4 billion Muslims of the world. In my opinion, those criminals needed to be dealt with in a manner with which you deal with all such perpetrators of such actions. However, to launch a world-wide media and military attack (which many see as a war on Islam as a religion) on vulnerable nations, killing hundreds of thousands innocent civilians (many of whom are women and children) is not a reasonable solution to the problem nor was it a sensible response.

Much has been written about the War on Terror and its repercussions. I do not wish to enter into the details. However the question needs to be asked: In order to avenge the deaths of 2,973 innocent 9/11 victims, is it justified to ruthlessly murder over 200,000 innocent civilians in Iraq, Afghanistan and Pakistan? Almost all of those innocent deaths and casualties are suffered by the poor and vulnerable who have absolutely no connection to the 9/11 attacks personally, then labelling them as 'collateral damage'.

In April 2013, it was estimated in a study undertaken by

scholars with the Eisenhower Research Project at Brown University's Watson Institute for International Studies that the cost of wars in Afghanistan, Iraq, and Pakistan are estimated at 225,000 lives and up to $4 trillion in US spending. The group's "Costs of War" project has released new figures for a range of human and economic costs associated with the US military response to the 9/11 attacks.

In recent years we have heard the media reports about the US financial Government shutdown, austerity measures with budgets not being approved by Congress and CEOs of major banks asking Obama to raise the debt ceiling. Therefore again returning to my inadequate GCSE mathematics score, even I can see that $4 trillion that has been earnestly wasted on a war that simply cannot be won, could have been saved and spent efficiently on domestic affairs in order to provide more jobs and financial security to the American people. Unfortunately, what the US governments fail to comprehend or acknowledge is that their fledgling wars in Iraq, Afghanistan and now Syria are having a long-term counter-productive effect on both the financial stability of the United States and its national security. It is most paradoxical and juxtaposed to see that the ultimate purpose for which the war on terror is being fought, is not being achieved and to add insult to injury it is creating more hardline anti-American sentiments and fuelling more extremism in the Middle East.

Furthermore the illegal deadly drone attacks on Pakistan and Yemen which were started by George W Bush and increased under the Obama administration have taken thousands of innocent lives. In February 2013, US Senator Lindsey Graham publicly admitted that 4700 people have been killed by their drones. This number is disputed and is rumoured to be much higher by Pakistani authorities. My argument is: I fully unequivocally condemn and share outrage at the 9/11 attacks and extend sympathies to the families of victims. However are the 4700 killed by drones also not human beings? Are the 200,000+ innocent lives taken by the Allied forces on the so called 'War on Terror' not people? Where is the justice? Where are the human rights? Where is the peace?

On this note, I would like to extend my limited knowledge of Islam, which in all practicality is a religion of peace. It has been categorically stated in the Holy Quran *(5:32)*, which we as Muslims believe to be the divine word of God, that *"He who kills one innocent person, is as if he has killed the whole of mankind, and he who saves one person is as if he has saved the whole of mankind"*.

This verse alone explains how killing any innocent human being regardless of race, religion, nationality or gender is forbidden in Islam. The religion of Islam, like all other religions promotes and seeks to deliver the message of Peace to all of mankind across the globe. It denounces hatred, violence and injustice in all shapes and forms. Hence the so called 'IS/ISIL/ISIS' or whatever the barbarians wish to call themselves are also *NOT MUSLIMS!* I would urge all readers to undertake their own independent study of the Quran in detail from reliable sources rather than the media in order to gain enlightenment.

Anti-American sentiments

The general animosity or suspicious view of the Americans by the average man on the street in the Middle East stems from the above descriptions of coups and covert practices which generated a feeling of distrust. This was also evident among the Egyptian people in Cairo who suspected the Americans of secretly interfering in the post-Mubarak era, as the majority still have vivid memories of the Iranian coup. On the contrary many ordinary Americans find it baffling as to why the Arabs would think such a thing and why their governments would want to interfere in other people's business. This is unfortunately the case since many of these ordinary Americans probably haven't studied history in depth. This is why John Cassidy, a writer for the *New Yorker* paper, stated in his excellent article that we should pay more attention to history: "In watching the events convulsing the Middle East, and thinking about how to react to them, it is essential to be aware of how we got to this juncture. Second, the official version of history is often very different from what really happened. During the Cold War, as now, the reality of what the US government was doing was often hidden in classified documents. In the case of the coup against Mossadegh, it's taken sixty years for the full truth to emerge. Doubtless, it will take almost as long for us to learn everything about the spying agencies' electronic prosecution of the "War on Terror." But thanks to Edward Snowden and journalists like Glenn Greenwald, we've at least had an advance briefing."

Cassidy touched on a very sensitive yet very relevant issue of Edward Snowden and the revelations that have come since the *Guardian* in the UK broke the story in early 2013 regarding the US breaching of civil liberties by accessing our personal emails and telephone calls. We will never really know the full story on the 'War on Terror' or the USA's role in orchestrating certain events which are held as classified until after we have lived out this generation. Then a century down the line media pundits and talk show hosts will discuss our period of history and try to embarrass governments of the day who will have no viable answers for actions that were committed by their predecessors a century ago. This is similar to what Obama did in Cairo in 2009 when he made a speech and referred to the Iranian coup. However he used a more diplomatic tone this time.

Across the spectrum, anti-American sentiments are increasing with each breadwinner of a poor family falling victim to American drones or a simply a misguided bullet. Take Pakistan again for example. On January 27th 2011, an undercover CIA agent called Raymond Davis unleased a flurry of bullets on the streets of Lahore only to kill two motorcyclists who attempted to rob him at gunpoint. Moments later a Toyota Land cruiser with backup appeared escorting Davis

I Love America, But Why Others Don't?

to safety and on the way killed an innocent Pakistani motorcyclist by running him over. The weeks and months that followed saw a frenzy of media coverage around the public outrage of this episode on the streets of Pakistan, along with a very strong effort by the American authorities to get Davis released and returned to the USA. After a lot of tension between Washington and Islamabad with many talks, including Joe Biden the Vice President of USA visiting Islamabad, Raymond Davis was forgiven by the victim's families in court (after being paid blood-money by the CIA) and then effectively left Pakistan scot-free.

In contrast, can you imagine a scenario where ISI (Inter Service Intelligence agency) officers of Pakistan's secret service would murder three unrelated men on the streets of New York or Washington in broad daylight and then later be pardoned by the US Justice system? Would the episode be brushed under the carpet so quickly in the US media? Would diplomatic relations be the same? I think not. Furthermore Obama had pressed for Davis's immediate release on the basis that he was a diplomat and be granted the same diplomatic immunity which all diplomats deserve. This was most definitely debatable given the reasons for which he was sent to Pakistan by the CIA. Yet, that is another episode which is not relevant to my story.

Mark Mazetti of the *New York Times* described in an article how Raymond Davis didn't stop there, in fact he was sentenced to two years' probation by a court after physically attacking a gentleman in a parking lot in Denver, USA. The witness had said she had never ever seen a man with such sheer rage before. The less said the better.

Furthermore the ultimate irony on today's 'War on terror' is that historically it all began as a result of USA's haphazard habit of unnecessary foreign intervention when the CIA funded, trained and armed Afghan soldiers who were called the 'Mujahideen' to fight the Soviets in the aftermath of the Soviet Union attacking Afghanistan. This operation was codenamed 'Operation Cyclone' that was signed by President Carter in 1979 but then accelerated

213

by President Reagan in subsequent years. It is well documented and common knowledge that Osama Bin Laden was recruited, trained, funded and groomed by the CIA and USA itself to carry out their dirty work against the Soviet Union. These were the same 'Mujahideen' who the then-USA President famously welcomed into the Oval Office in Washington DC by saying: *"These gentlemen are the moral equivalents of America's founding fathers"*.

Once the job was done and the Soviets were contained and defeated, the CIA had no more use for these 'freedom warriors' and many felt betrayed and used by the USA for fighting their 'proxy wars' and giving them false incentives as the USA shifted its interests. The Hollywood movie starring Tom Hanks called *Charlie Wilson's War* gives an illustrated yet fairly factual viewpoint and rhetoric of the mood and feelings of all within and outside the American camp during this volatile period of the operation between 1979–1988. Operation Cyclone leaned heavily towards supporting militant Islamic groups that were favoured by neighbouring Pakistan, rather than other, less ideological Afghan resistance groups that had also been fighting the Marxist-oriented Democratic Republic of Afghanistan regime since before the Soviet intervention. Many political commentators believe that Charlie Wilson's Operation Cyclone was one of the main catalysts that created defected elements within the 'Mujahideen', gave birth to Al Qaeda and nurtured repercussions which eventually led to the horrific 9/11 attacks on the Twin Towers. The fact that the hijackers were Saudi nationals, and not Afghani, Iraqi, Iranian or Pakistani also mesmerises many people, however this is another issue altogether.

In any case, Operation Cyclone was one of the longest and most expensive covert CIA operations ever undertaken; funding started with $20–30 million per year in 1980 and increased to $630 million per year in 1987. Some of this funding is apparently said to be channelled through BCCI and other banks according to the CIA, however BCCI management had no knowledge of any such transactions moving through its banking network. Even if it was

214

true, the CIA needed a banking institution to transfer money and weaponry to the Mujahideen Afghans who were fighting their war on their behalf. BCCI would merely have been a mechanism for them to further their interests on that region.

Finally in my opinion one of the most shocking revelations and discoveries of all thanks to Julian Assange and his Wikileaks team among others, even more so than Edward Snowden's NSA whistleblowing episode, was the proposal for 'Operation Northwoods' in 1962 to 'fake' a terrorist attack on American soil.

In the 1950s and 60s, the US was in the grip of the Cold War and terrified by the threat of Communism. Cuba, a Communist nation right on the doorstep, was deemed such a threat that a huge amount of intelligence and military activity was devoted to finding ways to depose or assassinate Fidel Castro. After the failure of the Bay of Pigs invasion, these activities were collected under a CIA programme known as Operation Mongoose, also called the Cuban Project. It was led by General Edward Lansdale of the US Air Force.

In 1997, the John F. Kennedy Assassination Records Review Board released a pile of records from the Kennedy era. Among them was a 1962 document titled "Justification for US Military Intervention in Cuba." The memorandum concerned something called Operation Northwoods, a plan to create fake attacks on "friendly" defected Cubans, US military bases, and US citizens – all designed to appear conducted by Cuba. This action, known as a "false flag" operation, would be used to garner the public and political support necessary for direct military intervention against Cuba. And the plan wasn't some crackpot scheme devised by a minor official – it was sent from the Joint Chiefs of Staff to the Secretary of Defense, Robert McNamara.

Ultimately, Operation Northwoods never went beyond planning stages. Nevertheless, it's impossible to escape the feeling of creeping horror when you realize that such a plan was even considered at such high levels of the US government. Again, when you think about plans like these, the now increasingly evident plan for BCCI's closure might also have existed as some say and seems like child's play compared to the larger scale CIA top-classified operations. Only time will tell, if ever, such classified documents relating to BCCI will become available to the public.

The only known secret document to have been available in recent times is the PriceWaterhouse's 'Sandstorm report' which apparently was the reason why the Bank of England changed its direction and moved swiftly to close BCCI in coalition with the US Authorities in July 1991.

My wish along with many others in this world is to see world peace on a global scale. Our planet Earth along with its inhabitants over thousands of years are miniscule and tiny beings in a vast universe of countless galaxies. We are on this Earth for a limited time only, if we are lucky enough we will live until one hundred but then even with advanced medical treatment, regardless if you are a King or a President, we will all die. War and hatred is simply not worth it. Love one another and be good to one another regardless of religion or cast. Be human first, which is what you will be remembered for.

Chapter Sixteen

Conclusion

My final thoughts are pretty straightforward. During eight years of research I was quite sceptical that I would be able to find a definitive answer due to the complexities of the case. Furthermore I must admit that the sheer nature and vast amount of negative news media content surround the BCCI 'scandal' had instilled in my mind that BCCI was possibly the worst ever bank in the world and proving otherwise would be a fruitless exercise. I have hopefully provided enough material evidence to prove otherwise in the minds of the reader so that you are able to make your own independent and informed decision after having reviewed and verified the facts.

BCCI, a bank with roots in the Middle East and South Asia, created with a vision and objective to bridge the gap between the third world and the west and elevate poverty on a global scale seemed to have been committing all the age-old crimes which every other bank in the world is doing today (and had been for decades before BCCI even was born).

To wrap up BCCI was accused of:

1. Creative accounting and manipulation – This was correct and has been addressed in detail in Chapter 5.

2. Links with intelligence agencies like CIA, MI5 and ISI

   I love this Hollywood-style story which always tends to come up in the previous four BCCI books written by the likes of Peter Truell and co.

   It has been reported and documented that the CIA had used BCCI itself to fund its various covert operations worldwide, but this was without BCCI management knowledge. The CIA must have used a variety of channels to transfer funds for their activities and probably still do. But BCCI is no longer around so they must be using other methods. The most famous two cases were cited in Chapter 15 where we learnt that CIA sold weapons to Iran in the seventies under the leadership of President Ronald Reagan in exchange for US hostages. George Bush Sr. (then Vice President) denied all of it but later it was discovered to be true. BCCI was apparently used as a financial vehicle by the CIA to channel funds for the so-called 'Iran-Contra affair'.

The bank was probably again used to send funds to the Mujahideen in Afghanistan to arm them against the Soviets. The CIA was tangled in so many covert operations throughout the seventies and eighties that BCCI had become a huge mess for them naturally with so many transactions involving their name would be incredibly damaging and incriminating especially if they were denying it in public.

3. Terrorist Financing

This again has not been proven to date. If we examine point 2) above then the CIA funds used to arm the Iranians and then again to arm the Afghan 'Mujahideen' against the Soviets can be seen as arming military personnel which some might call 'terrorists' and others may call 'freedom fighters'. It is open to interpretation. The main point being that BCCI was a bank, not a political organisation, however it was used by all sorts of organisations, corporations, governments and individuals to process their financial transactions.

On a note of record, the famous Abu Nidal is always mentioned by BCCI-bashing enthusiasts. The reality was that Abu Nidal was suspected of having two accounts in London and this was brought to the attention of BCCI management including Swaleh Naqvi by the UK authorities themselves in the eighties. Naqvi said: "Abu Nidal is a very interesting story, we did not even know he was even a customer until the UK authorities informed us of their suspicions. The authorities told us not to do anything except watch those accounts and keep an eye on them."

It was later confirmed by the governor of the BofE Robin Leigh-

Pemberton at the Treasury Select Committee that BCCI themselves alerted the BofE of suspicious accounts such as these. This confirms that the bank was never purposely funding or facilitating terrorist related accounts and was not complacent either.

4. Money laundering – Again this was dealt in detail in Chapter 5 and Lord Bingham confirmed in his report in 1992 that BCCI was never found to have any money-laundering activity in any of the regions it operated especially the UK. The 1988 Tampa indictment was a result of an undercover sting operation used to entrap BCCI and was the only isolated incident of 'laundering' ever to be found to-date. It is reassuring to see that even the main 'infiltrator' Robert Mazur himself has suddenly had a re-awakening of his moral conscience. As of late recently he has been giving interviews about how disappointed he is in the regulatory and enforcement agencies as they did not follow through on to other banks after incriminating BCCI. When asked whether he felt guilty about what he was doing as an undercover agent coercing innocent bankers into committing a crime he said he felt bad for the officers and their families.

"I completely agree that all many other banks, which have been found to be involved in money laundering, should have been shut just like BCCI. But I really feel ashamed that government of my country lets these bankers go scot-free."

—*Robert Mazur, in an interview given to Saad Hasan of the Express Tribune paper in Pakistan in April 2015.*

His book The Infiltrator is now being made into a Hollywood movie starring none other than Breaking Bad's Bryan Cranston.

As a result of my extensive research, I was surprised about the amount of false reporting and lies that were exposed in books released by mainstream publishers like Bloomsbury in the USA like Peter Truell's *False Profits* for example. A story fabricated by one Tariq Ali, who seems like a disgruntled BCCI hater, in his book *A Banker for All Seasons* involved a former BCCI employee named Masood Asghar. In Tariq Ali's narrative, he tells us how when Masood Asghar left the bank he expected a large pay cheque but was disappointed to receive a low amount and so threatened the bank to 'expose' them. Soon after his 'threat,' armed military personnel broke into his home and raped him.

This was a story repeated in Peter Truell's book published by the USA. It was such a shocking story that one actually began to suspect BCCI of having a military wing and that it used terror and thuggery to push its weight around (as per John Kerry). Hence a leading banker in Pakistan Mr. Khurshid Hadi (of KPMG Taseer & Hadi Pakistan) tracked down Masood Asghar and asked him about his ordeal.

Masood Asghar categorically denies to this day that anything of the sort ever took place. How did this story come about then and managed to find its way into two books and various other print media?

Asghar says: "I was on the phone to a colleague saying that the bank is *buggering me around* regarding my final pay cheque." That is how the story started and made its way into published books and world media by so called respected journalists who *vow to tell the truth and verify their sources.*

A former executive from the First American Bank Khusro Karamat Elley had written an article of which I would like to include an excerpt:

"Bernie Madoff might be the single individual associated with the most evil scams, but the legal ones of the Banking sector, abetted by the (US) government, eclipsed his crimes."—Nomi Prins

BCCI was structured in a way that it had no credible lender of last resort. All who dealt with it knew of this and they dealt with it knowing this fact. It was a handicap that BCCI had chosen and they reserved the right at some stage to opt for a lender of last resort. In fact it was an unspoken assumption that the lender of last resort was the Sheikh of Abu Dhabi and when the time came, which it did, the Sheikh came forward with the money to bail out BCCI.

That this money was not accepted because a decision had already been taken to close BCCI come what may, is proof of the double standards of the Western Regulatory authorities. Everything that BCCI was accused of money laundering, reckless lending, use of undue influence, creative accounting and many more "crimes" all were committed by large American Banks in amounts so large that they are to this day mind boggling and unimaginable and these institutions got away with not even a rap on the knuckles. In fact most of them receive billions of dollars in taxpayer money and were bailed out.

Consider the following unimaginable numbers:

Fifty trillion dollars of global wealth was erased between Sep 2007 and March 2009. In the US seven trillion dollars was wiped from the stock market plus six trillion from the housing market plan. The hedge funds represented one and a half trillion dollars of unregulated assets. No one knows the leverage behind creating these Assets. (It is thought that these were leveraged to $140 trillion).

The US government had to spend $13.3 trillion on bailing out their Banks as follows:

Source	$'s in Trillions
From the Federal Reserve Bank	7.6
From The Treasury	2.5
From FDIC	1.5
Joint Effort	1.4
Housing Bill	0.3
Total	13.3

This was a situation brought about by a collusion between the Federal Reserve Bank, US regulators, the rating agencies, other agencies of the US government including regulators and Wall Street. The idea was not necessarily to commit a crime but to serve an ideology. This ideology could be summed up by a quote from the Chairman of the Senate Banking Committee in 2001. "Some people look at subprime lending and see evil, I look at subprime lending and I see the American dream in action"—Senator Gram.

Based on such thinking, a whole series of laws were passed which set up what I call the greed structure. This structure came about through taking the steps listed below;

- Repeal of the Glass–Steagall Act – late 1999.
- Allow Bank Holding Companies to acquire non-Banks
- Increase the leverage ratio of Investment Banks from 12:1 to 30:1 – 2004
- Allow creative accounting in the form of derivatives
- No strengthening of regulations happened with the spiralling deregulation
- The Federal Reserve Bank flooded the market with soft money b bringing down the discount rate to zero – 2007/2008
- The Banks handed out huge bonuses for creating assets (Loans) which later turned out to be bad.

These and other laws eventually created Banks that became too big to be allowed to fail because their failure could take down the entire system.

On Oct 22, 2008, The House Committee on Oversight and Government Reform held a hearing in a report entitled, "Credit Rating Agencies and the Financial Crisis." Chairman Henry Waxman (D-CA) in his opening statement remarked, "The credit rating agencies occupy a special place in our financial markets. Millions of investors rely on them for independent, objective assessments. The rating agencies broke this bond of trust and federal regulators ignored the warning signs and did nothing to protect the public. The result is that our entire financial system is now at risk" (Page 60 of report).

The rating Agencies have come out of this whole system unscathed. Robert Farzad writing in Business Week in 2007 says "The Rating Agencies, despite having contributed to the global economic meltdown that impacted the greater public, didn't consider themselves responsible for any of it."

Nomi Prins, in her book, 'It Takes a Pillage,' (Behind the bailout, bonuses, backroom deals from Washington to Wall Street) outlines with immaculate research what I cannot and do not wish to duplicate, the story of this collusion. I quote below from her book,

"History particularly the great depression, has taught us that the desire to make money or gain power breeds bad habits. Yet our country is built on the premise that making money is on a par with our inalienable right to pursue happiness. And the recent actions of our government have only strengthened the urge – and the ability – for financial firms and the political leaders who stack the decks in the financial firms' favour to make money and become very very happy."

If you truly want to understand how crooked the system was that sat on judgment on Abedi, read Nomi Prins and other books that bare the sad partnerships of government and business in the US. It is not my intent to go into details of this system. People more able than myself are already doing it, but it is my intent to point out that these very people who excuse their excesses because they are a part of their ideology never gave Abedi a chance because he took some shortcuts to serve his ideology. Perhaps I do a disservice to the financial crises of 2008/2009 by using it to mitigate the wrong doings of BCCI but I sincerely believe that the punishment meted out to BCCI (closing it down) was far in excess of the irregularities that may have been committed by them.

It wasn't as if BCCI received bad advice about US laws. They were represented by people like Clark Clifford and Robert Altman. If men like Clark Clifford, decided to work for Abedi, it was not because of the money. Clifford was a man who, advised five US Presidents. He had a reputation to protect and he had made it clear to Abedi, that he was laying his reputation on the line in representing him or his supporters. Men like Clifford do not do that for ordinary people. If Jimmy Carter gave his time to Abedi, he did it only because he thought there was merit in the vision and ideology that Abedi espoused. Abedi wore his ideology on his sleeve. He lived, talked and breathed it. Clifford was not a man who could be fooled by idle talk.

The only case that was ever brought to trial in a court of law was the case brought by the Manhattan District Attorney against Robert Altman, Clifford's law partner and the Manhattan DA lost that case. They lost the case because they never had a case and because Altman was well represented. In many cases where the prosecutor was judge and jury and could intimidate the accused, the prosecutor was able to do deals in which the accused pleaded guilty for promises of lighter sentences. This happened in the Tampa case and in the case against Naqvi where both parties could not afford to be properly represented by legal counsel.

Khusro Karamat Elley expressed his views and frustration with great accuracy and I echo his thoughts. But history has been made and the textbooks have been written. Agha Hasan Abedi is dead and so are his dreams along with him.

His legacy however does not have to die however and can be celebrated. It is unfortunate that a man that was once received by Presidents, Prime Ministers and officials at airports around the world had only a handful of people clustered around his coffin in Karachi at his funeral on 5th August 1995. It is because as I stated at the beginning of the book, Pakistan has an uncanny knack of shaming and forgetting her heroes and those who would normally ignite a sense of pride for any nation.

One similar example to Abedi would be the shameless expulsion of Pakistan's first ever Nobel Laureate the late Professor Dr. Abdus Salam who was awarded the Nobel Prize for Physics in 1979 for his contribution to the electroweak unification. In addition he achieved the Pati–Salam model, magnetic photon, vector meson, Grand Unified Theory, work on super symmetry along with magnetic quantum theories. He was a mastermind scientist and like Abedi favoured to strengthen the scientific progression and development in third world countries. Shamefully he left his home country to pursue his science all over the world due to prosecution in Pakistan of the *Ahmadi* sect to which he belonged under the Bhutto and Zia regimes. This was a man who served his country his entire life as an advisor to the government on science and laid the foundation work for Pakistan's nuclear ambitions yet he has been erased from the history books in his country as if he was a disgrace, merely because of his religious beliefs. Pakistan shunned him yet he was welcomed and celebrated worldwide and respected by the likes of Albert Einstein and Stephen Hawking who used Salam's work also. Pakistan has never produced a scientific genius like Dr. Salam nor a banking genius like Agha Hasan Abedi since but many millions have the potential to become the next Dr. Salam and Abedi.

Unfortunately the state of affairs in Pakistan, no matter how patriotic one may be is the blatant reality that there is no equality and discrimination both on grounds of religious beliefs and sectarianism is rampant. This is not only confined to the 'mullahs' or extremist clerics, but is deep rooted in the educated class of the country too. Whether one defines Dr. Salam as a Muslim or a non-Muslim, this is irrelevant to his outstanding contribution to Physics whilst representing Pakistan as a nation – both Muslims and non-Muslims. Why do people play the religion card and shun successful achievements of patriotic citizens?

Although not the business of anybody else except between me and my creator, I consider myself to be a Muslim by reading and obeying the Quran (commandment of God), believing in the oneness of God and in his last and final Prophet Muhammad but above all this trying to be a good human being to others. The best quality of any body is good manners and how you behave with others regardless of what religious beliefs they may have. My parents and their extended families both hail from different Islamic sects. I was brought up with a free will to read, educate and decide for myself which path I wish to follow. I read and studied them all and now I refuse to subscribe to any sect or sub-sect, whether Shia/ Sunni or others. Instead just be a 'Muslim' or try to be a good human being. Problems should be dealt with love not hate.

This reminds me of my favourite saying of the Holy Prophet Muhammad (PBUH), the last and final Messenger of God is when a funeral procession was passing by, and he stood up immediately as a mark of respect. But then he was told by one of his companions to sit down as the funeral was of a Jewish man. The Prophet immediately responded: "Is he not a human being?"

Hence Agha Hasan Abedi included people of all races, religions and colours in his bank. BCCI was a true multi-national and multi-cultural organisation in the real sense. But why was he abandoned by those who were with him during the good days? It is a tragedy of all sorts but his good deeds and the effect he had on people will remain forever. The lives he touched and changed will continue to praise him and continue to do so.

The United Bank Limited (UBL) which he founded in the sixties is still alive and flourishing with a UK subsidiary also. It is one of Pakistan's largest banks. But more importantly the charitable trust he started called the BCCI Foundation in the eighties is still operating today but under a new name called the Infaq Foundation. Abedi said he would use all profits derived from BCCI's Pakistan business and donate them to the BCCI Foundation which would then distribute funds to various charitable projects and to those who needed them most.

The profits and amounts of BCCI's profits to the BCCI Foundation were so impressive that the Infaq Foundation is still using the same funds injected by the bank over two decades ago

226

without ever having a fear of a real shortage. A.B. Shahid, a former colleague of Abedi said that millions of rupees every year are donated to dozens of hospitals and schools.

The prominent projects BCCI financed and founded are the GIK (Ghulam Ishaq Khan Institute of Technology), the BCCI FAST Colleges for Advancement of Science and Technology (now known as just FAST) along with NUST (all brainchilds of Abedi) and the Orangi Pilot Project which manifested his vision of Corporate Social Responsibility (CSR). A.B Shahid further added that the desire to share amongst others was institutionalised as in 1980 Abedi addressed a letter to all BCCI employees emphasizing their obligation to share the benefits accrued to them with those who less fortunate. This could be offering their time and energies as well as financial help because employees were offered a sum along with their monthly salaries specifically for this purpose of 'giving'.

BCCI Foundation (Infaq) also provided substantial funding for the Shaukat Khanum Memorial Hospital in Lahore and is acknowledged by Imran Khan that Abedi supported him from the very beginning. Abedi also initiated the Third World Prize to recognise outstanding achievements in the socio-economic field by individuals in developing countries. Nelson Mandela was also a recipient of the prize. To free the developing countries from the shackles of debt and poverty and as an alternative to the World Bank and IMF, he projected the idea of a 'Third World bank' – an idea which China is now progressing with their AIIB (Asian Infrastructure Investment Bank) which the UK has welcomed but as usual the Americans have boycotted.

As they say better late than never, the Government of Pakistan awarded Agha Hasan Abedi the highest civil award 'Hilal-i-Imtiaz' for his contributions to public service posthumously on 23rd March 2015.

Also recently in 2015 a lot of talk and focus has been applied by the Financial Conduct Authority (FCA), the PRA and the Bank

Of England around the notion of 'Conduct Risk' and how it is extremely important to be vigilant of this. This means the regulators are bumping up their efforts to crack down on mis-conduct at financial institutions with hefty fines and DPAs and seemingly the regulatory environment is fiercer now than ever before.

I strongly disagree as the regulatory enforcement was never as strong as in 1991 when they shut BCCI down for wrongdoing.

Plus when there is an instance of fraud, somebody usually benefits financially or otherwise. In BCCI's case – nobody in the bank itself benefited from senior management who were involved. Abedi died a poor and simple man. Naqvi lives an extremely humble retired life in Karachi, Pakistan and never amassed a fortune.

In light of my findings and conclusive evidence outlined in previous evidence I think it is now fitting that serious consideration may be given to re-writing new editions of academic textbooks at universities globally as clearly it can be argued that the Bank of Credit and Commerce International is no longer the 'largest bank fraud in world history' as described by Robert Morgenthau.

Certainly no media outlet, website or newspaper can factually describe the BCCI as 'collapsing' as there was never a collapse. The correct phrase should be used henceforth: "forcefully shut down" or closed. One should focus on factual and historical accuracies especially when citing past events.

To sum up, let me assume or accept for a moment that BCCI was the most crooked, corrupt and filthy organisation on this planet. That the bank was dirty from top to bottom and was a 'financial cesspit' as per the New York Feds. I am sure that the informed reader of this book will be able to come up with his/her own conclusions on whether the decision to shut it down was correct/fair or not based on the punishments meted out to its competitors by the regulatory authorities in recent years.

To quote the *Governor of the Bank of England Robin Leigh-Pemberton's* response to a question posed by the Chairman at the UK Treasury Select Committee on Tuesday 23rd July 1992:

> *"I hope it does not shock you too much, it is only a matter of realism that we do have occasions of fraud in banks, not all that often, but if we close down a bank every time we find an individual act or two of fraud we would have rather fewer banks than we do at the moment."*

Not much else to say really. You are free to make your own mind up after that one.

Epilogue: By John Hilbery

Humility and Giving

"There are two who are never satisfied — the lover of the world and the lover of knowledge."

— *Rumi*

One can learn immensely from the teaching and vision of Agha Hasan Abedi.

We did not need to own anything. Our desire and purpose was to teach and practise Global Management and to develop people through work. We had little or no desire for great personal wealth. Of course some, if not many of our colleagues expected a good and comfortable life from all our efforts. Some even wanted to be very very rich. But that was not our philosophy. Our philosophy was to maximise the potential of the human being through work and experience. Our philosophy would have made it very clear none of us owned anything, ever, in the final analysis. All we had to pass on was our experience and knowledge and to better the condition of as many people as we could.

We had great desire for quality and aspired to become it. If you could see how I for example live, you would see the result of our Philosophy and my wife's deep love of Jesus Christ who for her is God's representative on Earth. Simplicity and modesty do not exclude quality but it seems materialism and the current way of living cannot and will not understand this fact. So. It all ended in tears but hope remains for that which we believed in and trust that time and the development of Science and Faith together will reveal the truth ultimately.

The underlying theme is of course that with a deep and genuine practise of real management one does not need to own anything at all. What did Abraham, Mohammad, Moses or Jesus own? Nothing. What influence did they have? Today's modern shareholders who possess so many shares in the largest of companies have failed to influence management in any way. Truth, Real Management and Faith are far more powerful than monetary assets in the long long term and Real Management was our aim our objective and purpose. John Kerry would not have understood that in three life times . At the last count he was worth 175 million dollars and that is not taking into account his wife's Heinz assets.

John Hilbery, 2016.

Acknowledgements

There are many people without whose help this book would not have been possible. However I would like to thank the following which is not conclusive or exhaustive – and there are too many to list but they all know who they are – I am very very grateful and indebted to all.

My late father, who instilled the qualities of humility in me and taught me how to be a gentleman, a son, brother, helper, leader and above all a better human being.

Numerous interviews have taken place over many years and I have attempted to be as neutral as possible in my writing whilst highlighting the facts only based on evidence and face to face interviews. Former BCCI employees have been extremely helpful in interviews including: Swaleh Naqvi, Zahid Kasim, John Hilbery, Dildar Rizvi, Zafar Iqbal Chaudhry, Ameer Siddiqui, Amjad Awan, Basheer Chowdry, Kamran Rizvi, Khusro Elley, Munib Burney, Mohammad Qayyum and Qaiser Malik to name just a few.

Other friends, former colleagues and journalists who have been extremely instrumental and supportive throughout my journey include: Dan Ghaney, Farrah Mahmood, Mashaal Gauhar & Humayun Gauhar, Urfi Jafri, Faiza Butt, Dr. Junaid Ahmad, Sirajuddin Aziz, Hussein Lawai, Tariq Fuad, A.B.Shahid, Saad Shafi, Zara Jawad, Sundus Sheikh, Azeemeh Zaheer, Souad Al Hosani, Sheikh Mohammad Al Hosani Eyad Ajaj, Raza Piracha and Rahul Kochhar.

Utterly thankful to all my friends and family for believing in me along with those that have not been mentioned – apologies for missing anybody out!

Note on Sources:

The BCCI story has been told with over 8 years of research including first-hand accounts from ex BCCI staff and customers/ clients who have given me detailed interviews face to face. The instances where various bank scandals have been outlined in the latter chapters, have all been quoted from publicly available sources like the Financial Times, Reuters, Wall Street Journal/New York Times. All credits and sources of information have been listed wherever possible within the text.

Contact:
   Twitter: @mubashir_malik
   email: malikmbm@gmail.com

Bibliography and Websites accessed

The Lord Justice Bingham report, 1992

False Profits, Peter Truell / Gurwin, 1992

Outlaw Bank, Jonathan Beaty, S. C. Gwynne 1993

Too Big to Fail, Andrew Ross Sorkin 2010

http://business.time.com/2012/08/15/the-accounting-trick-behind-thirty-years-of-scandal/#ixzz2hstgkowW)

fas.org/irp/congress/1992_rpt/bcci (Kerry Report)

www.bbc.co.uk

www.reuters.co.uk

www.wsj.com

www.ft.com

www.nytimes.com

www.bankofengland.co.uk

Shredded: The Rise and Fall of the Royal Bank of Scotland. (Ian Fraser.)

CPSIA information can be obtained at www.ICGtesting.com
Printed in the USA
LVOW10*2207210316

480172LV00009B/47/P